WHEN YOU GREET ME I BOW

When You Greet Me I Bow

NOTES AND REFLECTIONS FROM A LIFE IN ZEN

Norman Fischer

Edited by Cynthia Schrager

SHAMBHALA

Shambhala Publications, Inc.
4720 Walnut Street
Boulder, Colorado 80301
www.shambhala.com

Cover photo: Renshin Bunce
Cover design: Daniel Urban-Brown
Interior design: Gopa and Ted2, Inc.

8 7 6 5 4 3 2 1

First Edition
Printed in United States of America

∞ This edition is printed on acid-free paper that meets the
American National Standards Institute z39.48 Standard.
♻ This book is printed on 30% postconsumer recycled paper.
For more information please visit www.shambhala.com.
Shambhala Publications is distributed worldwide by
Penguin Random House, Inc., and its subsidiaries.

Library of Congress Cataloging-in-Publication Data
Names: Fischer, Norman, 1946– author. | Schrager, Cynthia, editor.
Title: When you greet me I bow: notes and reflections from a life in
Zen / Norman Fischer edited by Cynthia Schrager.
Description: Boulder, Colorado: Shambhala, 2021. | Includes
bibliographical references.
Identifiers: LCCN 2020027636 | ISBN 9781611808216 (trade paperback)
Subjects: LCSH: Zen Buddhism.
Classification: LCC BQ9266.F57 2020 | DDC 294.3/927—dc23
LC record available at https://lccn.loc.gov/2020027636

Longtan made rice cakes for a living. But when he met the priest Tianhuang, he left home to follow him.

Tianhuang said, "Be my attendant. From now on, I will teach you the essential dharma gate."

After a year, Longtan said, "When I arrived, you said you would teach me. But so far nothing has happened."

Tianhuang said, "I've been teaching you all along."

Longtan said, "What have you been teaching me?"

Tianhuang said, "When you greet me I bow. When I sit you stand beside me. When you bring tea I receive it from you."

Contents

Editor's Foreword

O N A GIVEN week in the Bay Area, you can sometimes attend one of Norman Fischer's Dharma seminars in Tiburon one evening, hear him read poetry in Berkeley the next, and the following weekend join a Jewish meditation gathering he's leading in San Francisco. While marveling at his energy, I have happily run into overlapping circles of Norman's friends, colleagues, students, and fans at all of the above, watching Norman segue comfortably between events, exchanging a Zen robe for a kippah or pair of jeans, depending on the local custom.

A transmitted teacher in the Soto Zen lineage of Suzuki Roshi, Norman served as coabbot of San Francisco Zen Center from 1995 to 2000, before leaving to lead the Everyday Zen Foundation, a string of sanghas on the west coast of North America stretching from Vancouver, Canada, to Chacala, Mexico. Norman has simultaneously remained deeply engaged with his Jewish roots, founding with his friend, the late Rabbi Alan Lew, the first synagogue-based meditation center, Makor Or. And ever since he graduated with an MFA from the University of Iowa Writers' Workshop, poetry has been both vocation and passion, a steady counterpoint to his Zen practice. He has published twenty poetry volumes, as well as numerous prose works on Zen.

Norman first approached me about this collection because he needed someone to track down and organize his body of Buddhist magazine writing. As he is a prolific writer, Norman's copious output of articles was scattered, with no reliable inventory either on paper or in his head. I came to enjoy my task as a treasure hunt. Many of the journals I searched (*Buddhadharma*, *Inquiring Mind*, *Lion's Roar*, *Tricycle*, and *The Sun*) have extensive online archives, and even more articles came online during the several years we contemplated this collection. I also spent a pleasant afternoon digging through the entire output of *Turning Wheel* magazine in a couple of bankers boxes that Susan Moon, its former editor, unearthed from the attic of her North Berkeley brown shingle. There were also serendipitous finds made possible by the internet, such as the short piece Norman wrote for the fiftieth anniversary of Berkeley Zen Center, a tribute to his teacher Mel Weitsman, which I turned up while engaged in a completely unrelated search. In the end, I sifted through more than seventy-five pieces to cull this collection, listening carefully for the themes that Norman kept returning to again and again. What resulted is a record of his insights, musings, and preoccupations over three decades of Zen practice.

The first section, "A Buddha and a Buddha," contains essays that explore Zen as a practice of intimate encounter and speak to the centrality of relationships: teacher and student, marriage, parenting, spiritual friendship, communities of practice, and the relationship with practice that is simultaneously a relationship with oneself and with all things. In one essay, Norman presents himself directly and humorously as a reluctant teacher of Zen, reinforcing his bona fides as an heir to this paradoxical, irreverent tradition. Other essays in this section explore renunciation, celibacy, sexuality, love, and spiritual friendship as fundamental aspects of human experience.

The next section, "Form Is Emptiness," includes discussions of more philosophical Zen teachings on impermanence, suffering, and emptiness of self, traditionally known as the three marks of existence. Very personal essays on suffering the loss of loved ones, including his mother and his best friend, speak to the grief and beauty of impermanence. Other essays in this section consider the imagination as an expression of Zen mind and speak directly about Norman's twinned spiritual practice and writing practice.

The third section, "East/West," takes up the issue of cultural encounters: between Zen in Japan and Zen in the West, between Judaism and Zen, and between contrasting philosophies of the self. Some of these essays pose questions about how Buddhist traditions are transmuted as they pass from one culture to another, both shedding and gathering dimensions. Others mash up Zen and Jewish traditions to produce an entirely fresh, syncretic style of commentary that explores the existence of God, the texture of suffering, and the path of spiritual liberation.

The essays in the last section, "Difference and Dharma," all speak to a common paradox. Zen is a practice of nonduality, and yet we live in a world divided by difference and conflict. These are also the essays in the collection that turn most directly to questions of social activism and social engagement. Several demonstrate Norman's decades-long commitment to racial justice and his efforts on behalf of gender inclusion in Buddhist communities, which he contextualizes in terms of an honest reflection on his own identity as a Jewish white man. In this, he anticipates and champions conversations that are only now getting their fuller due. Other essays turn to social justice issues more broadly, addressing ethnic conflicts, violence, and war; our terrifying climate emergency; and the problem of evil as a fundamental aspect of human expression. Collectively, these essays ask of us: what types of social engagement are appropriate responses in our broken world?

The collection also includes new writing. Norman's "Notes" introduce the book and precede each section, offering present reflections on the themes that have interested him over a lifetime of practice. One of the great pleasures of working on this book has been participating in the unfolding of Norman's dialogue with his previously published writings (in addition to the notes, some of the essays were substantially revised for this collection). The pieces that resulted are not definitive statements, any more than the original essays were. They are fresh glimpses into the imper-manent thoughts and perceptions of a wide-ranging and original writer, thinker, and transmitter of dharma.

———— ▶◀ ————

Students of a Zen teacher, especially one as well known as Norman, make up a far-flung community and often share a special bond without even knowing it. One year, I attended the Everyday Zen *jukai* ceremony, at which students officially take the Buddhist bodhisattva vows and receive Buddhist names. The ceremony represents the culmination of a year or more of studying the Buddhist precepts and sewing a *rakusu*, an intricately stitched blue bib that is a representation of Buddha's robe. As part of the ceremony, Norman gives each student receiving the precepts a four-character Japanese name, which speaks to both spiritual realization and aspiration on the path.

Among the familiar local faces receiving jukai that year was someone from far away whom I didn't know. Norman presented her with the name On Shin Dai Ji (Profound Gift Great Healing). And he tenderly and tactfully acknowledged her grief and courage in bearing the most difficult loss of all, that of a child. Afterward, I was introduced to this woman, whose name was Anne and who was visiting the Bay Area from Wisconsin. Anne was overjoyed to meet me, because as it turned out we had been engaged for some time in a joint project together with Barbara, another local sangha mem-ber. Anne, who lived far from any Zen community, had found the Everyday Zen website and began transcribing Norman's recorded talks as part of healing her grief. Eventually she contacted someone to see if these transcriptions that she had made for herself would be of interest to the Everyday Zen community. So Barbara began to edit the transcriptions for the website and asked me to do a final editorial review.

I had taken some small pride in thinking that I was helping Nor-man with this editorial service, but now my thinking was turned completely around by Anne's presence at the ceremony. Far from it being about Norman as I had supposed, I now saw that my task was in the service of a larger community of people—people I didn't know, who might be living far away from me. What I in the San Francisco Bay Area had taken for granted through proximity had been a rare and precious resource for Anne. The many Everyday Zen students who helped to create and populate the website all had a part in helping her and others access these teachings, ease their suffering, and find their way to our community. Similarly, the many, many hands who helped bring the essays collected here to a wider audience have joined, often without knowing one another directly, in the labor that resulted in this book.

May this collection also be of benefit to you who are reading this volume wherever, however it finds you. If you do not already have the good fortune of being one of Norman Fischer's students, turn the page. You are now.

Cynthia Schrager
Oakland, California
January 2020

NOTES ON LOOKING BACKWARD WHILE WALKING FORWARD

BACKWARD AND FORWARD. In time, in space. Is there any difference? Are we getting anywhere, going anywhere?

All my life I have been obsessed with time, even as a child, and death, of course death: How does a day arrive and pass by? Where does it go when it's done? And a person (like my grandfather, with whom we lived, and who died when I was seven): where does he go when he no longer appears in this sad world? Such lunatic musings drove me to poetry and to Zen, and a lifetime of more musing, scribbling, and sitting for hours, days, maybe years, decades, all told, in deep silence. What is language? What is thinking, feeling, seeing, hearing? What is going on here?

So now at a relatively advanced age (or so they say, and so it seems) I can read many decades of my own writing about these matters.

After all this time, what do I find? How do I feel about it? And what's next? Is being old enough to be coaxed by time and others to look backward just rummaging around in the debris of your past? Do you suppress or not suppress a certain disappointment over your "legacy," the smallness of what has occurred and been accomplished? And that's it?

What a fantasy! And how odd! Looking backward at a life lived, walking forward into more life to live built on all that, trying not to be too much influenced by what's already been said and done, not to be held to a point of view or an identity previously expressed, trying to be surprised and undone and maybe even dismayed by what lies ahead.

Reading these essays, some published so long ago I barely remember having written them, is an interesting experience. Sometimes I am impressed to find more wisdom than I expected from the young man I once was (I know how foolish and mistaken about so much I have mostly been, or so I remember); sometimes appalled by his cavalier shallowness (the most flagrant of such essays have not been included!); and sometimes have the impulse to tinker (which I have done when I couldn't bear the clumsy prolix writing: apparently my prose skills have improved).

In any case, what you read here is the record of a certain category of the thinking of a certain person who has never been stable, sensible, or coherent but has rather (like any of us, if we were to notice closely enough!) been in constant flux, shift, and burble: a changeable if discernible (to others, if not to himself) shape defining an empty space. Should I be embarrassed? Should I congratulate myself? Should I accept (with horror? with joy?) that it will be up to others, my editors, readers, and listeners, to fill in the cipher that is suggested by the echoing four syllables of my name?

PART ONE
A Buddha and a Buddha

Notes on the Joy and Catastrophe of Relationship

I BEGAN ZEN PRACTICE some fifty (??!!) years ago as a callow yet stubborn and arrogant student of literature, philosophy, and religion on a quest, not a "spiritual" quest but, as I saw it, a truth quest. The reason I was so driven in that quest is that I was in great pain. Unlike so many people I have met over the years—nearly everyone!—I had no good reason for my pain. I had led a modest yet privileged life: my parents were decent people, they did not drink or rage; they did not abuse me in any way; they provided a roof and food and a simple upbringing in our traditional family faith, Judaism. No, I couldn't blame it on them. It was the times: the horrible Vietnam War (which I was about to be drafted into, though, as it turned out, I was not), fear of the world-destroying atom bombs that, during the Cold War, could be dropped at any time by us or them. Also ruining my life were the time question and the death question that obsessed me and would not let me rest; I took them quite personally and desperately. In that desperation I stumbled into Zen, looking for, I suppose, something like metaphysical relief.

So it is quite surprising that the opening section of this book, its bedrock, is about relationship. Because this is what I have discovered after many decades of Zen Buddhist practice: that the religious life isn't about truth as much as it is about relationship. Or that, perhaps, truth and relationship are one and the same. In other words, from the standpoint of Zen practice, "relationship" doesn't mean what we normally think it does: boy meets girl, person meets person; parents and children; friends, relatives, associates, colleagues. It does mean all that, of course, but that only as a vehicle for some truth beyond them. Relationship is not something that happens (or doesn't happen) in a life: it is life, it is life's truest truth. We live in relation to other human beings, of course—but how, and at what level of depth? But we live also in relation to ourselves, to our own thoughts and feelings, to our body, our breath. We live in relation to the whole of the physical world. We pick things up, we put them down, we see the sky and the sea, we hear the waves and birds, we taste and smell and touch and are touched: these things make us what we are; we are nothing without them. Understanding this, fully appreciating it at its depth, goes to the heart of Zen practice.

None of this is, as it turns out, metaphysical. It is exactly the opposite of metaphysical: it is being alive, as best you can, in the midst of whatever relation is occurring, moment after moment as moment after moment. (Because, yes, there is no time: just the relation between the mind and what it meets—the thought, sensation, person, feeling—arising and ceasing in this now that we think of as the time of our life: but it never happened!)

Relationships between human beings are, as I have found, poignantly warm and fulfilling. I found this to my surprise, having, at the beginning of my Zen life, imagined myself to be a romantically tragic American loner. All forms of human caring and interaction—including sexual relationships, marriage, monastic living, and spiritual friendship—are essential; they form us, they sustain us. I have been lucky to have had many close relationships in spiritual practice, as you will see in the pages that follow. Of all of them I am most grateful for my good fortune to have been married for more than forty years to the Zen priest Kathie Fischer. Zen priests-spouses: sounds good, but naturally, as with any human interaction, there are pushes and pulls, mostly, I am afraid, because of my having remained, in my imagination, despite myself and my better intentions, the romantic loner who sometimes can't penetrate his own thoughts and vague impulses long enough to pay attention to someone else. (I apologize for this sometimes, but apologies without deeply changed behavior are weak.) I am quite sure I would not have survived all these years without Kathie, and while we don't often engage in extensive Zen conversations, we do meditate together, and see more or less eye to eye on most things in the practice, and in life in general, although we have sometimes shockingly different perspectives too.

The essays "Leaving Home, Staying Home" and "Stages of Monastic Life" extend the question of relationship to religious community. I have rewritten the former to make it less abstract (the original was way too theoretical), but it still retains a good dollop of my wanna-be-philosophical mind. I wanted to include it for its retelling of an important alternative (yet canonical) version of the story of the Buddha's awakening in which it is clear that the Buddha's story is not (as I had thought) the story of a romantic loner/quester but half of a whole human story—the other half of which is the story of his wife Yasodhara's giving birth to their son Rahula. While on one hand this version may still strike some as sexist (as is so much in the Buddhist canon)—it is after all the guy, not the girl, who gets enlightened; the girl stays home—to me it isn't: male and female together make a whole human story. (And male and female aren't specific person-genders, they are roles, positions: we are all male and female; or, maybe, there is no essentially male and female.) Anyway, this is how I read the story. And I hope that as time goes on more people will tell this version, rather than the well-known but no more "true" Theravadin version, of the Buddha's journey. It may be that this story's inclusion here is the most valuable contribution this book makes.

"Stages of Monastic Life" was written long ago, when I was immersed in the communal life of San Francisco Zen Center, and often lived at the monastery, Tassajara Zen Mountain Center, deep in the Los Padres National Forest, inland, as a crow flies, from Big

Sur. Though it has been two decades since I have lived in religious community full time, that experience is so engraved into my heart that it seems to me that I have never left, and when I meet a monastic comrade from those days, it is as if we are still young monks together and no time at all has passed. It is hard to describe how valuable, poignant—and sometimes exasperating!—is this life and, as I say in the piece, I really do recommend it to everyone, at least for some period of time in the course of a life. Nothing changes you more for the better. So I appreciate this piece today for its evocation of that life more than for its definitive, and perhaps suspect, description of stages; and also because it may say something to anyone on the human journey—monastic or not.

Reflecting on this essay reminds me of the days long ago when I led family retreats at Green Gulch Farm Zen Center. We would divide the group in three: two groups of parents and one group of children. While one group of the parents took care of the children, the other would meditate; after lunch the parent groups would switch positions. The theory was that every parent is also a monastic and needs some time to live that. I firmly believe it! We all need time to sink back deep into the soul and try to remember who we actually are.

A word about the essay "Wash Your Bowls," which ends with what seems to me now, from the perspective of 2020, a rather naive and too-hopeful view of capitalism's "invisible hand." In 2020, with so many severe economic and environmental problems before us, it seems pretty clear that market forces per se are insufficient to repair what needs to be repaired in our economic lives. We still and probably will always have to depend on "the sum total of human goodness," but it seems now that unbridled free-market capitalism can't be the form that such dependence should take.

———— ▶◀ ————

In Mahayana Buddhist texts spiritual teachers are called *kalyanamitras*, spiritual friends. And yet the relationship with a spiritual teacher includes, perhaps, more dimensions than does ordinary friendship, spiritual or not (and perhaps leaves out some dimensions). I have been lucky in my life to have had many spiritual teachers, to whom I have felt and still do feel close (even when, as in several cases, they have passed from this world).

Kathie and I were ordained Zen priests in 1980. Both of us received *shiho* (dharma transmission, full priest ordination and permission to teach) from our teacher Sojun Mel Weitsman, I in 1988, she in 2011 after a full career as a middle school teacher. (Our ordination teacher in 1980 was Zentatsu Richard Baker, to whom we are deeply grateful for his sponsorship of us and our twin sons at the Zen center.)

I met Mel before I met Kathie, in the early 1970s. I had just moved to California with the idea of doing Zen practice. I looked up "Zen" in the Berkeley phone book (yes, in those days you looked things up in the phone book). I had no expectations, so I wasn't surprised that the place I found looked so ordinary, just a small Victorian house. A tiny plaque by the front door said it was the Berkeley Zen Center. There was a small front yard with a young monkey puzzle tree on one side and a young yucca tree on the other. (I recently drove by: these trees are gigantic now.) A man was raking leaves, obviously the gardener. I asked him who the roshi was. He said there was no roshi, but that if I wanted to sit *zazen*, I could come back the next morning.

At 5:00 A.M. I climbed the steep, narrow stairs to the attic *zendo*. I could see as I ascended a priest in robes sitting next to the altar, first the lower part of him, the middle part of him, and finally, as I got to the top steps, his face. It was the gardener! Mel.

He was very low key. He worked around the place, especially in the vegetable garden in back. There was a clothesline with clothes flapping and a leaning plum tree that flowered loudly in the springtime. During all-day sits we'd work back there. I also remember sitting with Mel in the garden, having green tea, saying very little.

Mel wasn't a teacher in those early days and wasn't trying to be.

He was just taking care of the place. His style was precise but not fussy.

A student will always be, whether they know it or not, deeply influenced by their early training with their teacher, and I am no exception (though Mel is different now, ninety years old as I write this). I find it impossible to think of being a Zen "teacher," as if there were any such accomplishment, occupation, or real designation. Although I have been at this business ("teaching" Zen) for more than thirty years and have ordained and given shiho myself to many people, I still think of myself as not defined or limited by that role or designation. I am a reasonable person who cares about his friends and associates, so I do with and for them what I am obligated to do: with joy (or anyway mostly with joy). I do have empowerments to be exercised and I exercise them as needed. Since I like to read and write and think about things, I am happy to give talks and write books, which I often do. Since I like people, love them in fact almost always, I am happy to meet with them and offer my honest impressions. But "teaching" Zen! What Zen?

In any case, I am having a good time of it, I feel very lucky to do what I do, whatever you call it, as long as I can. The hardest part is knowing that people will inevitably think you are something you are not and that you will therefore often disappoint them. This is a cause of some anguish to me, but who in this crazy world lives without at least some anguish?

For better and worse I am deeply formed as an American person: I grew up in America, studied and became a poet here, and have practiced Zen here with mostly American teachers. So I have had no choice but to try to understand and practice Asian Zen in an American, or Western, context. Though I didn't choose it, it seems that working out how to teach and practice Zen in America has been one of my chief occupations. There is, I have found, a lot of subtlety and difficulty in the attempt to transpose the ancient Asian practice of spiritual teacher and student to the West. Anyone who has followed Western Zen at all will be aware of the many scandals involving teachers (including my own teacher, Zentatsu Baker) who one way or another failed to observe what we now call "proper boundaries" and ended up hurting themselves and many others in the process. These events, it seems to me, are sad but completely understandable. We have learned from them—I have learned from them—and they shouldn't happen again. Of course, they will anyway, not only in Zen, and not only with Western teachers but with all clergy in all religious traditions (the Catholic Church is a particularly toxic and horrid example) because religion is powerful stuff and gives rise to all sorts of confusing passions and distortions.

The conclusion that it is all and only about hierarchy and abuse by males overly enamored of their own power is sadly too true, yet not complete. There is and ought to be (there can't not be) an erotic element in religious practice, so there is always a potential dark side. There is power too: more potential darkness. If it could be shown that getting rid of religion in all its forms would once and for all eliminate sexual and power abuse by males, I would quit my job and do something else, gladly participating in the dismantlement of my own and all other religious establishments. But I think these problems would persist, as they already do, in other institutions. And whatever benefit there is in religion (and I hope this book stands as an argument that there is benefit in religion) would be lost.

———— ▶◀ ————

I'm writing these words in May 2020, in the middle of the Covid-19 pandemic. Like many others, Kathie and I have been "sheltering in place," seeing no one and going nowhere. In these times the importance of others in our lives, our children and grandchildren, relatives, sangha friends, and many others, becomes desperately and poignantly clear. Not a day goes by when we are not thinking of the many people we cannot see in person, speaking with them on the phone or in videoconference. This is a necessary blessing, but it is not the same as being in one another's presence. We are living like hermits, but (perhaps like all hermits) our hearts are aching with love for people everywhere. I am these days literally praying that when this pandemic is over (and I hope it is by the time this book is in your hands) our world will be overcome with a moral imperative to take care of one another, ensuring that no human being will have to needlessly suffer for want of food, housing, education, or medical care. Compassion—feeling the suffering of others and caring for their spiritual and physical well-being—is surely the heart of all religious teaching.

1

When You Greet Me I Bow

OST PEOPLE COME to Zen practice not quite knowing what to expect. Popular images of tough Zen masters, rigorous retreats, and hard-won enlightenment experiences may obscure the fact that, when you come down to it, Zen is as much about relationship and interaction as anything else. Think of the koan literature for which Zen is famous. On the surface, these stories flash with enigma and a wonderful patina of the exotic (to Westerners anyway). But scratch the surface and you realize that the stories are basically about encounters between people.

Zen koan literature is essentially dialogic. The typical Zen story involves two or more people, who seem to be on intimate terms with one another, bringing up the teaching in dynamic, even amusing, ways. Because the protagonists know each other so well and share a serious and long-standing commitment to the dharma, they don't need to stand on ceremony. Their discussions (which are sometimes wordless) are always laconic, rough, and full of affectionate slang and jokiness, and relationship itself—with all its glitches and contradictions—is often the subject matter. So, contrary to expectations, Zen stories may have something fresh to say about the tricky and problematic nature of relationship. Here's one:

> Longtan made rice cakes for a living. But when he met the
> priest Tianhuang, he left home to follow him. Tianhuang

said, "Be my attendant. From now on I will teach you
the essential dharma gate." After a year, Longtan said,
"When I arrived, you said you would teach me. But so
far nothing has happened." Tianhuang said, "I've been
teaching you all along." Longtan said, "What have you
been teaching me?" Tianhuang said, "When you greet me
I bow. When I sit you stand beside me. When you bring
tea I receive it from you."

And another:

One day, while Guishan was lying down, Yangshan came
to see him. . . .
   Guishan said, "Let me tell you about my dream."
   Yangshan leaned forward to listen.
   Guishan said simply, "Would you interpret my dream
for me? I want to see how you do it."
   In response Yangshan brought a basin of water and
a towel. Guishan washed his face and sat up. Then
Xiangyan came in.
   Guishan said, "Yangshan and I have been sharing
miracles. This is no small matter."
   Xiangyan said, "I was next door and heard you."
   Guishan said to him, "Why don't you try?"
   Xiangyan made a bowl of tea and brought it to him.
   Guishan praised them both, saying, "You two students
surpass even Shariputra and Maudgalyayana [intimate
disciples of the Buddha] with your miraculous activity!"[1]

These are wonderful stories about people who know each other
so well and whose minds and hearts are in such harmony that they
don't need to explain or discuss. They are so close they can communicate everything with a bowl of water or a bow. Simply appreciating being together, sharing life basically and intimately, they

understand one another at a level far beyond ordinary needs and wants and arguments. Of course, not all Zen stories illustrate this perfect accord between practitioners, but those that do are eloquent in just this way; they are saying that simply being together with warmhearted kindness, dropping story lines, and appreciating each other's profound human presence is the whole of the teaching. No mention here of meditation insights, esoteric ritual, or fancy Buddhist doctrine. Intimate and caring relationship is the miracle that moves Guishan so much.

Someone said to me recently, "I know your feet." This is a funny and intimate thing to say. In Zen practice we spend a lot of time in the meditation hall together, doing things in unison—sitting down and getting up, standing, walking, and eating. It is not unusual for us to spend a week together in retreat like this, with no speaking or looking into each other's faces. But we appreciate and recognize each other's presence. Some of us wear robes, and our feet are bare. We see each other's feet and hands, and we acknowledge with a bow each other's bodies in passing.

In the world at large, we can know someone quite well—they can even be a good friend—but we might not know their feet or their hands or fully take in the sense of their body as they stand near us. Though we know what they look like, we may not really have taken in their face, or their voice, or the way they move when they are deeply connected to their feelings. Yet what are we if not our feet, hands, face, voice, and the way we move?

Instead of our bodies, what we know of each other in the ordinary world is our stories, our social words and beliefs, our wants and needs and complaints. A relationship operates across the divide of two people's needs and wants and opinions, which may or may not, at any given moment, harmonize. And when they don't harmonize, then what? No wonder relationships are so rough!

In contrast, the relationships in these Zen stories are pristine in their clarity and simplicity. Whatever conflict or controversy there may once have been has been worked out through years of mutual practice. Willing, finally, to be present with what is, the protagonists can be perfectly present with one another as they are. Sharing mutual commitment, they can share life. They can know each other with an intimacy that goes beyond the abstraction of story line and desire. They seem to appreciate each other enough to feel comfortable bringing up life's most challenging questions.

In his book *The Social Animal, New York Times* columnist and television commentator David Brooks summarizes the plethora of recent studies about the brain and emotion. He quite wisely finds this research germane to his interest in politics and society. Most of what goes on between us, he says, isn't what we think is going on. Unconscious and unintentional, our interactions are subtle and by and large unknown to us. Our relationships really are as mysterious and resistant to explanation as the Zen masters of old understood they were. We stand in each other's presence; we drink in each other's being; we know and influence each other; and we turn each other inside out simply by being in each other's presence. We are always breathing, sitting, walking, and standing together—the togetherness is just more noticeable in quiet meditation halls.

It's true that the Zen masters of old lived lives of silence, meditation, ritual, lore, and teaching that created a nonordinary atmosphere in which their needs and desires could be clearly seen and seen through. So over time they could realistically hope to come to a feeling of living at a more basic, visceral level, and, at this level, relationship is heartfelt and clear. You drink in the other's presence, hands, feet, face, voice, until, over years and decades, friendship ripens and deepens into brotherhood and sisterhood—true kinship of the spirit. You are living the same dream, and you know it. You don't need to explain or contend.

———— ▶◀ ————

Recently, I attended a funeral at the San Francisco Zen center for the priest Shuun Mitsuzen, Lou Hartman, who had died at the age of ninety-five. He had been married for sixty-three years to Zenkei

Blanche Hartman, who was coabbot of the center with me more than twenty years ago. To open the ceremony, as is the Zen custom, Blanche carried Lou's ashes into the Buddha hall and placed them on the altar. Though there are probably very few people who appreciate the Buddhist teaching of impermanence as much as Blanche does, she cried quite a bit as she placed the ashes down. So did I.

Lou had been quite famous around the Zen center as a talker, curmudgeon, and great doubter. He was absolutely faithful to daily meditation and ritual practice and he took care of altars and small repairs constantly, but he was outspoken in his scorn for any sort of falseness or cant, was almost incapable of taking anything on faith alone, and didn't have a pious bone in his body. His manner was gruff and probably a little scary to new students, and in some ways, despite his long marriage, fatherhood, and many years living communally in the temple, he was a loner. So the expressions of love and tender regard for him that were made at the funeral were eloquent testimony that what counts in human interaction isn't outward sweetness, polite solicitude, or fulfilling others' needs and expectations. It's the capacity to show up intimately and honestly, with one's whole self, for and with each other, over time. It's not necessary that the people we love be perfect or even overcome what might be serious personal defects. Living together for a long time with practice as a backdrop, we can get over our need for others to be as we wish they were, and appreciate them as they are.

The celibate monks of old China and the married priests of San Francisco Zen Center may be living in unusual situations, but the basic template of what they have learned from the Zen tradition about relationships is useful for the rest of us. Though we may not be able to replicate their lives, we can, I am quite sure, find a way to capture the essence of the practice that they've done, and it can help us with our contemporary relationship problems. There is, of course, some serious effort involved—meditating on one's own and at group retreats, listening to teachings, and the daily effort of paying attention. But these are efforts that can realistically and successfully be made, if you feel it's a priority.

The most important thing is coming back to presence every day, back to the breath, to sitting, walking, and standing, and remembering that this is what we are. It's a practice we can do with as much integrity as Guishan, Longtan, or Lou Hartman. We can remind ourselves that when our passions are aroused, or when we feel our needs are unmet, we can return to presence and just feel whatever we feel, with some forbearance. We don't need to make it go away and we don't need to insist that others do what we think we need them to do.

Of course, we can't expect our lives to go as smoothly as those of the ancient Chinese Zen masters whose stories I have used here (and remember, these are stories, yarns, not memoirs). Real-life relationships will involve negotiation, push and pull, and, sometimes, a necessary parting of the ways. But it makes a difference if all of this is done with some deeper basis, some deeper knowing and appreciation of one another, rather than simply needs and wants.

I have found over the years that when a couple practices together, there's a basis or grounding for their relationship. Even if there are tough times, somehow the return to basic human presence—their own and that of others—brings them back to appreciation and affection.

In relationship, as in spiritual practice, commitment is crucial. In both Zen and marriage there's the practice of vowing, intentionally taking on a path, even if we know we won't get to the destination. Vowing is liberation from whim and weakness. It creates possibilities that would not occur otherwise, because when you are willing to stick to something, come what may, even if from time to time you don't feel like sticking to it, a magic arises, and you find yourself feeling and doing noble things you did not know you were capable of.

Real love can include desire, of course, and desire is touchy and powerful—it can even capsize the boat of a great Zen master! But desire is not the only thing, nor need it define or limit our love. Insofar as loving another is being there for that person, come what may, we always have to go beyond self-interest and desire, though, paradoxically, love itself, as ultimate selflessness, may be the most personally satisfying experience possible. On the whole, when people get together in intimate relationships with some serious spiritual practice as a common basis, their chances for success as a couple are maximized, and, as with Blanche and Lou Hartman, that success can deepen and be enriched with time.

In our story, Tianhuang says, "When you greet me I bow." Bowing is an ancient form for showing reverence and respect. In our culture we have the handshake. Maybe it is more intimate than a bow because we touch one another, warm hand to warm hand. But they say that the origin of the handshake is suspicion and wariness. The handshake is a gesture of peace and harmlessness because it demonstrates that we aren't holding a weapon in our hands. Our hands are empty of aggression and we show this by offering our hand and taking the hand of another. So the handshake is more intimate than the bow, but the intimacy is predicated on the possibility of aggression. In contrast, by bowing we are acknowledging a friendliness and respect, but also a distance. A bow expresses our love and respect, but the space between us when we bow also expresses that we understand our aloneness, and that we can never assume we understand one another. We meet in the empty space between us. A space charged with openness, silence, and mystery.

A while ago I met two middle-aged people who had recently gotten together as a couple. Each of them had had nothing but troubled relationships their whole lives through, starting in childhood, but they were hopeful this time around. Given their past conditioning, they were understandably nervous and were seeking help. They'd already ordered several books, were looking into couples therapy, and wondered what Zen relationship advice I had for them.

"Practice this every day," I said. "Do it first thing in the morning (or, preferably, second thing, after meditating together): Sit facing each other and say to one another, 'I am grateful today that you are in my life.' Say the words, even if you find it difficult. If you don't believe them, say so. Say, 'I just said that I was grateful that you are in my life, but I don't really feel that this morning, although I would like to feel it,' and then try it again; if you still don't mean it, you can say so and give up until tomorrow. Then try again the next day, preparing yourself in advance by reminding yourself that you really are lucky to be alive, to be whole and healthy, and to have someone willing to share their life with you."

None of these things is automatic; none of them is permanent. To be alive with others—nothing could be more basic, yet there is no greater spiritual practice.

2

No Teachers of Zen

2014

ONE OF MY favorite Zen stories is about teachers. The great Zen teacher Huangbo strides into the hall and says to the assembled monastics, "You people are all dreg-slurpers! If you go on like this, when will you ever see today? Don't you know that in all of China, there are no teachers of Zen?"

A monastic comes forward and says to him, "Then what about all those people like you who set up Zen places that students flock to like birds?" Huangbo replies, "I don't say there is no Zen, only that there are no teachers."

As an independent-minded (some would say stubborn) person, I find this story appealing. I have never been attracted to Zen masters or gurus, powerful and charismatic spiritual guides. There may or may not actually be such special people, but in any case I have never been interested in them. I assume that I know what I need to know for living my life, and that when I need to know more, I will find it out for myself. No wisdom or experience that isn't my own is worthwhile.

So I have asked myself, what's the point of spiritual teachers? What benefit could possibly be gained from hanging around some supposed sage if somebody else's enlightenment is never going to rub off on me?

When I began my Zen study, I wanted to learn how to do zazen so I could find out firsthand what Zen was all about. I was happy to listen to talks and instructions that might help orient me to the practice. But the idea that following a Zen teacher and hanging on his every word and deed (in those days, Zen teachers were men) would somehow help me become enlightened seemed not only unappealing but also wrong.

My thoughts resonated with Huangbo's: there is Zen, but there are no teachers of Zen. Of course people with credentials set up shop and welcome students. We all need some structure and a place to practice. But the teacher can't teach you. Your practice is up to you. Good old American individualism. I believed it so much that I had no interest whatsoever in encountering teachers, though at the time there were several storied Asian Buddhist teachers in America. Though I first came to San Francisco Zen Center in the summer of 1970, about a year and a half before the passing of the center's great founder, Shunryu Suzuki Roshi, I made no effort to hear him speak, never saw him, and was not interested in attending his funeral nor the installation of his successor, the first American Zen master, that preceded it. Looking back at this now, I see it as a missed opportunity. But that's how I was at the time.

All this might imply that I was a rebellious Zen student. But I wasn't. I had no problem respecting my teachers, listening to their talks, going for regularly scheduled interviews. To reflexively rebel, challenge, or deny a teacher is to set up a teacher in your mind who fulfills the ideal requirements the teacher in front of you is failing to fulfill. If you feel compelled to rebel, it is probably because you actually do believe in an idealized almighty Zen master. I had no such belief and no such compulsion. I was at the Zen center to study Zen. I had my reasons for wanting to do that. Since the teachers were in charge, I would cooperate with them. But whatever benefit or understanding or enlightenment I got was my own affair. No one else could give it to me or even lead me to it.

———— ▶◀ ————

I recount all this not because I entirely agree with it now, but to give a sense of how I was thinking about teachers and Zen practice in my early years. I certainly did not think that I would become a Zen teacher myself. My thought was simply to get what I needed from the practice and move on with my vague life as a poet, surviving somehow. My wife, Kathie, and I were ordained as Zen priests in 1980 because our teacher required us to either do that and continue to practice full time at the center or move on and get a life (we had two children by then). We weren't ready to go, so we agreed to ordain, a step Kathie was much more ready for than I was, but I managed.

In 1988, when my teacher offered me shiho (dharma transmission), which would give me full ordination as a Soto Zen priest, I was surprised. In those days in American Zen, shiho was rare (though it was not rare in Japan). People presumed that only deeply enlightened people could receive it, which is why I was surprised. Nevertheless, I went ahead with the process and became a Zen teacher, a role I found at first disturbing, being so ill prepared and ill suited for it. But eventually, thinking of Huangbo, I came to accept the social designation "Zen priest" or "Zen teacher," and since then I have done my best to try to help people practice.

There is more to "no teachers of Zen" than meets the eye. I still believe that students are responsible for their own practice and their own awakening. No one can communicate a truth worth knowing; the only worthwhile truth is the one you find uniquely, for your own life. On the other hand, Zen is not Lone Ranger practice. Zen teachers are important to the practice, as the tradition certainly indicates and experience proves. Yes, there are no Zen teachers because Zen isn't a teachable subject matter or skill. There are things to be learned, such as Zen liturgy, how to comport oneself in a zendo, and how to strike a proper bell at a proper time, but it is clear that Zen itself, while not exactly something other than these things, isn't the same as them. Zen is much more slippery than that. The *Heart Sutra* says, "All dharmas are empty." Zen is empty—empty of content, empty of doctrine, style, or faith that can be codified and defined. So what is there to teach?

But yes, there are Zen teachers because Zen practice is not nothing: real transformation occurs. Zen teachers can't show you how to effect this transformation, they cannot cause it to happen in you, and they are not "masters" of it (no one could be a master of an indefinable, empty feeling for living). But they do play an essential role.

In the ordinary educational model, there are teachers who teach, students who learn, subject matter, standards of knowledge, and an educational institution that contains and certifies the educational process. While in some ways Zen might look like this, in fact Zen is not an educational process but rather a transformational one in which both teacher and student fully engage, each playing his or her proper role. The process itself effects the transformation.

Think of it as a machine with many moving parts that interact in a complex system, each part affecting every other part. No one part "teaches" while another "learns." Yet run the machine for a while and something happens: a product is produced, in this case a seasoned Zen practitioner who embodies, in their own unique way, the values, the commitments, and, mostly, the feeling and vision of a life of practice. So it's just as Huangbo says: there is Zen but, strictly speaking, no teachers, although yes, the machine won't turn unless all the parts function fully in their proper places. The teacher, not actually teaching anything, must occupy their place in the process. Another analogy might be a mandala: each element has its crucial place in the overall design, but no element is sovereign. Only the overall design matters. So yes, in just this way, teachers are important.

In order to effectively take their place in the pattern, the teacher, ideally, has certain capacities. Faith in the practice, especially. And not just enthusiastic faith, but faith grounded in experience over time—faith that is not only spoken of but also demonstrated in action. Experience in the lived reality of the practice is the source of this kind of faith, that certain knowing, to the very bones, that the practice is the truest way to live. "Practice" doesn't mean only formal practice that happens in temples and meditation halls. It means understanding and living a human life among others. Meditation is fairly new in Western culture, and naturally we have overemphasized it, romanticizing the mystical experiences intensive meditation can produce. Such experiences are just a matter of course. They are among the least important things for a teacher to have experienced, but any Zen teacher will have experienced many such things. Sit there long enough and everything is bound to occur. But it isn't the experiences that matter as much as the folding of them into a whole life and a whole view.

But even this depth of faith, though essential and basic, is not sufficient. Ideally, a Zen teacher is also willing and able to share life completely with others. This takes a wide and deep acceptance of and interest in the many wily and wild manifestations of the human heart that arise in the course of practice over time. Practice with people for a while and you will bear witness to births, deaths, marriages, divorces, love affairs, enlightenment experiences, endless tears, tragic illnesses, angry feuds, breaches, collapses, and surprises of all sorts. A Zen teacher will eventually live through with others almost everything human beings perpetrate, so he or she needs long patience, deep forbearance and forgiveness, and a healthy sense of the immense tragedy and beauty of human life. The more the teacher has an idea of "Zen" that students must conform to, the more everyone (teacher included) will suffer, if not at first, then later on as people who were initially inspired by that idea come to feel oppressed or even betrayed by it. No doubt there are many important skills people would like their Zen teachers to have, but deep faith and a willingness to share your life honestly are the core of what I have come to feel is most important after having been in this business a long time. But I have also seen Zen teachers who seem seriously lacking in these capacities still be of benefit to others. There seem to be no universal prescriptions in Zen or in life.

Zen practice is dialogic, interactive. Compared to other forms of Buddhism it is, classically, "together practice." In a formal Zen meal, for instance, everyone starts and ends together. In Zen walking meditation, everyone walks together in single file, evenly spaced. Meditation is done side by side, in a hall, with each period of meditation starting and ending with everyone together. The form of the characteristic literature is also dialogic, with short verbal or nonverbal encounters between teachers and disciples, or disciples and disciples, presenting rough-and-tumble back-and-forth conversations in which the teachings are explored not so much discursively but dynamically, using as few words as possible. And one of the characteristic and essential Zen practices is the one-on-one meeting with the teacher, which is viewed not as reporting in or asking for advice but as "dharma encounter"—a chance to meet oneself by meeting another.

Given this radical "together" style, it's clear that a Zen teacher has to be ready, all the time, to let go of their life and enter the life of the other. This deep mutuality is the essence of the Zen process. It's been wonderful training for a stubborn person like myself, softening me considerably over the years and expanding my horizons. But it took me a while to be ready for this or even to know that it was required. Soon after my shiho ceremony in 1988, I read a line in one of Thich Nhat Hanh's books to the effect that "if you can't find a true teacher, it is best not to study." This tangled me up for a while in the net of my unacknowledged preconceptions about Zen teachers. I found it very upsetting because it seemed to imply some exalted state of being a "true teacher," a state unknown to me.

Yet here I was, one of the few American Zen people in those days with full dharma transmission, and what did I think I was doing? It took me a few years to finally catch up with Thich Nhat Hanh to ask him about this, and he told me something like, "Don't worry, we all help each other. The one-day person helps the one who just came in the door. The five-year person helps the one-year person. Each one helps according to their experience." That made me feel much better.

Still, it took me years to feel comfortable in the teacher's seat.

(And being a so-called Zen teacher is, in many ways, literally that, feeling comfortable in the seat you are sitting in, facing the altar, at the front of the zendo.) For a while I was unconsciously caught by the idea that I was supposed to be someone that others expected me to be, and I couldn't help straining a bit to be that person. But the truth is, there was no one in particular I needed to be.

A formal Zen talk isn't conceived of as a lecture on Zen; it's called "presenting the shout"—that is, expressing the teaching just by speaking in your own voice. I have always appreciated the fact that when you give a Zen talk, you make three prostrations to the Buddha before and after the talk. These bows are meant to indicate that it isn't exactly you giving the talk. The Buddha is giving the talk using your body and voice. Bowing is praying to Buddha to help you do as good a job at channeling him as you possibly can, with the faith that whatever you say, right or wrong, will be of some use if you are sincere and try your best. After some years I came to see that this applied to anything I did as a Zen teacher: if I was honest, tried my best, followed precepts, and didn't pretend to be anyone, everything would be OK. This sounds simple-minded enough, and it is, but it is actually not so easy to do.

And what does "everything would be OK" actually mean? It certainly doesn't mean that things won't ever go wrong. In fact, things will certainly go wrong. Maybe another capacity a Zen teacher should develop is the resilience and breadth of view that will enable them to live with the fact that they are going to fail. At least, this has been my experience. Occupying the teacher gear in the whirling Zen machine requires that you receive everything with an open heart and have the willingness and stamina to take full responsibility for each and every relationship you enter, which means to care and try your best to help.

———— ▶◀ ————

People come to Zen practice, as they do to any spiritual practice, with plenty of human needs. They come with trust, mistrust, and hidden expectations. Of course, the Zen teacher, an imperfect human being, is going to disappoint a fair number of them. Some will be disappointed on the first day, others only after many decades. You, the teacher, will misunderstand them and they will misunderstand you. You will say and do things that are hurtful, even if you never intended to. Meaning to straighten someone out (always a dubious proposition), you will completely botch the job, reinforcing the behavior or view you were trying to soften. Students who have practiced faithfully with you for years will realize it has all been wrong and leave, creating confusion and dissension. Your public words and actions will, in being variously understood and misunderstood, create confusion among sangha members, who will act out their confusion in sometimes painful ways. You will have all kinds of complicated and contradictory feelings about people who come to practice with you—loving them, worrying about them, dreading them, seeing them make terrible mistakes you can't prevent, watching as they manipulate you and set you up for all sorts of falls. In the end, you will realize you can't help them at all and will have to watch them suffer, or watch them make you suffer, and maintain your composure even so.

I have spoken to many Zen teachers who are trying hard to get better at what they do—to see where they make mistakes and to correct those mistakes, maybe even to get some psychological or other training so they can understand the various twisted ways students sometimes present themselves. I have learned from commiserating with other teachers (something I think is essential) and from my many mistakes. Ultimately, I think Zen teachers can no more learn than teach. Each situation, each person, is unique, and one's own response, at that time, to that person, must and will inevitably be unique. I always trust my response and am, of course, willing to change or be corrected when proven wrong. But in the end, I know I'll never get it right. Sometimes getting it wrong is the best thing anyway.

It's true that everything always turns out OK. When you really trust the process of the practice more than you trust your limited self, the limited sangha, or what happens in the short run, you realize that the magic of the practice is much stronger than you thought. It is not limited to what you or anyone says or does; it is not limited to meditation or what takes place in meditation halls or on temple grounds.

I have seen how after students leave a place of practice in a huff or not in a huff, their lives miraculously turn around, sometimes five, ten, or twenty years later, because of unexpected circumstances that Buddha somehow placed in the middle of their lives long after they left. Sometimes the perfect priest you thought you were ordaining needs to fall apart, leave, and go through many ups and downs for decades before she finally emerges as the buddha you always knew she was. Or the wreck of a human being who was so disruptive and annoying and hopeless comes back to visit you decades later shining with love. And the crazy mixed-up young woman who seemed headed for certain doom returns with her three lovely children, grateful for the practice she seemed to have resisted mightily at the time.

Seeing things like this happen over and over again, you do come round, finally, to trusting the practice—and life.

———— ►◄ ————

This fundamental trust is the magic of the teacher-student relationship and is, I think, the goal of the practice: it is liberation itself. Having confidence in someone whom we look toward as an example, an inspiration, and coming to trust that person completely—even when they seem not to be cooperating with our ideas about who they should be and how they should behave, and even when they make mistakes—is the path toward deep trust and confidence in ourselves, our true selves, and in life, no matter what it brings. In the end, "teacher" and "student" are fluid roles—positions, not persons. Sometimes the student is the teacher and sometimes the teacher is the student. In the Soto Zen dharma transmission ceremony, this reality is ritually enacted, and in Zen lineage charts the red line of succession goes from Buddha, down through the generations of teachers, to the present disciple, and then back up to Buddha. So each one of us, when we find our feet in the dharma, are not only the teacher of our own teacher, but the teacher of Buddha and his successors. Such radical independence, which is identical with interdependence (for our True Self is No Self and All Selves) is what both student and teacher hold as their common treasure. Once someone asked a monastic, "Do you agree with your teacher or not?" And the monastic responded, "I half agree." "Why only half?" "If I agreed completely then I would be ungrateful." We must trust ourselves; we must trust each other: we and everything that exists are teachers of Zen, which is why there are no teachers of Zen.

3

Falling in Love

1999

THERE IS NOTHING more miraculous to me than the experience of looking at a baby, especially if the baby is your own, but any baby will do. The perfect fingers and toes, with their tiny precise nails, the intense face with its soulful expression devoid of defensiveness or posturing, the round soft body always alive with motion or utterly in repose: a picture of pristine humanness that delights the eye and heart.

Parents can spend hours gazing at their babies with endless fascination. How could such a creature exist and where could it have come from? How is it that it seems to look exactly like so many different relatives at once? How can its personality be already so clear and at the same time so unformed? The very nature of our lives seems to be called in question by this small person, whose fierce impulse simply to exist makes everything pale by comparison.

To really look at a baby in this way is to feel with immediacy a powerful, selfless, healing love that astonishes you with its purity and warmth. Overcome by it, you easily lose yourself in wonder. This is because the baby evokes an experience of pure human possibility. She, having only recently come up out of emptiness, bears still the marks: pure skin, soft limbs, perfect features; clear and unadulterated karma before the formation of self, with all its messy anxieties and complicated desires.

The same feeling comes over us when we fall in love. The beloved doesn't appear as simply another person: they are rather the occasion, the location, of something unlimited, a feeling of connection and destiny that dissolves our habitual selfishness and isolation. We are overcome with a warm and enthusiastic feeling that cannot be denied and that will distract us day and night. We exist in a special zone of delight as a result of this encounter with the unexpected force of love. All songs, soap operas, and most stories feed on whatever memory or longing we have for this feeling.

It seems to me that these experiences (which are always fleeting, though the commitments and consequences that flow from them can last a lifetime) are flashes of enlightenment, or, more exactly, of what is called in Buddhism *bodhichitta*, the oceanic impulse toward enlightenment not only for ourselves but for all beings.

Unlike anything else we think or experience, bodhichitta is not a creation of ego: we don't decide to fall in love with our mate or our child; it is something that happens to us willy-nilly, a force of nature whose source is wholly unknown. The sutras call it "unproduced," which is to say, unconditioned, unlimited. We can't even say it exists, in the ordinary sense of that word (and this is why many people doubt that it exists as anything more than a youthful delusion). It lifts us up, releases us from all that holds us to earth. Love occurs, we now know, although we don't know what it is. We only know that we have been overcome by it.

———— ▶◀ ————

Love is generated from twin impulses. Buddhism calls them emptiness and compassion; we could also call them wonder and warmth. Emptiness points to the miraculous nature of phenomena: that things are not what they appear to be; that they are, rather than separate, connected; that they are, rather than fixed and weighty, fluid and light. When we see a baby, when we look at the face of our beloved, we know that the way we've been conditioned to perceive the world isn't right: the world is not a fearful and problematic challenge; it is, instead, a beautiful gift, and we are at its center always.

This comes to us primarily not as a thought or even as an emotion but as a physical experience so compelling we are overcome with an impulse to merge with another, and through that other, with the whole world. We want to pour ourselves out of ourselves and into the beloved, as if our body were water. Love, then, is quite naturally and positively connected with the sexual. Minds don't love, nor do hearts. These are abstractions. Whole bodies love, and naturally we want to cuddle, kiss, touch, hold, and feel the literal warmth of the other penetrate our body.

It is a wonderful and a necessary thing to hold your child next to your cheek or heart, to lie down with her at bedtime, kiss good night, perhaps fall asleep together. Such a thing is wonderful for parent, wonderful for child, this big feeling of peaceful security, of belonging and of transcendent warmth. A person can spend a lifetime longing to return to this feeling. In the same way, it is utterly relieving and necessary to fall into the sexual embrace with the beloved, to enter each other with warmth and delight and finally, peaceful release. It takes enormous trust to give yourself in this way, with nothing held back. It's a form of liberation. There's no sense of control, reserve, or separateness. There's no one there who could stand aloof.

I am sure that what I am saying here is so, but I also know that it is not what most of us experience most of the time. Sexuality may be the natural expression of a pure and selfless love, but it is also, in the deep economy of human emotion, chameleonlike; according to inner conditions, it takes on many colors. Clearly, the body only seldom operates in the pure service of selflessness. More often the liberative signals that are always potentially present, because we can at any moment fall in love with the whole world, get distorted by confusion of ego. We become conditioned to see sexuality as a replacement for so much else in our lives that we need but are unable to come into contact with. So sexuality becomes, among other things, a way to express a need for power, a way to avoid loneliness, frustration, or fear. Probably nothing produces more self-deception, and when sexuality is deeply self-deceptive, it becomes dark and is the source of enormous suffering.

The Buddha respected sexuality very deeply, I think, and saw its potential for disaster. He felt that though the spiritual path naturally and beautifully contains an erotic element, the chances for perversion of the erotic are very great. Because of this he taught the practice of celibacy as the path toward love. In fact, I would say that if celibacy is not a loving and warm practice it is not a true celibacy, it is only a justification for a coldness or distance that one naturally prefers, perhaps out of a fear of others. But a true celibate practitioner, because they are not attached to any one or several particular persons, is free to develop a universal love and warmth that includes self and everyone, all held in the basket of the Way.

For those of us who do not or cannot choose a path of celibacy, the challenge is to include our beloved or our family as a part of our practice, as exactly an avenue for the development of wide and broad love for the whole world. The fact is that there is no way that love can ever be narrow or exclusive. There is a tendency to see love in a limited way, as if loving or being loyal to one person or group means we cannot love or be loyal to another. But this is a perversion of love's real nature. Love's salient characteristic is that it is unlimited. It starts locally but always seeks to find through the local the universal. If that natural process is subverted, love becomes perverted: it must either grow or go sour. It can't be reduced or hemmed in.

It is very common, of course, for the initial pure impulse toward love to become reduced, to find ourselves domesticating the beloved, as if they were known and predictable, subject to our needs, possessable. Once this happens there is jealousy, selfishness, disappointment, the desire to control, and the fear of change. What was once love becomes a mutual conspiracy of smallness, and nothing is more common among long-lasting and seemingly successful relationships than this embattled holding on to the past in a way that is usually quite unhappy. It is debatable whether this is preferable to the endless seeking for the perfect mate that goes on among those who see divorce or breakup as the better remedy for inner restlessness.

These are, unfortunately, the usual paths that intimate relationships take, and it is astonishing to me that the power of love and longing for love is such that people keep trying in the face of such painfully poor odds.

The alternative is to see that it is absolutely necessary to practice renunciation within the context of loving relationships. This means that we are willing to give the beloved up, to recognize that we can never really know them, or, in any absolute sense, depend on them, any more than we can depend on our own body or on the weather. They are a mystery and as such unpossessable, so giving them up is not a matter of sacrifice.

If we had our eyes open from the start, we would have seen that the real vision of love was showing us this all along. All things are impermanent, created fresh each moment, and then gone. This being so, the miracle of love between two people, or within a family, is something precious and brief. In fact, any human relationship is brief. We are together for a while and then inevitably we part. To love someone truly is to recognize this every day, to see the preciousness of the beloved and of the time we have together, to renounce any clinging need for or dependency on the other, and to make the effort to open our hands, so that instead of holding on we are nurturing and supporting.

People often wonder how it is possible, in the face of impermanence, to make a commitment to a relationship. It certainly seems logical that we either deny impermanence and assert our undying vow, or accept it and move on as soon as things change. But it is exactly impermanence that inspires commitment. Exactly because things always change, and we cannot prevent that, we give rise to a vow to remain faithful to love, because love is the only thing that is in harmony with change. Love is change; it is the movement and color of the world. Love is a feeling of constancy, openness, and appreciation for the wonder of the world, a feeling that we can be true to, no matter what circumstances may bring.

Although this may sound impossibly idealistic, I believe it is quite practical. To respect the beloved, to give and ask for nothing in return, in faith that what we ourselves need will be provided without our insisting on it too much, may seem like the work of a saint. But I do not think there is any other way. In order to do it we will have to condition our ego, soften its edges, so that it becomes pliable and fearless enough to be open to what comes, and to be permissive, in the best sense of that word, for another. This is the basic spiritual practice.

It seems to me that for most of us, the journey of loving relationship, though quite difficult, is our best chance to develop bodhichitta. In Mahayana Buddhism, this seemingly impossible and unlimited aspiration for the enlightenment of all is the heart of the practice, the beginning and end of it. And it seems only logical that in order to develop a love that big and thorough, it is good if we have somewhere to start, someone to practice on. To really love your lover, partner, husband, wife, or child, taking that on as the most challenging and worthwhile of life's projects, is a noble thing, and it is possible. We know it is possible because we have all felt the compelling force of love at one time or another, even if we have forgotten it.

4

Leaving Home, Staying Home

1997

In the middle of the night, Siddhartha prepares to leave the palace. But as he passes his wife Yasodhara's room and sees her sleeping figure, he is overcome by her beauty and his love for her. He can't leave. He goes to her, without telling her of his resolve, and they make love, conceiving their only child. Yasodhara senses Siddhartha's impending distance. "Lord, wherever you go, take me with you," she pleads. "So be it," he replies, "Wherever I go, I will take you." By morning, he is gone.

From that night on, Gautama's spiritual quest is mirrored by the course of Yasodhara's pregnancy; both go on for six years and culminate during the same fateful night. Both Gautama and Yasodhara, in their very different circumstances, practice austerities, eating only one sesame seed, one grain of rice, and one pulse pod a day. And for both, the period of asceticism is grim and unsuccessful: Gautama nearly dies and Yasodhara almost loses the child. When Gautama accepts solid food again, Yasodhara does too, and the child is saved. Gautama sits under the Bodhi tree full of strength and determination; Yasodhara enters labor. Gautama is then tempted by Mara while Yasodhara, in the palace, receives a messenger from Mara who tells her that her husband has died, and she, overcome with grief, again almost loses the child. But at the moment when the former prince is about to enter enlightenment, Yasodhara hears the truth, recovers, and gives birth to their son, Rahula, at the eclipse of the moon.[1]

B EING HUMAN is a tough proposition. The world is wonderful, colorful and bright; we love it; we want more and more of it. But it is also overwhelming. And embedded within it, as the very essence of its beauty, is the seed of suffering. As the Dhammapada says, the flower is beautiful, but within the flower is an arrow. The world is painful, distracting, seductive. It pulls us in and pulls us down.

But we can't get away from it. Even if we could somehow live in an imagined Shangri-la where we could be quiet, peaceful, and fulfilled (supported, I suppose, by an inheritance), we would still have ourselves to contend with. We would have escaped the outside world, but not the many worlds inside our minds. Wars, frustrations, disgusts, and rage would still be with us, even if the world was not. And even assuming we could somehow subdue all of this and find contentment, I think we would soon discover that that contentment was shallow—and, ultimately, boring. Which would soon turn us toward the world again, but maybe now, wiser and deeper, we would understand the world differently: perhaps as, potentially, a sacred place, a field for the activity of our deeper life, our spiritual practice.

Sacred means set apart. Special. Exclusive. Different. There's a built-in difficulty here: for it seems as if the sacred, to be the sacred, must scapegoat the profane. This is what we object to in the idea of the sacred: its inherent elitism, its demonization of the ordinary, the regular.

But perhaps there is another way to look at it. What is separate or exclusive is also particular and distinct. It has a strong integrity in and of itself. It is this thing, not some other thing. So perhaps the essence of sacredness is particularity rather than specialness. Perhaps sacredness implies a powerful sense of commitment to something very concrete and specific, involving a certain sense of devotion to that specific thing, of vowing, of letting go of things outside the vow, outside the particular, of giving ourselves completely to one thing.

Through such devotion to the particular, the sacred, we open up our lives: this is, I think, the secret of spiritual practice. Following what might appear to be a narrow path of particularity, we open out at last into the wide field where we can meet everything. Powerful practitioners I have met over the years achieve union with the universal in just this way. These people, through total dedication to a particular thing throughout the course of a lifetime—a relationship, a skill or an art, a practice tradition, or perhaps, most radically, each and every moment of living—have been able somehow to transcend that particular thing. In other words, they've been able to include everything within it, acquiring in the process an ease and a graciousness that looks almost transcendent.

The Sanskrit Buddhist term *tathata* means "thus," "just," "merely," or "as it is" and indicates just the sort of particularity I am talking about. Tathata implies real, true: things as they are, without projections, elaborations, wishes, lies, or dreams. Living in the world as it really is sounds like a good idea—we all aspire to truth rather than falsehood, to accuracy rather than fuzziness—but it is a radical idea that requires more of us than it seems to at first sight, because the world as we know it is nothing other than the world of our projections and confusions, our wishes, fears, lies. The very idea of "myself" is the biggest projection of all, the distorting image through which I see everything.

"Things as they really are" is constantly fading, passing away, coming and going, free of our desires. Things as they are, from a human perspective, require an acute appreciation of loss—total loss, loss of self and loss of world. Buddhism calls this liberation: to be free of clinging to illusions. And this is the shape of the world's sacredness, the union we find within the particularity of each moment of our lives, when we are able to really give ourselves to it. In other words, it is not a question of holding on to the world or transcending it. The real world is its own transcendence, and our human dilemma is conceptual. It is language and thought that imprison us, not the world, not even our own desire. In order to be free, we need to be free in relation to this transcendent world, because there isn't any other way. There isn't anywhere else to go.

———— ▶◀ ————

A monk once asked Yunmen, "When there's no thought inside and no thing outside, what is it?" Yunmen replied, "Upside down!"

What thought inside? What world outside? We long for peace, but there's no peace outside activity. We want to hold on to the world, but the whole world in its real form is nothing but loss, fading, moment by moment. And there's no hope that this is going to be different. There's only the appreciation of it as it is. With this appreciation we can once and for all respond to conditions as they arise. With this point of view the whole world and our particular place within it is the field for our practice.

So what do we do with this world? What do we do in it? Didn't the Buddha, facing a choice, leave home, renounce the world and his family, and devote himself to a life of dedication to dharma? And what about us? Are we as serious about our lives as he was about his?

The story of the Buddha's renunciation comes to us through the Theravada Buddhist canon, one of several versions of the canon that were handed down in the various schools that existed after the Buddha's time. That this particular version of the story is the one that has been given to us in the West is simply a historical accident. It is not the "official" version, nor is it in any way the best or the truest version. It is simply the one we happen to have given our attention to over the years.

There's a radically different version of the renunciation story (condensed above, to open this essay), which exists in the canon of the Sarvastivadins, another major early school. In the Theravadin version of the story the Buddha leaves home disgusted with the worldly life of pleasure and debauchery. In the Sarvastivadin story he leaves with great reluctance. Far from oppressed by his family, he is, instead, deeply in love with his wife, and sad to part from her. And so, on the night of his departure, he cannot help making love to her one last time, and they conceive that night their only child. From that night forth, the story proceeds remarkably and mythically along a dual track. All of the events of Buddha's quest are matched exactly by the course of Yasodhara's pregnancy, which, like Buddha's journey, lasts for six years! In the Theravadin version of the story the word *rahula* is etymologized as "fetter," but in the Sarvastivadin version the word is said to derive from the word meaning "moon god," because the dual climax event of the Buddha's enlightenment and Rahula's simultaneous birth takes place on the night of the lunar eclipse.

This story, as I understand it, is about sacred particularity and the loss—and the great gain—it entails. The Buddha must leave home; Yasodhara must stay. They give each other up, so that each might pursue their own path with full devotion. Inner birth and outer birth ensue. In translating this story, John Strong comments that its literary structure makes it clear that it is not simply about, on one hand, the Buddha and his solitary heroic spiritual quest and, on the other hand, the woman he leaves behind. The story, Strong contends, is clearly presented as a single whole, a narrative with two halves joined. The implication is that the Buddha's spiritual achievement isn't something that happens to him or is effected by him alone. Nothing in the way the story is structured privileges Siddhartha over Yasodhara. What's being indicated is that it is the whole narrative—the outer physical birth and the inner spiritual turning—that describes the path in its fullness. Leaving home and staying home, renouncing the world and accepting the world, must go together. Any life is a single particular life. One stays home, one leaves home. And yet both include the other. And must. Our human path is particular, and it must involve renunciation: I will be myself, not you; I will walk where I walk, not where you do. And yet my particularity can and must include all of life.

In the story, the Buddha is a renunciate. But so is Yasodhara. The Buddha gives up the home life, but Yasodhara gives up the homeless life. Together, through loss of each other and devotion to the particularity of their own paths, they create the whole of the great Way. Both appreciate and express the world as it really is.

5

Stages of Monastic Life

1997

RELIGIOUS TEXTS make monastic life sound deep and constant, a life that has been the same for a thousand years, timeless and seamless. Of course, this can't be true: everything changes. Traditions aren't eternal. However slowly, they always change, even when no one wants them to. On the other hand, maybe there is a reason we think of monastic life this way: maybe underneath who any of us are is another person, the monastic, who is living—or who, at any rate, aspires to live, imagines it is possible to live—a true and perfect human life. I believe all of us have this monastic in us. However noisy and excitable we are, I think we all have, someplace in us, a deep longing to live this life of silence and perfection. What a relief—and how beautiful—it would be! When we're completely out of touch with this wish, as most of us usually are, we suffer. We run around looking for something we can't seem to find, and our lives don't work out. When we are in touch with it, as we are in a retreat or even in a few moments of meditation practice or at the beach or alone under the stars, we feel whole. And we can approach others and the complicated world with a measure of equanimity.

So this monastic life, this way of silence and wholeness, this sacred way, this ideal, lives at the bottom of our hearts and is reflected back to us in reverie, religious experience, and religious literature. But ideals, when we mistake them for concrete realities, can be poisonous. Ideals inspire us to surpass ourselves; to be fully human we need them, but of course we never do surpass ourselves, we remain imperfect. Religious ideals inspire us to keep on trying, and failing, with sincere good spirit. The fact that we have so often missed this point accounts, I think, for the sorry history of religion. In the name of ideals, we berate ourselves and others for not measuring up. We even kill people to improve their chances of becoming perfect!

The monastic life appears in the texts of religious traditions as the ideal way to live. In perfect obedience. Perfect peace. Perfect gratitude and silence. In deep meditation or prayer, in harmony and calmness in the quiet mountains among the clouds and forests, or in rolling hills under sunny skies.

Maybe it really is like this someplace on earth—or someplace inside our imaginations—but in conscious life it never is.

What is the monastic life really like? I spent many decades living in semimonastic compounds at the San Francisco Zen Center temples. Our communities are not monasteries in the traditional sense: we do not take lifetime vows of celibacy, poverty, or stability. But over the years in conversation with many monastics from other traditions, I have found that the rhythms, issues, joys, and sorrows I have experienced in these communities are virtually identical to those of traditional monastics.

Here is what I have discovered as possible "stages" of monastic living over time, the changes that occur, the problems that arise. Of course, none of what I am about to say is true: there are no stages that occur in precise sequence, and no two communities or individuals are alike. No setting-forth of stages or general descriptions of what happens could possibly do justice to the variety of people's experiences on the path; yet, systematic thinking has its virtues, and there are some general tendencies most of us can notice and recognize.

———— ▶◀ ————

So: eight stages of monastic life. First, the honeymoon; second, the disappointment or betrayal; third, the exploration of commitment; fourth, commitment and flight; fifth, the dry place; sixth, appreciation; seventh, love; and finally, letting go of monastic life altogether.

The first stage, the honeymoon, is probably typical of the first stage of almost anything we are attracted to, a time when we're really thrilled with the life of the monastery. It's moving; it's perfect; we can't believe how lucky we are to have found such a place. The contrast with what we had become used to in the world, or what we're fleeing from in the world, is so great that we're in a state of constant delight. Our fellow monastics are so kind and wonderful! The sounds of the monastery bells, the simple hearty food, the early morning meditation, the landscape, the weather, the brilliant teachers and teachings, nothing could be better. We're learning every day so much about ourselves; we are delighted by the teachings we hear, they seem absolutely true, they reflect what we have always sensed inside ourselves all our lives without ever really being aware of it or having words for it. We feel relieved and renewed, as if suddenly and unexpectedly, perhaps in the midst of a great sorrow, we turned around in the middle of our life and found to our amazement a new life in which all the old assumptions and behaviors were turned upside down.

This stage may last for some time, but it usually comes to an end in fairly short order and we enter the second stage, the stage of disappointment or betrayal. This stage commences when we start to forget about what we are escaping, the craziness of the world, and begin to get used to this new world in which we are living. All the problems we thought we had escaped—because we thought they were problems in the world and not in ourselves—now appear all over again. This is a shock. And rather than see these problems for what they are, our own internal contradictions, we are so disappointed that they have not disappeared—when we were sure they would, and had—that we don't take them as our own: we project them outward onto the community.

We begin to notice the community's many imperfections and limitations. The food gets tiring. The work seems repetitive and boring; no creativity, no challenge, no appreciation from others for what we do. The people aren't as nice as they seemed at first. They are grumpy, inscrutable, imperious, and worse. Many of them seem clearly disturbed: and how is this possible in a pure monastery? The early rising, the sleep deprivation, the many large and small restrictions on our lifestyle—there's no space! no time!—become grating, we seem to be literally wearing down to a nub. We notice a lack of creativity and energy in our fellow practitioners, especially in some of the old-timers. And we begin to notice many baffling and unacceptable aspects to the teachings. In fact, on the one hand, the teachings sound purposely confusing and incomprehensible, and on the other hand, they may sound suspiciously like the religion we grew up with and fled from. And the teachers turn out to be a lot less fantastic than we first imagined. We're seeing them stumble and make mistakes, and if we haven't seen it we've heard about it. If we haven't heard about it or seen it then the teachers appear a little too perfect—there's something suspicious and even coercive about their piety. Are they really real? Little by little a sense of disillusionment, of betrayal, comes over us. We thought this was something it turns out not to be. And why didn't anyone warn us?

All of these perceptions, as disturbing as they are, have some truth to them, so when we bring them up, no one tries to talk us out of them. Old-timers in the community may become defensive, but they can't really disagree. Yet the truth of all this doesn't really account for what we're feeling: cheated and disappointed. The only thing that accounts for that is our inner pain. We were feeling, for a moment, better, as if finally we had found what we were looking for, and now we feel worse than before. Because if this doesn't work as the perfect life, what does? If we are lucky, we eventually realize that shabby though the community is (and it may in some ways even be toxic), it's us, not the community, that is the source of our present suffering. This will be harder to see if there are, as there have been in many communities of all religious traditions over the years, flagrant cases of betrayal by leaders, and we come to realize the obvious fact that the whole community, knowingly or unknowingly, must have colluded in that betrayal.

Whether it comes soon or only after many years, and whether its causes are spectacular or quiet, this sense of betrayal and disappointment is something we have to come to on our own. Because when we're deeply disappointed with the community, it's hard for long-term committed community members to point out that it's our eye, not the visual object, that's cloudy. They can't tell us this because they know we won't hear it; they also know that if they tell us this, they will appear to be defending the status quo and we will mistrust them for it. And besides, many of them don't understand that this is the case anyway; many of them are themselves confused about the community and where it and they begin and end. So, for all these reasons, the older members of the community tolerate us and our views, and there is very little they can do to help us through this stage. If we feel this sense of betrayal or disappointment acutely enough, and especially if a difficult personal incident happens to us when we are in the midst of it, we may very well leave the community in a huff, which happens, though seldom, and when it does it's a real tragedy. If this doesn't happen and enough time goes by, we usually realize what's really going on.

We begin to see that a lot has been going on in our lives that we were simply unaware of. We came to the community to find peace, to live in a kind of utopia where we will become enlightened and our problems will end. Few of us actually think these thoughts this baldly, but most of us have some unexamined version of them in our minds as we arrive. But instead of utopia we find an extremely flawed community; and instead of the imperfect people we figured we were, we find, in the stillness and intensity of the practice, that we are a raging mass of passion, confusion, hatred, and contradiction. Enlightenment—or whatever illusions we had about such a thing—is very far away. In other words, we feel worse off now than when we began, and we have to acknowledge that the job we've undertaken is much larger than we thought.

So we enter the third stage, to explore honestly, and without our former idealism, the actual nature of our commitment to the practice and to the community. This is a very difficult thing to do because we now have access to our mind much more than we did before, and we can see the full extent of our doubt, grief, and confusion. Some days we are sure we want to practice forever, to take vows as a lay or priest practitioner, to devote ourselves completely to the path—there's absolutely nothing else to do. Other days we can hardly wait to get out of this crazy place. There are so many other things we want to—need to!—do.

This is really a difficult stage, and it can go on for some time. In fact, it *should* go on for some time. If we commit ourselves to that path too soon, it may well be because we haven't listened to ourselves enough. Sometimes people leave at this stage and really shouldn't have; sometimes they make commitments that they regret having made. So it's good to take your time, be willing to live in the uncertainly for a while, and seek advice from teachers and other senior and junior students. Even though the advice doesn't help all that much: we've got to come to what we come to on our own. Sometimes following the view of someone else whom we admire can be a big problem, so our elders have to be careful to be sensitive to what they're hearing from us, and not to impose their wishes and views on us. Nevertheless, their advice can serve as a useful, and probably a necessary, mirror.

The fourth stage I call commitment and flight, which sounds like an oxymoron but is, I think, a good name for it. In this stage we have come to find solid ground under our commitment. We accept our wobbling and human mind and know now that underneath it there is something reliable, although we are often out of touch with it. Looking back, we can see how much we've changed since we entered the practice; we see how much we are the same too, of course. We are calmer. We are quieter in our spirit and less apt to fly off the handle inside or outside. Not as solid or as calm as we had hoped to be, but we have by now given up that hope as unrealistic and we are more able to settle for how it actually is with us, and to find it good, or at least acceptable, with a degree of joy. So we feel ready to make a commitment to the practice and the community.

This commitment can only take one form: renunciation of some sort, a giving-up of self and personal agenda, as we see that self and personal agenda don't, in fact, help us to get what we want and really need in our lives. They only cause suffering. As this becomes more and more apparent, we are more willing to enter into a serious commitment to the practice. In fact, after a while we feel that without even choosing to do so we have already done so. There isn't any other way. We are committed; we have renounced our life. At this point we find ourselves chosen to take on responsible community positions; we make practical commitments to stay in the community for some time; we take initiation as a priest or lay practitioner. We feel responsible for the community.

But as soon as we feel settled in our commitment, particularly if that commitment is marked by a particular event such as ordination or entering the monastery on a long-term basis, the demons of confusion return. Immediately our old interests and desires come back in force. Maybe we fall hopelessly in love the day before we are to go off to the monastery for an indefinite stay, or maybe we find ourselves roaring drunk two days after our ordination as a priest. Such things happen. They catch us quite off guard. We had thought we had the thing figured out, but there were still a fair number of unopened doors in our heart. The power of the commitment we are now making is such that it violently throws open those doors, and we are shocked at what we find inside. We are humbled by the sheer power of our own, and therefore of human, passion. Humbled, shocked, and amazed.

Sometimes our teacher and elders seem very knowing when this happens to us. They may even have a chuckle over it. This can be either comforting or maddening, depending on our temperament. At this stage sometimes there literally is flight. People take off, disappear overnight, run off with a lover, leave the monastery in the middle of the night. But more often it's an internal drama. You see it in people's faces, a kind of grim determination mixed with a very pure innocence, even if the person is middle-aged or older when this happens. The power and surprise of these feelings is enough to send any of us back to square one, with almost no identity left. In fact, the work of this stage is the reconstitution of identity. This is why we often feel like children now, like babies; and this feels wonderful and terrible at the same time. Because we thought we were grown up, we thought we were advancing.

This uncomfortable state is cured only with the passage of time. Time heals, as the old saying goes. Unless we stick obsessively to a bad or limited past, and stop time from doing its work. But those who get this far in the practice usually have enough awareness inside and enough support outside to avoid this trap, and do allow time to soothe and smooth, so that after a while they settle into their new commitment, go beyond the childlike stage, and begin to mature. They reconstitute their lives. They take on new practices, new studies, deepen their dharma relationships, let go of aspirations, fantasies, and illusions. More time passes.

The fifth stage, the dry place, we get to bit by bit without knowing it. Because we are never perfect in our letting-go to the healing winds of time. In a subtle way we hold on to our life even while we have given it up entirely in renunciation. We don't really escape our ancient conditioning. This subtle fact is not announced to us in a dramatic way, and we may not notice it. We go on practicing sincerely, seemingly going deeper and deeper with our renunciation, becoming more and more settled in the life of the dharma. But this becomes exactly the problem. We are too settled. We seem to be getting a little bit dull, a little bit bored. We've lost the edge of our seeking and searching mind and are feeling fairly comfortable. We have a position in the community, we are an experienced person, a respected member. We have a good grasp of the teachings, or at least we have heard them so often that we seem to grasp them. We can't go back into our old life, and yet there seems nowhere to go forward to. We are stuck.

Fear arises. Fear of never realizing or even glimpsing the path; fear of the world we have left behind; fear of what we ourselves have become. Sometimes none of this surfaces. We go about our business in the monastery, feeling OK, but actually dying a little bit more every day. Up until now our path may have been difficult at times, yet we have always been growing and learning. But at this point we have few difficulties and we have stopped growing and learning. This is exactly the problem. And we have mistaken the laziness or dullness that covers our fear for the calmness that comes of renunciation. It's true that our mind is calm, but it is a dark rather than a bright calm. Our creativity, our passion, our humanness, is beginning to leave us, little by little, and often we have no idea that this is happening.

This is the hardest stage to appreciate and cope with. Often no one, not even the elders and teachers of the community, can recognize that this is happening to us. Indeed, those very elders and teachers may themselves be in the midst of such a stage and be unaware of it. In this stage what we have seen as the cure for our lives, what everyone in the community has affirmed and has devoted their lives to, now becomes the very poison that is killing us off slowly.

I have tried to discern the signs of this stage in myself and in others, and it is not an easy thing to do. In oneself it may be too subtle to notice, and though it is easier to see in others, they do not want to hear about it from you. To overcome this stage might very well mean leaving the community or otherwise doing something very radical to shift the ground. And most of us have a hard time, after going in a particular direction for ten or twenty years, a direction that has involved great effort and sacrifice, changing direction. Our fear, acknowledged or not, holds us back. And we may stay this way for a very long time, perhaps for the rest of our lives. This kind of thing can happen to anyone in any walk of life.

Still, a religious community, unlike many other communities, has a strong and explicit commitment to awareness and truthfulness, so when it happens within such a community, even if only to a few individuals, it is like a disease infecting the community. The effect of the disease can be felt in many ways. There can be a subtle occlusion in the flow of communication, an almost imperceptible dishonesty, a jarring or not so jarring disjunction. Even though no one may recognize that a failure to discern the effects of this stage in a few community members is the cause of the disjunction, people can feel it. So it is very important for each individual to remain open to the possibility that this dry place may be arising in their life, and to have the courage to address it when it comes, so that it will become an opportunity to go deeper, and open up to time's healing power, and the love that comes only in this way.

If we can pass through the dry place—which is always done in the company of and with the help of others, and usually occurs spontaneously, for no reason at all—there is an opening into the simple joy of living the religious life every day. Even when the monastery has great controversies and problems, as any group of people will have, these no longer have a stickiness that catches us. We can enjoy being with the others but don't need to feel compelled by them. The quiet meditation periods, the daily work, the sky and earth of the place where we live and practice, all of these things take on a great depth of peacefulness and contentment. We come to appreciate very much the tradition to which we now truly belong, we feel a personal connection to the ancients whom we see as people very much like ourselves. Texts that formerly seemed arcane or luminous now seem biographical. We are grateful for the place where the monastery is located, for the people now and in the past who founded and support it. Our life becomes marked by gratitude. We delight in expressing it wherever and in whatever way we can. This is the sixth stage, the stage of appreciation.

Little by little this appreciation, which begins as a religious gratitude and is private and quiet and joyful, becomes more normal and ordinary. We begin to take a greater interest in the practicalities of caring for the monastery, and in doing so we begin to notice how marvelous are all the people with whom we are practicing. We see their many faults, of course, just as we see our own faults, which remain numerous. But as we forgive, and are even grateful for our own faults, we forgive and are grateful for the faults of others. We see others as they are, but despite this—or because of it—we love them, as we love the sky and the trees and the wisdom of our practice tradition. This love is different from the love we have known before, because this love doesn't include much attachment. We are willing to let people, places, and ideas go. In fact, this willingness to let go is the most essential part of our love. We know that we will eternally be with these people and that wherever we go we will see these same people, even if we never see them again. So we don't need to fear or worry. We are willing to see them grow old or ill, and die, and to care for them and to bury them and to take joy in doing this. We cover the grave with some dirt and chant a sutra and walk away full of the joy of knowing that even in the midst of our sadness nothing has been lost, no one has gone anywhere. A beautiful life that was beautiful in the beginning and in the middle has become even more beautiful in the end, even to the point of perfection. The brother or sister whom we are burying is Buddha, and how privileged we have been for so long to have lived with them, and to be able to continue to live with them in memory and in the tiny acts of our own lives in the monastery. And we know that soon we will go that way too, and that in doing so we can benefit others, and give to others what we have been given in the passing of this brother or sister. This is the seventh stage, the stage of love.

The eighth and final stage—although I must repeat here that there are, in fact, no neat stages, that the stages are simultaneous, spiraling, both continuous and discontinuous—is the stage of letting go of everything, even of the practice. At this stage there isn't any practice or teaching or monastery or dharma brothers or sisters. There's only life in all its unexpectedness and color. We can leave the monastery or stay, it doesn't matter. We can be with these people or any people or no one. We can live or die. We clearly want to benefit others, but how could one not benefit others? We certainly have plenty of problems, a body, a mind, a world, but we know that these problems are the media of our life as we live it. There isn't much to say or do. We just go on, seeing what will happen next.

———— ▶◀ ————

Perhaps the foregoing imaginary sketch of the stages of monastic life is also a sketch of the human heart on its journey to wholeness, whether we live in a monastery or not. Yet monastic life brings the journey more sharply into focus, for that is what it is designed for. I believe that monasteries should be open to all of us for at least some time in our lives, because, as I said at the outset, all of us have a monastic inside us, who is essential to our being who we are, and if we don't find a monastery for her to live in, for at least a week or a month some time in her life, we might miss her altogether, and that would be a shame. If you are lucky enough to spend some time in a monastery to internalize and make your own the schedule and the round of monastic life, you take that deep pattern and rhythm with you wherever you go. The world itself can be your monastery when the monastery is within your heart. But this takes time, patience, luck, and the kindness of others, and the world.

6

Wash Your Bowls

2005

THERE'S AN OLD Zen story that I like very much: A monk comes to the monastery of the storied master Zhaozhou. Diligent and serious, the monk asks for instruction, hoping for some esoteric teaching, some deep Buddhist wisdom, or, at the very least, a colorful response that will spur him on in his practice. Instead the master asks him, "Have you had your breakfast yet?" The monk says that he has. "Then wash your bowls," the master replies. This is the only instruction he is willing to offer.

Although the Zen master's response might seem gruff, odd, and cryptic, it actually makes a fundamental point. Zhaozhou wants to bring the monk back to the immediate present. "Don't look for some profound Zen instruction here," he seems to be saying. "Open your eyes. Just be present with the actual stuff of your ordinary, everyday life"—in this case, bowls.

Like the monk in the story, I came to San Francisco Zen Center years ago with huge metaphysical concerns. A student of literature, philosophy, and religion, I was full of questions about what was real, what was right, what was enlightenment, what was consciousness. The world that I had inherited from my parents, in which so much was taken for granted, no longer seemed tenable. Everything was up for grabs. I came to the Zen center propelled by this spirit, and I was willing to go to almost any length, do anything—meditate, read texts, practice austerities, listen to lectures—to answer my all-consuming questions.

But my questions seemed to have little to do with Zen as it was presented to me. Instead of engaging in study and discussion (the only modes of discovery I knew at the time), I learned how to mop the floor, wash the dishes, tend the garden. It was good training for me. Actually, it was exactly what I needed. As this experience grounded me, my metaphysical concerns began to be settled. The answers I was looking for were not to be found in spiritual teachings, enlightenment flashes, or meditative states—although there were enough of these over the years to keep me going. Little by little, through tending to the daily life of the temple, I began to breathe and feel my answers bodily instead of knowing them intellectually.

I did receive some Buddhist instruction, of course. I heard about impermanence, about emptiness, about nirvana. But more often I heard about simply being present, with body and mind fully engaged. Once, during a meal in the middle of a long retreat, my teacher began speaking in a grave tone, as if he were about to explain the secrets of the universe. "When you eat the three-bowl meal during retreat," he intoned, "you should eat a little out of the first bowl, then eat some from the second bowl, then eat from the third bowl, and then go back to the first bowl. This is the best way to eat."

Over and over again throughout Zen literature, we read of students approaching their masters with complicated matters, only to be brought down to earth. "What is Buddha?" a student asks. "The cypress tree in the courtyard!" the master replies. "What is the Way?" "A seven-pound shirt!" Like the teachers of old who saw that their students' existential concerns could best be met here on earth rather than high up in the clouds, my teachers grounded me and helped me to keep my balance. "It's right here in front of your nose," they told me.

——— ▶◀ ———

The word *Zen* means meditation, and meditation is certainly the best-known Zen practice. But meditation is not mere spiritual contemplation. In the Soto Zen tradition that I follow, teachers continually stress the actual mechanics of sitting on the cushion. We are not given lofty objectives, mantras, or deep koans on which to meditate. Instead the instructor talks about the details of physical posture, the alignment of ears and shoulders, the correct position of hands and arms, the placement of hips and knees. The instruction is so physical, so specific, that one might well wonder when the "Zen" part begins. But this is the Zen part. To pay attention to the body in all its details, to be present with the body in its physical immediacy—*this* is the practice, and the depth of the practice derives from it.

This emphasis on the physical as the fountainhead of the spiritual extends to all aspects of Soto Zen monastic life. "Careful attention to detail" is the motto of the school. As Zhaozhou instructed, monks are to be careful of their bowls, their robes, their shoes. The temple work is considered not a necessary and unfortunate series of chores, but rather an opportunity to realize the deepest truths of the tradition. Zen monastics clean the temple inside and out daily, wet-wiping the wood of the pillars and floors, raking leaves, cutting wood, drawing water. None of these maintenance jobs differs in any way from sutra chanting, text contemplation, or meditation itself. All is physical; all is immediate; all is the stuff of enlightenment. Meaning comes not so much from what you understand as from the way you do whatever it is you are doing.

The daily schedule usually calls for a period of mindful, silent cleaning immediately following meditation. Even the maintenance shop has a Buddhist altar in it. Tools are to be handled with respect and put away in their proper places—not *after* the work is done, but as an integral part of the work. Monks sew their own robes and are enjoined to care for them as sacred vestments. Bowls used for eating in the meditation hall are to be handled "as if they were Buddha's own head." The head monastic not only gives lectures and meets privately with students; he or she is also in charge of taking out the garbage and cleaning the toilets. These traditional assignments are seen as holy tasks to be undertaken with full respect and honor. (An old koan: "What is Buddha?" "A shit stick!") For students in training, the sight of the head monastic diligently carrying garbage pails or wielding a toilet brush is as much a part of their teaching as the words uttered in the dharma hall.

Soto Zen temples are especially devoted to kitchen work. In our center, for instance, there is a "knife practice": knives are always washed immediately after use rather than being placed in a sink for washing later on. (Someone might get cut.) There is also a "counter-cleaning practice" (wiping down with vinegar at the end of each work period), a "cutting-board practice" (different boards carefully stacked in different locations for fruit, onions, and other foods), and a "chopping practice" (specific ways of holding the knife and the food to be cut for various styles of chop). All of these teach the practitioner that the manner in which something is accomplished is just as important as the result—if not more so.

In the training period, too, Zhaozhou's words about bowls are taken quite literally in *oryoki*, formal Zen eating practice. Monastics take all of their meals with great formality in the meditation hall, eating out of a set of three bowls, which are wrapped ceremonially in cloths, often hand-sewn by the practitioner. The choreography of managing the cloths, laying out the chopsticks and spoons, receiving the formally served food, chanting, eating, and, yes, washing out the bowls with the hot water offered, is truly prodigious. It takes years to master and feel comfortable with the practice, but when one does, one finds the movements enjoyable and beautiful. What previously seemed fussy, complicated, and arbitrary, now, having fully entered into the fingers and palms of the hands, seems lovely in its quiet grace. Like playing the piano, which requires much clumsy exercise before fluency is achieved, the physical acuity of simply eating a meal is transformed through oryoki into a profound religious act.

Far from offering a means to transcend the material world, the process of Zen practice deepens and opens the material world, revealing its inner richness. This is accomplished not by making the physical world symbolic nor by filling it up with explanations or complications, but simply by entering it wholeheartedly, on its own terms. When you do that, you see that the material world is not superficial or mundane. What is superficial and mundane is our habit of reducing it to a single dimension. Dissatisfied with this flat view of the material world, we look elsewhere for depth.

Seeing the material world as it really is, we recognize that it's no different from the highest spiritual reality. For where is spiritual reality if it isn't right here in the material realm, bleeding through space and time at every point? Zen training is an effort to enter the material world at such a depth and to appreciate it. As the story of Zhaozhou indicates, the way to see the material world in all its fullness is to be present with it and to take care of it: "Wash your bowls!"

———— ►◄ ————

Once, not long after I was ordained as a Zen priest, I visited my cousin in Miami. An oral surgeon, my cousin is good at what he does and consequently rather wealthy. He is also quite enamored of cars. When he takes a fancy to a particular kind of car, he buys several, so that he typically has a small fleet of the same model, in different colors and with slightly different features. On this particular visit, he was taken with the Chevrolet Corvette. Tentatively he asked whether I'd like to take a ride in one, and I said sure. He rolled the convertible top down, and we went speeding along in the wonderful warm south Florida weather. I was impressed with the automobile's smooth handling and considerable power, and I enjoyed the ride thoroughly.

On our return, when I expressed my enthusiasm for the car, my cousin was surprised at my reaction. He'd expected that, as a religious person, I'd disapprove of his conspicuous consumption. And maybe I did. But apart from any ideas I had about consumption, I told him, I could appreciate the actual experience of riding in the automobile. "In experiencing the material world," I explained, with all the didactic authority of a newly ordained priest, "there are always two elements at play: the material object—in this case the car, the highway, the scenery going by—and the sense organs and mind that apprehend that object. So-called materialists emphasize the object; so-called nonmaterialists, or religious people, emphasize the sense organs and the mind. But we need both. The key point is, though, that if the mind and the sense organs are acute enough, even a fairly humble object can bring a great deal of satisfaction. Think of how much money I save by practicing Zen: I can get all the satisfaction I need out of just one ride; I don't have to buy the car!"

The truth is, what we call "materialism" isn't really materialistic; it is idealistic. In other words, it is not the objects that we are after in our consuming; it is the ideals those objects represent. Just consider advertising, the function of which is to create an aura of emotion and ideology around an object, so as to make it more desirable than it actually is. In a magazine ad, a van is parked on a gorgeous beach. On one side of the van, a man is reclining. On the other side, a beautiful woman in a bathing suit is lying on the sand with her feet in the sea. A luminous, almost ethereal shaft of sunlight shines through the open doors of the van and onto the woman's face. The setting, the man, the woman, the light—all of this has nothing whatsoever to do with the actual van.

This is a far cry from "wash your bowls," which makes a humble object magnificent not by associating it with desirable images but simply by the act of taking care of it mindfully. Once, the twentieth-century Japanese Zen master Nakagawa Soen Roshi gave a retreat in America. The retreat took place in a rented school building, and there wasn't much kitchenware available for serving meals. The daily schedule included a tea service, and since there were no teacups, paper cups had to be used. On the first day of the retreat, after the tea service, the students began to throw the cups away, but Soen Roshi stopped them. "No!" he scolded. "We need to use these same cups each day. You have to save them." For seven days the students used the same paper cups for tea. When the retreat was over, Soen Roshi said, "OK, now you can throw away the paper cups." But the students wouldn't hear of it. They couldn't possibly throw away the cups. They had become too precious.

My friends are always astonished when I tell them how much I like going to shopping malls, especially at Christmas. I enjoy being around people who are looking for gifts for their loved ones, anticipating a festive meal, happy to be spending lots of money in a celebration of life. I am, of course, aware of the waste and misery that also accompany the holiday season. Yes, the parking lot is too crowded, and yes, the amount of merchandise in the stores is overwhelming. But I can't help it; I still have a good time.

The contemporary American shopping mall may seem like a blight, but such shopping districts are as old as human civilization. I have visited Jerusalem several times and walked through the narrow streets of the Old City. They are now, as they have been for millennia, crowded with shops overflowing with merchandise. I have also spent many happy hours at the great market in Oaxaca, Mexico, where vendors sell all manner of clothing, jewelry, liquor, and food, including that Oaxacan specialty, peppered grasshoppers. Although I don't buy much at any of these places, I enjoy the spectacle of people coming together in one teeming location to purchase material goods they hope will bring pleasure, comfort, and sustenance.

In the end, commerce is a way of helping each other fulfill our human needs. Thirteenth-century Japanese Zen master Dogen says in his essay "The Bodhisattva's Four Methods of Guidance": "To launch a boat or build a bridge is an act of giving. . . . Making a living and producing things can be nothing other than giving."[1]

It is possible for us to buy and sell in a spirit of participation and compassion. We can recognize in material goods an opportunity to meet each other on the ground of our shared human needs.

When you do business with someone, you are entering into a relationship with that person. You could see the relationship as adversarial (who will get the best of whom), but you could just as easily see it as mutual, each of you providing, as fairly and as pleasantly as possible, what the other needs. We could see our customer, our supplier, our shopkeeper, and our banker as friends, people who, like us, want to be happy. To look at commercial life in this way takes sensitivity and mindful awareness. This we can develop by paying attention to our thoughts and responses just as we pay attention to our breath on the meditation cushion.

Paying attention requires that we be honest and realistic about our greed, fear, and confusion. To what extent is our attitude about money connected to our sense of self—our sense of being powerful and important, or weak and unimportant? Clearly, whatever self-esteem, or lack of it, we may have probably exists independently of money. We project these feelings onto money and likely conduct our financial lives in a distorted, or at least an unconscious, way. Perhaps we are just playing out our childhood conditioning. Having grown up deprived, we may worry that there won't be enough. Or, having grown up with plenty, we may feel guilty about owning too much. By observing in detail what we do, say, and feel as we deal with money, we can bring these unconscious and dysfunctional feelings to conscious awareness. Eventually we might be able to view money less as a source of worry, pride, or guilt and more as a means of exchange between people, a convenient device for the distribution of the material goods necessary for living, a way for us to share life together.

To conduct our economic lives mindfully requires us not only to be mindful of our attitudes, the goods we buy, and our relationships to the people who supply these goods, but also to be as informed as we can be about the possible exploitation involved in our purchases, and to use our purchasing power to reinforce justice. When we know that a company is harming its workers, its competitors, or the environment, we simply don't buy its product. When we know that a company is making a conscious effort to offer something useful in as harmless a way as possible, we go out of our way to buy what it sells. When this is our consideration, price and convenience become less important than relationship. We want to give our business to people whose efforts we are interested in encouraging.

Companies change policies constantly, however, and are bought and sold with alarming frequency. The effort to keep informed about the companies we do business with could become too much in the context of the complicated lives we all lead. Knowing that it is impossible to do it perfectly, we can nevertheless do it as perfectly as possible, trusting our intention more than our information. Information in the modern age goes out of date almost as soon as it's gathered. Intention, on the other hand, can remain firm and help keep us on a wholesome course. Although it is shortsighted to trust to intention alone, intention's power to transform the world should never be underestimated.

It seems to me that the world is in need of a new economic theory to replace unrestrained free-market capitalism, which operates on the faith that an "invisible hand," as economist Adam Smith called it, will see to it that things don't get out of control. Free-market capitalists trust that somehow the market (which often seems to take on the proportions of a deity) will, in the end, serve us as well as anything else could, and is less subject to corruption and disaster than other, more rational systems.

In fact, the "invisible hand" has been relatively reliable. Although our world economy is in terrible shape (especially when you consider its ecological costs), it is in miraculously good shape considering its complexity and the fact that it is ruled by people who are motivated by self-interest. Many people starve, but more are being fed every day. And little by little, some of the more enlightened nations are joining together to cooperate for the collective good of the planet.

I don't know if Adam Smith ever proposed a definition of the "invisible hand," but here's mine: it is the sum total of human goodness, of our love for ourselves and each other, and of our hopes for a future that will be more humane than the present or the past. Perhaps we can trust this unseen hand to inspire us to more mindful consumption and production as time goes on, and to discover, eventually, some new organizing principles for our economic life.

7

On Spiritual Friendship

2016

Once the Buddha's disciple Ananda asked him about friendship. Ananda knew that having good and encouraging friends was very important for the path. He even wondered whether having good friends is half the path.

"No, Ananda," the Buddha told him, "having good friends isn't half of the Holy Life. Having good friends is the whole of the Holy Life."

The *Meghiya Sutta* is my favorite Pali text about friendship. It tells the story of the eager young monk Meghiya, who wanted to practice meditation alone in an especially peaceful and beautiful mango grove. But Meghiya's meditation was anything but peaceful and beautiful. To his shock, he found his mind a snarl of malicious, lustful, and confused thoughts—probably because his practice was too self-involved. When Meghiya rushed back to report his confusing experience, Buddha was not surprised. He took the opportunity to give Meghiya what he must have hoped was a relevant teaching.

"Five things induce release of heart and lasting peace," the Buddha told him. "First, a lovely intimacy with good friends. Second, virtuous conduct. Third, frequent conversation that inspires and encourages practice. Fourth, diligence, energy, and enthusiasm for the good. And fifth, insight into impermanence."

Then, for Meghiya's further benefit, and to cement the point, the Buddha goes through the list again, this time preceding each of the other items with the first: "When there is a lovely intimacy between friends, then there is virtuous conduct," and so on. In other words, friendship is the most important element in the spiritual path. Everything else naturally flows from it.

I appreciate the truth and beauty of this teaching more and more as the years go by. To be able to practice with good friends for five, ten, twenty, thirty, or forty years is a special joy. So much comes of it. As you ripen and age, you appreciate the nobility and uniqueness of each friend, the twists and turns of each life, and the gift each has given you. After a while you begin attending the funerals of your dearest friends, and each loss seems to increase the gravity and preciousness of your own life and makes the remaining friendships even more important.

When long friendships with good people along the path of spiritual practice are a central feature of your life, it is almost impossible —just as the Buddha says—for spiritual qualities conducive to awakening not to ripen. For those on the bodhisattva path, loving and appreciating your friends, even when they are difficult, as they sometimes are, is the path's fullness and completion. Friendship ripens and deepens our capacity for compassion.

These days we talk a lot about "relationships." The word usually suggests romantic relationship, but we might also mean our connections with parents, children, siblings, and colleagues. But we don't hear so much about friendship.

Yet friendship may be the most wonderful form of human relationship. Emerson called it "the masterpiece of Nature." That we and our friends can communicate intimately with one another and support each other unselfishly come what may—this truly is a masterpiece of nature, and one of our brightest human achievements. It is also, I believe, our best hope in troubled times. When things are tough, having a trusted friend to help shoulder the burden makes survival not only infinitely more possible, but also much lovelier.

In his essay on friendship, Emerson writes, "The laws of friendship are great, austere, and eternal, of one web with the laws of nature and of morals . . . but we seek our friends not sacredly but with an adulterated passion."[1]

In other words, most friendship falls short of the spiritual friendship the Buddha is referring to in the *Meghiya Sutta* and Emerson takes as his ideal. We are looking for something from the other person—entertainment, sympathy, some kind of support. Unable to stand the fullness of the other, we don't want to discover and offer our own.

"Almost all people descend to meet," Emerson says. "What a disappointment is actual society!" Real friendship, he says, includes the depth of solitude of each of us. Real friendship is profound. Real friendship is always spiritual.

Perhaps Emerson is a bit too idealistic. I feel that ordinary friendship is good, as far as it goes. We come together out of mutual interest, attraction, or social necessity. We need people to talk to and to play with. This is normal and healthy. There's joy in it. And we do care about one another.

Yet spiritual friendship—the friendship the Buddha called the whole of the Holy Life and that Emerson considered true friendship—is different.

—————— ▶◀ ——————

In the Buddhist path, spiritual friendship takes place in the context of community. Life in a sangha is built on teaching, dedicated meditation practice, and a shared commitment to going beyond self-interest and personal need.

Spiritual friendship is less about personal connection than it is about helping one another grow in faith and goodness—to realize, as we say in Zen, our true nature. Sangha friendships are forged and grounded in silence. This is especially true in the Soto Zen tradition I practice, which emphasizes meditation as a shared activity over a long period of time.

In ordinary friendships we might connect right away, with lots to share and learn from one another. In sangha life, friendship develops much more slowly. It may take years to share backgrounds and personal stories. Maybe we never do.

But in the meantime, we slowly get to know one another intimately in the silent space of the meditation hall. We know each other's hands and feet and facial expressions, how we walk and stand and sit. We see the suffering and the triumph expressed in body language and facial expression. We share the sound of our voices joined in chanting. We hear our groans, our fatigue, the ways we cope when we don't have our usual social strategies available.

Often the most unlikely people show up in Buddhist communities, people who under ordinary circumstances would never meet and spend weeks, maybe years, together. Yet this disparate group of people manages to find harmony, commonality, and deep mutual appreciation despite their differences. They come to share something more fundamental than their interests and affinities.

It's not unusual to be in a community with someone who pushes all your buttons. Exactly the sort of person you'd avoid at all costs in ordinary life will appear in your sangha. There he or she is—your father or sister, childhood nemesis, or ancient school or workplace enemy—sitting right across from you in the meditation hall. You will have to deal with this person in ways you never would have if left to your own devices. And eventually, they become a valued friend.

Emerson and the Buddha both believe that spiritual friendship requires two elements: truth and tenderness. Spiritual friends are honest with one another. They have courage, they take risks, and they speak from the standpoint of truthfulness, not expediency. When my friends go astray, at least as far as I can see, I must speak up. And I expect the same from them as well.

Yet tenderness is equally important. Dogen writes of the power of kind speech: "Speak to sentient beings as you would to a baby"—speak with that much tender love and sweetness. I can receive a true friend's criticism with loving-kindness because it comes from a loving heart seeking only my benefit and well-being. And if I find

I am lacking in tenderness, speaking what I consider to be truth out of defensiveness or separateness, I have to discern this. I have to work on healing the causes within myself of this breach of kindness. I need to keep my peace until I am ready to speak with love.

We often think of spiritual teachers as parents or authority figures. Maybe we think of them as coaches or trainers. But in the Mahayana sutras, teachers are referred to as kalyanamitras—spiritual friends. They are people who see us as we are, love us anyway, and care absolutely for our ultimate welfare.

A teacher's job is to model spiritual friendship. While at first we may be intimidated by the teacher, imagining them to be far more spiritually developed than we are, as time goes on the teacher transforms from a scary boss to a trusted friend. And over time in community life we come to have such inspiring friendships with others who support and love us in the same way. No matter what their background or personal style, anyone with enough proximity in sincere practice becomes a sangha friend. You will treat them with full respect and affectionate regard, and they will treat you the same way.

The Buddha thought of the sangha as a harmonious group of spiritual friends looking out for one another's welfare, living together in full equality for the spiritual development of each one. The early Buddhist sangha was radical in its insistence that anyone, prince or pauper, could join and be fully accepted and equally loved. Rank was established solely on the basis of seniority, without regard to wealth, social position, or even skill in practice.

To this day, Buddhism retains this emphasis on equality and inclusion. To be sure, this ideal isn't always practiced very well. As is well known, women were and still are not included as equals with men in nearly all forms of Asian Buddhism. Convert Buddhist communities in the West are far from free of sexism and are overwhelmingly made up of white middle-class people. We notice this, hope that it will change, and work to make it happen. But it will take time, and many more women teachers and teachers of color.

Still, even as things stand now, we can rejoice in the wholesomeness and inclusivity of our sangha friendships. We can depend on them to support us in hard times. Sometimes we might expect or ask for more emotional or material support from our community than we seem to be getting. But the more we are established in our practice, the more we understand that the support our spiritual friends provide is the most fundamental and the most healing kind: gentle encouragement to awaken.

This is the seventy-eighth case of the *Blue Cliff Record*, a classical compendium of Zen stories:

> In olden times there were sixteen bodhisattvas. When it was time for monks to wash, the bodhisattvas filed in to bathe. Suddenly they awakened to the basis of water. All you Chan worthies, how will you understand their saying, "Subtle feeling reveals illumination, and we have achieved the station of sons of Buddha"?[2]

In big Chan monasteries of China, there were no private bathrooms. The monastics went to a common bathhouse to bathe and use the toilet. The schedule provided for bath time, when everyone filed into the bathhouse to take a bath together in the big tub. We still practice like this at Tassajara Zen Mountain Center. Bath time is late afternoon, after work and before evening service and dinner. Entering the bathhouse, we bow at the shrine and recite the bathing verse. Enshrined on the bathhouse altar is a picture of the sixteen bodhisattvas in the bath. We bathe silently and then put on our robes for service.

This is the only Buddhist story I am aware of in which a fairly large group of people realized awakening together, as good spiritual friends. Sitting chest-deep in the tub, they must have looked around at one another with beautiful smiles of acknowledgment, saying, no doubt, nothing at all.

Mostly we think of awakening as an individual affair. The teachings can make it sound like that. But in Buddhism we practice together, awaken together, and understand together. Together we go forth to do what needs to be done.

In the Mahayana Buddhist teachings, the bodhisattva clearly sees that no one can be happy or content while others are suffering. There is no individual awakening. No one can be happy, no one can be enlightened, unless everyone is happy and enlightened. Self and other are not two truly different existing entities. They are mutually conditioned positions or concepts.

What we call a person is in reality a series of interactions and relationships. There is no atomized, freestanding person. This is completely obvious to the bodhisattvas. That is why love, compassion, and friendship are at the center of the bodhisattva path. That is why the buddha of the coming era is called Maitreya, the buddha of the practice of friendship.

―――― ►◄ ――――

In his essay on friendship, sixteenth-century French writer Michel de Montaigne compares friendship to all other human relationship and finds it superior. Siblings usually fight with one another. Spouses are too emotionally entangled to support each other disinterestedly. Parents and children are too blinded by the psychological weight of their connection to see one another with fully open appreciation. But friends, he writes, share one mind, one heart, and one will. They are for one another even more than a person can be for themself. You can trust your friends to look after your interests more than you can trust yourself, he writes. Nothing is more intimate, nothing more lovely, than friendship.

Montaigne's essay is all the more poignant because in it he tells us that he is not merely theorizing. He is writing in testimony and memorial to the most cherished friendship of his own life—his relationship with the writer Estienne de la Boétie, whose death has left him "feeling like half a person."

In this essay about friendship, I too am giving testimony and memorial to my own great friend of more than forty years, the late Rabbi Alan Lew. We met on the first day of classes at the University of Iowa Writers' Workshop in 1968, before either of us had begun our spiritual practice. After Iowa we moved, independently, to California, where we practiced Zen together for a decade under our teacher, Sojun Mel Weitsman.

When Alan went on to become a rabbi we continued our spiritual friendship, founding a Jewish meditation center (that I still direct, in his name and memory) in San Francisco. For all those years, Alan supported, loved, and respected me more than I supported, loved, and respected myself. His practice and loving heart was, and remains, my inspiration.

In his essay, Montaigne argues that deep friendship is necessarily exclusive—it is only possible, he says, to have one such dear friend—and that exclusivity is its essence. But that isn't the case with spiritual friendship. We can have many dear spiritual friends. Probably the more such friends we have, the more we are capable of having—and the more enriched our lives will become.

Still, with luck, we may have, as I have had, a spiritual relationship that is uniquely precious to us. In an uncanny way, my friendship with Rabbi Lew was not exclusive. Our intimacy was one in which others were always welcome. Because we were such good friends, others were encouraged and inspired to be good friends too.

This is the nature of spiritual friendship. It never depends on division or discrimination between people. Love can't be exclusive. It is boundless, empty, open, and free. Spiritual friendship is too. No doubt this is an ideal we can never completely realize. But I believe it was what the Buddha had in mind when he taught that there is no element of the path more precious or more important than spiritual friendship.

PART TWO

Form Is Emptiness

Notes on Thinking, Writing, and Emptiness

I HAVE ALWAYS had a complicated relationship to thinking; on the one hand, like everyone, I am always thinking. Beyond this, I have been naturally drawn to thinking and reading and writing; it has been one of my lifetime's chief occupations, even though Zen tradition seems to denigrate such activities. As a young person I was interested in religion and philosophy, and have read quite a bit in religion and philosophy over the years, although I forget most of what I read, and have not read very systematically or, probably, carefully. I enjoy reading "difficult" texts (they preserve an aura of "depth"), because reading them feels important, as if I am getting someplace in my ongoing exploration, though I am not sure where. And yet I am quite sure I mostly make up what I read rather than actually understand the words of authors as they intend them. Maybe this is true of most if not all readers (including you, dear reader who is making up this book as you read), but perhaps my case is worse than most.

When I began my Buddhist practice I was, as I have said, metaphysically driven, in search of a truth that would solve my life's dilemmas. I had been pursuing that truth for some time through my various readings and conversations with friends who were also reading, which finally led me to the first English-language books about Zen, which eventually led me to practicing Zen. (It is hard to believe now, but in those days there were no known Buddhist centers in America, and meditation was obscure, so I thought Zen was a philosophy that one accessed through reading. I had been reading about Zen for some years before I discovered Zen meditation existed, and that you could practice it in California. Though many of my contemporaries were at that same time in Asia finding Buddhism, I was too small-town-minded to even conceive of such exotic journeys.)

I say all this because as I read through the essays in this second section, "Form Is Emptiness," I see how philosophical they are. Many of them make an effort to think through (or with) reality, to try to understand, through language and reason, what is going on in this human life, beyond the usual unexamined conceptions.

I wonder how many people find themselves, as I did, philosophically challenged. Perhaps not so many. But at some point I learned by observing my father that whether you think about things or not, everyone is a philosopher.

My father was not what we call an educated person. He graduated from high school in the "commercial" curriculum—not "college prep"—which meant he learned to type and do basic business math. Soon after high school he went off to war and came home several years later to start a family and find work. Like his parents, he had no interest in ideas or books, and when it turned out I did, he was suspicious. He considered that such interests were having a bad effect on me. So for some years I thought of my father as being a normal, well-adjusted person, and myself as being debilitated by my thinking, reading, and questioning. (My father never realized this because I was too stubborn to tell him; instead I resisted, even to the point of scorn, his point of view.) Eventually I saw that my father was also a philosopher, that of course he too had a point of view on life, a way of thinking about things that had been formed by ideas and attitudes beyond his own personal experience, however unexamined they may have been. He didn't need to read the books: their content, their assumptions, were in the air he breathed, and all around him. So yes, we are all philosophers. The question is, how is our philosophy working for us?

For me the emptiness teachings of Mahayana Buddhism were salvific. As soon as I read about them and contemplated them (at first as they appeared embedded in the Zen books I was reading, later in other more explicit texts) I felt cheered up—as if finally I had found a way forward into some kind of life. Philosophy isn't just a set of abstract ideas. It is a point of view. And point of view on life and reality, however much you think about it or don't think about it, matters a great deal. It conditions the way you think, feel, and experience the texture of your life. It conditions your relationships and choices, even your perceptions. This is what, for more than a thousand years, people thought education was for (before we began to think of it as a form of job training): developing your point of view about life, so you could live humanely. Buddhist practice is a fundamental form of education, which is what the essays in this section are about.

In saying all this I don't exactly mean that anyone is going to figure out a philosophy and then go on to live that philosophy. It is all much more vague and impressionistic than that. Long ago, for a master's degree in religious studies, I produced a thesis on the writings of Zen master Dogen, which consisted, in large part, of an analysis of one of Dogen's more difficult works. I remember wrestling for weeks with Dogen's text, trying to comprehend it. Finally I had a breakthrough that enabled me to write for several days without sleeping, certain that what I was writing was entirely correct and brilliant. After getting some sleep, I found that I could not understand my own text, and had to spend many more weeks or months deciphering it. In other words: sometimes it feels like you understand something, sometimes it feels like you don't. Sometimes you can explain and it seems to make sense. But it's not the understanding or the explaining that matters: it's the feeling and the experience of trying to understand, and the effect this has on you.

There were two other reasons the emptiness teachings appealed to me. I had, as I say, metaphysical concerns: I was not looking for a religion or a faith to depend on. I felt fine about the Judaism I was raised in (in no small measure because I had a great rabbi who spent a lot of time with me in my formative years), and although I was not actively practicing it, because it didn't seem relevant at the moment, I had no idea of rejecting it so I could "convert" to some other religion. The emptiness teachings seemed to state clearly that everything, including Buddhism, is empty, so there was no religion I was being urged to join.

The second reason these teachings appealed so strongly was that they were peaceful, noninsistent, unfanatical. Just before plunging full time into Zen I had been, like many others of my generation, intensely political. I was an antiwar activist, had been arrested in protests, fought with police, was on the point of becoming an outlaw; in other words, I had gone as far as I could go with my politics. What next? The emptiness teachings, which neither affirm nor deny, and which emphasize the futility of fixed viewpoints, gave me a way to hold what I saw as true, without obsession or confusion.

People think of the Buddhist emptiness teachings as being abstruse or scary. But to me they are friendly, and light as air. They say that life's heaviness, and the suffering that naturally occurs because of that heaviness, is a pernicious and persistent illusion. Life isn't heavy. We don't need to suffer in the way we think we do.

It's hard to accept this. Human beings seem to have a long-term love affair with personal suffering. As much as we complain about it, and seek all sorts of remedies, we come back to it again and again, because it seems so real to us, and so important. We are like tragically codependent lovers who can't stop coming back to a toxic relationship, no matter how many times it hurts us. I have heard of brain research showing that we're hardwired to react much more strongly to drama and difficulty than to peace and easefulness, though we think we are trying to avoid the former and develop the latter. I recently saw a Facebook post about Rwanda that may or may not be true, though it sounds true. The post said that in response to the trauma of the genocide that happened there, people went outside and spent a lot of time in the sun. They also did

a lot of communal singing and dancing. Then the Western therapists came to help. The therapists had them sit individually in small
dim rooms and encouraged them to recount, again and again, in
detail, the terrible things they had witnessed. The Rwandan people did not see this as a reasonable way to cope, so they sent the
well-meaning therapists home. Maybe they were in denial, I don't
know; certainly in our culture we would say they were. But who
knows? In any case, the emptiness teachings don't offer solutions
to problems we must solve; they tell us that these problems are illusions. This doesn't deny that problems can be solved, and it doesn't
brush them off as trivial or unreal. It simply takes the edge off our
desperation.

As I write in these essays, the emptiness teachings are an extension of the teachings on impermanence, and impermanence is
Buddha, which is love. Things don't last: you could either freak
out about this or embrace it and realize that impermanence makes
everything precious. In this section of the book, as in the last, I
write about my dear friend, my second rabbi, Rabbi Alan Lew, who
died all of a sudden in 2009. I still miss him, and feel in touch with
him; and he is not the only dear friend I have lost. At this point in
my life loss is basic, it is with me every day. Who can avoid loss? To
deeply reflect on and practice the emptiness teachings is to realize
that loss is tender, loss is love, the more loss there is the more love
there is.

And so after all these years it has turned out that the philosophical urges that plunged me into Zen practice were really leading me
back to the most basic of all human emotions, love, simple decency,
and kindness.

————— ►◄ —————

The emptiness teachings also shade necessarily into questions of
language and imagination, two other topics I seem to have been
thinking about for many decades. Things are mere designations,
say the emptiness texts; they are not really existing entities. So

we'd better question our words and resituate ourselves in relation to them! This is, unavoidably, my approach to poetry, odd as it may seem to some: to be aware of the fact that in writing words this is what is going on: the writing of words, which phenomenon is prior to anything one thinks to say in relation to the experiences or things the words propose to refer to. We are language-created creatures. What does that feel like in the midst of the process of language-making, which is self-making? There is something supremely ironic about this task, this writing of a poetry (or, indeed, essays or essay notes) that is at all points shot through with holes and not to be taken seriously as actually referring to something real outside the words themselves and the experience of understanding them.

It seems to me that all uses of language, including almost all thinking, produce imaginary thoughts and experiences; language is an act of imagination. We imagine, through our words and ideas, a world we can live in. We imagine ourselves and one another. And then we think about and write about this imaginary world. It is in some ways wonderful and in other ways dismaying that over these last few centuries of maximum comprehension and manipulation of the physical world, humans have invested so much in the scientific materialist worldview that we have forgotten it is a worldview and not a solid fact. (In saying this I do not, of course, deny scientific fact, which is basic; only the unexamined philosophical assumptions behind it.) And in doing this we have not only put ourselves and so many other creatures of the planet in jeopardy; we have also forgotten how to dream and wonder, how to believe in stories and myths in their true power. If things are empty, it means they are wide open. The great Mahayana Buddhist sutras, which all either are about the emptiness teachings or assume them, are clearly written with enormous expansive extravagance for the purpose of loosening our grip on reality, which is to say expanding us in feeling and view much, much further than the eye can see.

8

Beautiful Snowflakes

2006

FROM THE FIRST time I encountered the word in English, I liked the sound of it: *emptiness*. Some would find it chillingly abstract, even scary. But I took to it immediately. I chanted the *Heart Sutra* ("form is emptiness, emptiness form . . .") alone and with sangha every day for years before I ever bothered to find out what the great teachers of the past meant by emptiness. It didn't matter to me what they meant. I knew what emptiness was.

Of course, I had no clue. But intuitively I knew. I remember once, at the beginning of my practice, wandering in the woods during a blizzard, drifting snow piled two feet high, chanting the *Heart Sutra* over and over again. In the snow, with trees, bushes, and ground covered in white, white, white, and the sky white with whiteness falling down, the sutra's meaning was perfectly clear. It wasn't until much later that I plunged into the vast philosophical edifice of Mahayana Buddhism, from the *Diamond Sutra* and Nagarjuna on, that elucidates this saving and elusive teaching.

The logic of emptiness is wonderfully airtight. Like all simple truths, its clarity is immediately self-evident. We are: and this means that there is no moment in which we can be separate and apart, torn from the fabric of reality: we are always connected— to past, to future, to others, to objects, to air, earth, sky. Every thought, every emotion, every action, every moment of time, has multiple causes and reverberations—tendrils of culture, history, hurt, and joy that stretch out mysteriously and endlessly.

As with us, so with everything: all things influence one another. This is how the world appears, shimmers, and shifts, moment by moment. But if things always associate with and bump up against each other, they must touch one another. If so, they must have parts, for without parts they couldn't touch (they'd melt into one another, disappearing). But the parts in turn are also things in their own right (a nose, part of a face, is a nose; an airplane wing, part of a plane, is an airplane wing), and so the parts must have parts (nostrils, wingtips), and those parts have parts, and so on: an infinite proliferation of parts, smaller and smaller, clouds of them. (This is true of thoughts and feelings as well as physical objects.) If you look closely enough and truly enough at anything, it disappears into a cloud, and the cloud disappears into a cloud. All is void. There is no final substantial something anywhere. The only thing real is connection: void touching void.

This simple but profound teaching is delightful. As a way of thinking and understanding, it is peerless, impossible to confute because it proposes nothing and denies nothing. Appearances remain valid as appearances, and there is no reality beyond appearances, other than the emptiness of the very appearances. So there is nothing to argue for or against! In being empty, everything is free of argument. Lighter than air.

But it is the taste of emptiness in the body, spirit, and emotions that has meant the most to me. Knowing that what happens is just what happens. My body, my thoughts, my emotions, my perceptions, desires, hopes, actions, words—this is the stuff that makes up my life and it is never desperate because I feel its cloud-like nature. That cloud is all I am: it is my freedom to soar, my connection to all. I can float in it, and watch it form and re-form in the endless sky.

This doesn't mean I am disconnected from life, living in a Buddhist nirvana of disassociation. Quite the contrary, I know there is no way not to be connected, no person or place that is beyond my concern.

When I practice meditation, I rest in emptiness: my breath goes in and out, a breath I share with all who have lived and will live, the great rhythm that began this world of physical reality and will never cease, even when the earth is gone. It's nice, in the predawn hours, to sit sharing that widely, knowing that this zero point underlies all my walking and talking and eating and thinking—all activity—all the day through; in fact, it is it.

They say that wisdom (the faculty that cognizes emptiness) and compassion are like the wings of a great bird. Holding both in balance against the wafting winds allows you to float, enjoying the day. Really, though, the two wings are one wing. Where you can appreciate the flavor of emptiness on the tongue you know immediately (without mediation) that love is the only way, and that everything is love and nothing but love. What a pleasant thing to hold in mind! All problems, all joys, all living, and all dying—it's love.

Traditionally, emptiness refers to the fact that phenomena have no "intrinsic existence." This means not that phenomena don't exist but that they don't exist as we think they do, as freestanding, independent, solidly real entities. This is as true of us as it is of the world around us: everything is contingent, not solid, ceasing the moment it arises, moment after moment. Everything is like space, real in its own way, and absolutely necessary, but not something you could put your finger on.

We, of course, don't know this. We are, according to the emptiness pundits of Buddhism, deeply ignorant of the one thing we should not be ignorant of: the real nature of ourselves and the world we live in. "Ignorance," unfortunately, doesn't mean we don't know. It would be better if we didn't know. Ignorance means we know something very firmly, but it is the wrong thing: we know that things are solid and independent and intrinsically existent. But they actually are not. So ignorance is not not-knowing; ignorance is a form of knowing, but it is a mis-knowing. And spiritual practice is the process of coming to see our mis-knowledge and letting it go: to begin to experience, accept, and live the truth about how we and the world actually are. When we begin to understand

and to live in this way, there is a great decrease in the fear and dread, so common in human experience, caused by the huge gap between our expectations and the way things actually are. With an appreciation of the empty nature of things, there are no more foiled expectations. There is a lot more joy, peace, and love.

———— ▶◀ ————

The Buddhist literature on emptiness, the Prajnaparamita, is vast. It includes many sutras that run to many thousands of pages. On top of that, the commentarial literature on the sutras is also vast and intricate, as are the scholastic treatises on the subject. So many words to discuss the voidness of all phenomena—and the fact that words do not actually refer to things the way we think they do! Why so much talk about all this? For most of us, who are simply trying to live our lives with less suffering, all this complicated philosophical discourse is really beside the point. The Buddha said, in so many words, I am not a philosopher; I am a doctor, and the purpose of my teaching is not to explain the nature of reality but simply to offer a path that will lead to suffering's end. Why then did the later Buddhists feel the necessity of producing such vast quantities of metaphysics?

Well, it turns out that it is naive to think that we can treat the human illness without having an accurate view of how things really are. Whether we are aware of it or not, we are all philosophers; we are all living our lives based on philosophical assumptions, however unexamined or even unconscious they may be, and this unconscious mis-knowledge is the root cause of our anguish. This mis-knowledge is not mere doctrinal incorrectness; it really matters to our lives.

In Buddhism, suffering means suffering of the mind, suffering that comes from the way we take things. Physical suffering is not preventable: if there is illness or injury there will be pain, and even the Buddha suffered pain. But pain is not suffering. Mostly what we call suffering is suffering of the mind. Even most of our seemingly physical suffering is mind-caused. It is emotional suffering, suffering due to our complaining and our disappointment and feeling of being cheated and ruined because we are experiencing pain. This suffering is worse than the physical sensations of pain, though we mistakenly think it necessarily goes along with the sensations of pain. Suffering is afflictive emotion—anger, fear, regret, greed, violence, and so on. When we exercise these emotions, no matter how justified they may feel, we cause suffering in ourselves, and that suffering has a way of spreading out all around us. But what's the root of these afflictive emotions? How do they arise in the first place? They arise out of clinging—clinging to the self and to our opinions and to all that is external to us that we identify with. We take all of this as intrinsically existing, and so are naturally—spontaneously and convincingly—upset when any of it is threatened. But the truth is that nothing can be threatened, because it doesn't exist in the way we think it does. Free of intrinsic existence, everything is free of all threat. When we really know this, through and through, down to the bottom of our souls, then the afflictive emotions don't arise. Instead there is peace and there is affection, even in tough situations. There is no sense of fearing or hating or desiring what is intrinsically nonexistent, empty.

That things are empty doesn't mean, as I have said, that they are unreal or that they don't exist. Here I think we can trust our common sense: we know that things are, we know that something is going on. We go to the movies, we read or hear stories of various kinds, and these matter to us. They are, in their own way, real, but we know the difference between stories or images and real life. The emptiness teachings are not telling us that things don't exist or that they are unreal. They are just telling us that things exist in a mode other than the one we think they exist in.

In Zen practice we are fond of not knowing. The not-knowing mind is the mind that knows that all phenomena, in being empty, are unknowable. Which means that all phenomena are marvelous, connected, magical. To see things in this way is to wake up from the dream of intrinsic reality: to walk out of the darkened movie theater into the light of day. In the dream, in the movie, various solid and menacing separate independent monsters are out to get us. When we walk outside, we see that this was never really true. We have awakened to the connectedness and indescribable meaning that is and has always been our real life.

The emptiness sutras speak of these things in magnificent ways and promise fabulous rewards once we become enlightened to this truth. In Zen practice too there's an emphasis on the experience of enlightenment, which is, more or less, the immediate experiential recognition of emptiness—seeing emptiness with your own eyes. All the things that are said about this in Zen and other forms of Buddhism are extravagant and idealistic. This extravagant idealism is perhaps helpful: it gives us some faith and enthusiasm. After all, if we stick too much to the so-called real world, to being mired in identity and all our emotional and physical problems, that's no fun, is it? Although all this is taken for granted as life, in fact it is a kind of narrow-minded and naive metaphysical assertion we could do without. On the other hand, to take literally all this talk about enlightenment and emptiness, about becoming omniscient buddhas (omniscience is a key concept in the emptiness sutras), may be going too far, especially if it causes us to be frustrated with our progress in practice or to imagine that other people have become enlightened and that we should therefore abrogate our personal responsibility and listen to what they tell us about our lives.

Practically speaking, there's a progression in our appreciation of the emptiness teachings. In Zen practice, we begin with some modest, everyday experience. We sit. We practice zazen. Maybe even one period of sitting is enough. When you sit, something always happens. Maybe you don't know what, maybe you cannot identify it, or you barely notice it, but something does happen. You can feel that sitting is real, powerful. I travel here and there and sometimes I go into a room in a hotel, or some other institutional setting, maybe with doctors or businesspeople, not faithful sutra-reading Buddhists, and I say, "Breathe and sit up straight and be quiet," and in a few minutes something happens; something always happens. There is some experience. What it amounts to is a faint glimmering that the world one has always assumed to be the world, the only world, the whole world and nothing but the world, may not be as it seems. The mind, the self, may not be as it seems. So our appreciation of emptiness begins with something that is really very common. It's common not so much because sitting is a magical practice but because it really is the nature of the mind to be empty of intrinsicality. So if you give it even a small chance, it will sense that, even if only a little bit.

The appreciation of emptiness begins there. Then you sit some more and experience it repeatedly. Possibly you sit long *sesshin*s and retreats, experiencing it more deeply and more frequently. Then you hear teachings and reflect on them, and little by little you become more and more convinced that this is really how it is. You may begin to notice—maybe with some frustration—that you persist in giving rise to afflictive emotions anyway, that you persist in seeing being as intrinsic. But still, you are beginning to know better. You are beginning to see how unsuccessful, how painful, that old knee-jerk way of living is. And so in this way you are beginning to train yourself in emptiness.

Then you might work directly with afflictive emotions, trying to let go of anger and greed and jealousy and so on, to begin to reduce their grip on you. Meanwhile you continue with your sitting and your study of the teachings and the verification of the teachings by your own experience. Someday you may or may not have a powerful experience of seeing directly, immediately, and powerfully that indeed things are empty, that they are like smoke or mist, like space, like the blue sky, like the movie, the dream: free and nondifferent from yourself. This would be lovely and it is certainly possible. But even if you don't have an experience like that, you continue to study and learn and experience; you apply the teachings of emptiness, of selflessness, of love and compassion, to your daily experience and to your relationships; and you see the results of this: that there is more peace, more affection, more happiness, more clarity in your life.

You probably still experience confusion and afflictive emotion, but after a while it doesn't bother you so much. You are not tempted to be caught by it because you know that just leads to suffering and you have gotten over your long-term love affair with suffering. In this way, little by little, you develop an understanding of and a grounding in emptiness. You don't need to call it emptiness. In fact, it's better if you don't. *Emptiness* is just a word you can repeat to yourself in a blizzard. But you know how things are and you are happy to live in accord with them.

9

What Is Your Body?

2013

W E THINK ABOUT our bodies all the time. How do they look? What is their state of health? Are they aging? Are they sufficiently strong, attractive, impressive? These questions churn out an almost endless stream of thinking, feeling, and spending. Consider all the clothing, beauty products, food products, accessories, books, equipment, therapists, health products, body workers, and so on that make up such a huge portion of our economy.

Everything depends on the body. Without it, we are literally nothing. Transcendent concepts such as consciousness, soul, higher self, buddha nature—are these meaningful realities or merely hopeful words? And whatever they are, how could they exist independent of a body?

The body matters. Yet what is it?

We take the body completely for granted, just as we do the sky and the earth. Yet the body, like them, is much more than we know. What we think of as our body—what we feel, imagine, and dream about it, what we unthinkingly assume it to be—isn't really what the body is.

The body is *more* than the body, and our feelings about it run deeper than we can know. The body, as it actually is, is mysterious to us.

We assume we know what the body is. But even a few moments

of examination will produce more fragmentation and uncertainty than clarity.

What self is there that is not the body? Yet where is the self that possesses a body to call its own? Who, outside the body, utters the words "my body"? Without a tongue, without a brain, I can't even utter the words.

Ask yourself: from what perspective do you look at your body? From inside, peering out from the body's eyes? Or from the outside, as if you were looking at it in a mirror? But how is it possible for the body to be external to itself? No, that can't be. The body must be contained in the experience of looking, so what you see and call "my body" must be something else.

Is the body the flow of its sensory experiences—seeing, hearing, tasting, smelling, tactile sensation? A closer look reveals problems here too. Where does a smell or a taste occur? In the nose, on the tongue? In the things smelled or tasted? In the brain? In all at once?

And what about awareness, the insubstantial, apparently nonphysical process through which anything we experience comes to us? Is awareness inside the body or outside it? If it is inside, how can we say "my" body? There is no one outside to say "mine." But if awareness is outside the body . . . no, that can't be right!

Yet awareness is foundational to experiencing oneself as a person at all. Without awareness there would be no smelling or tasting—and no body. There can be flesh without awareness, but a living human body, as we understand it, is aware of being a body.

The Buddhist teachings on the workings of mind, called *Abhidharma*, teach us that there isn't a body per se, just a variety of momentary mental events. Some of them we think of as "physical," even though they're not. When I feel an ache in my right leg, the Abhidharma analysis goes, this sensation is a mental event produced in consciousness when an object I call a leg activates inner sensors that awaken awareness in a particular way. Likewise, seeing, hearing, and all sense perceptions are mental events stimulated by apparently physical objects.

Contemporary cognitive science agrees. All experiences arise when consciousness is activated by a sense organ meeting an internal or external object. (Here, the mind itself functions like a sixth sense organ in relation to emotion and thought.) We assume we are "experiencing" the object that gave rise to the event in our consciousness. But the truth is that the only thing we can verify is the experience itself, however we may be misconstruing it. The idea of the body is like this. It is an idea based on unwarranted assumptions about the coherence of our conscious experience.

In Buddhist analysis, then, there is no body. What there is, is form (*rupa*)—some kind of illusory arising that appears to be solid and that forms a basis for experience we call physical. But in actual fact it's just a continuous flow of momentary conscious events.

Still, our idea that we have a body is powerful. Beyond our misinterpretation of our personal experiences, the idea of the body is reinforced by the social discourse we have all grown up with, which takes as an obvious fact that we "have" bodies. Our whole system of language is based on the metaphor of the body (which is more than anything else a metaphor). Most of our feelings and commonplace ideas about our lives are based on the metaphor of the body, a thought so foundational to us we can't even begin to know how to question it.

———— ►◄ ————

On the night of his enlightenment, the story goes, the Buddha was visited by the forces of Mara, the Evil One, who was determined to stop the Buddha from achieving awakening. Most of Mara's devastating and spectacular display of hopes and fears had to do with the body, either sensual allurements or threats of bodily harm. Declaring that the many threatening minions arrayed behind him were his army, Mara defiantly called out, "Where is your army, O Buddha?" In response the Buddha touched the ground and said, "The earth is my witness and support."

In touching the earth, the Buddha was not only calling on the earth goddess to be his protector. He was saying, the earth is my body. My body expresses earth, is produced and supported by earth, is made exclusively of earth elements. Nothing on earth, no matter how frightening, can threaten this indestructible earth body. Even if it is broken up into a million pieces it remains, going home to its Mother who gave birth to it, who embraces it now and always will embrace it.

With this gesture of truth, belonging, and ultimate invulnerability, born of surrender to and identity with the earth, Buddha expressed his absolute fearlessness, and in doing so defeated Mara. After this, his enlightenment unfolded.

And this is exactly true of all of us. Our bodies too are the earth. They rise up from her, and are nurtured, fed, and illuminated by her. Our bodies are in constant touch with earth, and they return to earth, from which they have never parted.

Our human bodies are expressions of the earth's creative force. Everything that makes human life—breathing, eating, elimination, perception, feeling, language—occurs only in concert with earth. No thought would ever take place without the prior existence of earth. No thought would be thinkable without air, water, fire, space, dirt. Even our most abstract ideas, like freedom, justice, and happiness, are nothing more or less than earth's urge, the thought of wind, sky, water, and light. Nothing we think or do could ever be more profound or true than these natural elements, which are literally nothing more or less than our own bodies.

Mahayana Buddhism was a philosophical and emotional reaction to Buddhism's earlier, more sober teachings, which often characterized the body as repulsive and a source of attachment. In Mahayana thought, the body as such is asserted and celebrated. It is transfigured, through art and faith, into the bodhisattva body, the buddha body, the perfect eternal beautiful body hidden in the earthly body of impermanence and decay.

The Buddha of the Mahayana sutras has three bodies: the *dharmakaya*, or truth body, measureless, all-encompassing and perfect, beyond perception and concept; the *sambhogakaya*, or enjoyment body, the purified perceived body of perfect meditation and teaching; and finally the *nirmanakaya*, the transient historical body that appears in our world for the purpose of teaching worldly beings. In Zen teaching, it is axiomatic that the ordinary human body that can be accessed in meditation practice is itself beyond the human body as normally conceived. The "True Body," as Dogen says, "is far beyond the world's dusts." Or, as Hakuin puts it in his *Song of Zazen*, "This very body is the Body of Buddha."

The actual biological human body really is (as we discover more and more every day) a marvelous and endlessly complex occurrence. Three hundred years of medical science has still only scratched the surface of its immense functioning. The brain, for instance: how does it regulate everything so perfectly, adjusting to any and all sorts of contingencies, producing thoughts, literary works, skyscrapers, cities, social systems, and so on? The heart, the lungs. Cells, DNA. The enormous knowledge and complex communication and movement that seem to occur effortlessly within every human body: walking, running, jumping, shouting, singing, playing the piano. There are twenty-five thousand miles of blood vessels in the human body. Stretched out end to end, they'd circle the earth. Blood flows through them ceaselessly, nurturing every organ in the body. The actual functioning human body is a marvel. No one manufactured it. No patents exist for it. No one knows where it comes from or exactly how it is produced. And the consciousness associated with it, the consciousness capable of knowing itself? About this we haven't a clue.

In the body scan meditation made popular in Jon Kabat-Zinn's Mindfulness-Based Stress Reduction meditation course, practitioners lie on the floor while an instructor walks them through forty-five minutes of detailed mindfulness exercises designed to bring awareness to various parts of the body, from head to toe. Simply applying awareness to the body in detail has a healing effect. No one knows why. Zen meditation, especially as practiced in the

Soto school, is a body practice, a process of paying attention to the body's detail. When you are taught Zen meditation, the lesson typically begins with instruction about how to walk into the hall to take your seat: you are to walk carefully, paying attention to each footfall, with your hands in a particular position, your body erect. You are then instructed to bow carefully to the meditation cushion (the form for bowing is also detailed for you), sit down, and arrange your posture carefully. Your spine should be erect, your chin tucked in, your hands folded delicately into a mudra—thumb tips just touching, palms curved. Breath should be smooth, natural, and deep in the belly.

All this physical detail is the focus for the sitting—not a teaching or a spiritual theme. Simply the experience of body itself is the focus of meditation. When the awareness wanders, as it will, this is fine as long as the practitioner is fully committed to coming back to the feeling of the body sitting and the breath moving. As with the body scan, there is an uncanny magic in this simple practice. Returning awareness to the body and the breath over and over again—over the course of one sitting, or many sittings, for years, decades, a lifetime—interrupts the usual flow of thinking profoundly based on the assumption of a discrete self inhabiting a unitary body. Once that flow is interrupted, and awareness is returned to the flow of lived experience in the present moment of being alive (a moment in which everything arises and disappears at once and seems to be both there and not there), life feels different. The body no longer appears to be the body per se. Somehow, within awareness of the process of living, the body becomes more than it is. It becomes identical with the awareness, and there isn't a beginning or an end to it.

After sitting practice, normal daily life in the body returns. But there's a lightness and ease that comes with the feeling of having been relieved, at least temporarily, of the confinement of your small life lived in a vulnerable body. You might feel "calmer," but the feeling is more than calm. It's the feeling of reality—of having left, for at least a little while, the stressful unreality of daily living and entered a larger space. This is calming. And if you practice for a lifetime, this temporary relief becomes more than temporary. The sense that the body is more than the body, and that your life is more than your life, becomes a conviction and a calm confidence in the body itself, and therefore also in the mind.

One of the deepest themes in Western philosophy, beginning with Plato, is that the world of appearance isn't real. So the job of the intellect, its spiritual assignment, is to carry us beyond this corrupt physical world to a perfected world of nonmaterial form, purely mental or spiritual. This was seen as the task of philosophy and religion until the twentieth century, when phenomenology, perhaps in part under the influence of Buddhism, which never did have a mind/body split, began to break it down. In our earth-threatened time, when we must think and care about the future well-being of the planet, it is fitting that we begin to learn and enact the truth that has always been engraved on our very skins: that body, mind, spirit, and earth are one expression, one concern, and one delight.

10

A Mother's Death

1992

AT FIRST it was a shock to see her. She didn't look the same at all. Her face was ashen and all puffed up from the chemotherapy or radiation. Her arms were huge from it, her hair was matted and a different color, her voice had gone all croaky and harsh, and the medication had got her mixed up and disconnected. She'd sit up in bed all of a sudden, beside herself with anger or frustration, and yell to my Aunt Adeline, "No, turn me over, not that way, this way, no, not that way, I said like this, like that." Adeline and my father and my Aunt Sylvia all looked at one another and at me.

She'd go in and out of consciousness. She'd see things. She'd say, "Don't let them make you do anything you don't want to."

She said, "You all think I'm crazy, but I know what I'm doing."

She said, "Throw away all the envelopes you can."

She said, "Why are you standing around here. It's ridiculous! Scram!"

And she said to me, "You're a cute boy in that shirt."

After a while it was very beautiful to see her living this simple, intense, painful, but somehow noble existence in the six-foot-by-three-foot space of hospital bed that had become her whole life. This bed, together with the unknown realms of space and time through which she was traveling.

She'd say, "Put my shoes in boxes over there." We'd take shifts staying with her around the clock, and I would look forward very much to being with her, to be as intimate with her as I had been as a child and to experience a clearer, purer relationship with her. For a long time I had been a disappointment to her. She loved me very much, and I think she felt frustrated in some area of her life and so needed me to afford her satisfaction.

But this never happened. I had had an unusual kind of life, and this was hard for her. But now I could stroke her forehead and release the tension building up around her eyes. And I could breathe with her, which would calm her down a little bit. Sometimes, if she was making noise in her breathing, I'd make noise in the same way. But I couldn't do that when others were around. Sometimes she'd sit up suddenly out of her unconsciousness and say to me, "Don't make fun of me." And I'd say, "I'm not making fun of you. I love you." Late at night I could look at her in the lamplight and think of the many ways I could have been nicer to her or how much she'd loved me and how much she had given to me, and I could tell her then how much I loved her and it would make me cry. When she'd suddenly sit up and say, "My hat," or "Get my shoes, we're going out," or "Where are the red and green charts, they should beep by now," I'd tell her, "Don't worry about that. Your life is very simple now. Just breathe." And she would lie back down, reassured and calmer.

Gradually, over the course of days and nights, she began to give up everything. First her body became more relaxed, as though it wasn't hers anymore. Then she stopped having any sense of whether she liked or didn't like anything. Then she couldn't tell who anyone was or recognize anything in the room. All of the worries and cares of her life began to mingle in her delirium: her clothes, things she had to do at home or for my father, things at the office where she had worked. One by one she put them down, too. Finally there was only a dim awareness that grew finer and finer as her breath seemed to go more and more deep—more and more inward. It was as if the heavy earth of her body were dissolving into water. Then this water of the moving of her blood dissolved into the fire of images that receded in the distance. The fiery images dissolved into air and the air into space, endless space and endless consciousness.

My father cried and said, "It isn't fair," just as my sons, arguing with one another or carefully watching each other divide some special food, might say, "It isn't fair."

I knew she was gone but it didn't really make any sense that she was gone. She didn't go anywhere. And the gone that she was, was really no different from the gone that she had usually been to me my whole adult life and even during my life as a child. In one way she was gone, but in another way she was very present. We stood there looking at her. She looked very noble, and we were all in awe of her. Then everyone wanted to leave, and I said, "Is it all right if I stay with her a while?" Yes it was, and they left.

It was nearly dawn. The light coming in the window was lovely and my mother looked lovely in the light. Her skin was a different color than it had ever been before. It looked very soft and gentle. I could see that she had many freckles on her face. I had never before noticed that she had freckles. I felt like talking to her. I said, "Don't be confused!"

Then quietly I recited the *Heart Sutra*: Form is emptiness, emptiness is form, everything that is form is emptiness, everything that is emptiness, form. Further, there is no eye no ear no nose no tongue no body and no mind. There is no color no sound no smell no taste no touch no mental object. And it says: There is nothing to have and the mind is no hindrance. It ends: Gone, gone, gone, completely gone, gone beyond everything. I have recited this sutra thousands of times but never had I felt so clearly what it meant.

I looked out the window. The Florida hospital lawns were pale green in the dawn light, very quiet and pure, as if brand new, with no one around. My mother was all right. She had everything she needed. Far away on the lawn a workman appeared and tried to start a lawnmower. It took many pulls to get it going. Then silently and slowly he began to push it back and forth across the lawn.

Mama was all right. But it was going to be hard for the world with all its struggle and fragility and beauty to get along without her. It was then that I cried a lot for the world that didn't know any peace and perhaps never would.

11

Impermanence Is Buddha Nature

2012

PRACTITIONERS HAVE ALWAYS understood impermanence as the cornerstone of Buddhist teachings and practice. All that exists is impermanent; nothing lasts. Therefore nothing can be grasped or held on to. When we don't fully appreciate this simple but profound truth, we suffer; when we do, we have real peace and understanding.

As far as classical Buddhism is concerned, impermanence is the number-one inescapable, and essentially painful, fact of life. It is the singular existential problem that the whole edifice of Buddhist practice is meant to address. To understand impermanence at the deepest possible level (we all understand it at superficial levels), and to merge with it fully, is the whole of the Buddhist path. The Buddha's final words express this: Impermanence is inescapable. Everything vanishes. Therefore there is nothing more important than continuing the path with diligence. All other options either deny or short-shrift the problem.

A while ago I had a dream that has stayed with me. In a hazy grotto, my mother-in-law and I, coming from opposite directions, are trying to squeeze through a dim doorway. Both of us are fairly large people and the space is small, so for a moment we are stuck together in the doorway. Finally we press through, she to her side (formerly mine), I to mine (formerly hers).

It's not that surprising to me that I would dream about my mother-in-law. Her situation is often on my mind. My mother-in-law is nearing ninety. She has many health problems. She is usually in pain, can't walk or sleep at night, and is losing the use of her hands to neuropathy. She lives with her husband of more than sixty years, who has advanced Alzheimer's disease, can't speak a coherent sentence, and doesn't know who or where he is. Despite all this, my mother-in-law affirms life 100 percent, as she always has. She never entertains the idea of death, as far as I know. All she wants and hopes for is a good and pleasant life. Since she doesn't have this right now (though she hasn't given up hope for it), she is fairly miserable, as anyone in her situation would be.

I, on the other hand, am fairly healthy, with no expectation of dying anytime soon. Yet from childhood I have been thinking about death, and the fact of death has probably been the main motivator in my life. (Why else would I have devoted myself full time to Buddhist practice from an early age?) Consequently, almost all my talking and writing, and much of my thinking, is in one way or another in reference to death, absence, disappearing.

So this dream intrigues and confuses me. Is my mother-in-law about to pass over from life to death, though temporarily stuck in the crowded doorway? If that's the logic of the dream, then I must be dead, stuck in that same doorway as I try to pass through to life. Of course, this makes no sense! But then, the longer I contemplate life and death, the less sense they make. Sometimes I wonder whether life and death aren't merely a conceptual framework we confuse ourselves with. Of course, people do seem to disappear, and, this having been the case generally with others, it seems reasonable to assume that it will be the case for us at some point. But how to understand this? And how to account for the many anomalies that appear when you look closely, such as reported appearances of ghosts and other visitations from the dead, reincarnation, and so on?

It is very telling that some religions refer to death as "eternal life," and that in the *Mahaparinibbana Sutta* the Buddha doesn't die. He enters *parinirvana*, full extinction, which is something other than death. In Buddhism generally, death isn't death—it's a staging area for further life. So there are many respectable and less respectable reasons to wonder about the question of death.

There are a lot of older people in the Buddhist communities in which I practice. Some are in their seventies and eighties, others in their sixties, like me. Because of this, the theme of death and impermanence is always on our minds and seems to come up again and again in the teachings we study. All conditioned things pass away. Nothing remains as it was. The body changes and weakens as it ages. In response to this, and to a lifetime's experience, the mind changes as well. The way one thinks of, views, and feels about life and the world is different. Even the same thoughts one had in youth or midlife take on a different flavor when held in older age. The other day a friend about my age, who in her youth studied Zen with the great Korean master Song Sa Nim, told me, "He always said, 'Soon dead!' I understood the words then as being true—very Zen, and almost funny. Now they seem personal and poignant."

"All conditioned things have the nature of vanishing," the Buddha said. What is impermanence after all? When we're young, we know that death is coming, but it will probably come later, so we don't have to be so concerned with it now. And even if we are concerned with it in youth, as I was, the concern is philosophical. When we are older, we know death is coming sooner rather than later, so we take it more personally. But do we really know what we are talking about?

Death may be the ultimate loss, the ultimate impermanence, but even on a lesser, everyday scale, impermanence and the loss it entails still happens more or less "later." Something is here now in a particular way; later it will not be. I am or have something now; later I will not. But "later" is the safest of all time frames. It can be safely ignored because it's not now—it's later, and later never comes. And even if it does, we don't have to worry about it now. We can worry about it later. For most of us most of the time, impermanence seems irrelevant.

But in truth, impermanence isn't later; it's now. The Buddha said, "All conditioned things have the nature of vanishing." Right now, as they appear before us, they have that nature. It's not that something vanishes later. Right now, everything is in some way—though we don't understand in what way—vanishing before our very eyes. Squeezing uncomfortably through the narrow doorway of now, we don't know whether we are coming or going. Impermanence may be a deeper thought than we at first appreciate.

———— ▶◀ ————

Impermanence is not only loss; it is also change, and change can be refreshing and renewing. In fact, change is always both good and bad, because change, even when it is refreshing, always entails loss. Nothing new appears unless something old ceases. As they say on New Year's Eve, "Out with the old, in with the new," marking both a happy and a sad occasion. As with the scene of the Buddha's passing in the *Mahaparinibbana Sutta*, there's despair and equanimity at the same time. Impermanence is both.

In one of his most important essays, the great twelfth-century Japanese Zen master Dogen writes, "Impermanence is itself buddha nature."[1] This seems quite different from the classical Buddhist notion of impermanence, which emphasizes the loss side of the loss/change/renewal equation. For Dogen, impermanence isn't a problem to be overcome with diligent effort on the path. Impermanence *is* the path. Practice isn't the way to cope with or overcome impermanence. It is the way to fully appreciate and live it.

"If you want to understand buddha nature," Dogen writes, "you should intimately observe cause and effect over time. When the time is ripe, buddha nature manifests."[2] In explaining this teaching, Dogen, in his usual inside-out, upside-down way (Dogen is unique among Zen masters in his intricately detailed literary style, which usually involves very counterconceptual ways of understanding typical concepts), writes that practice isn't so much a matter of changing or improving the conditions of your inner or outer life as a way of fully embracing and appreciating those conditions, especially the condition of impermanence and loss. When you practice, "the time becomes ripe." While this phrase naturally implies a "later" (something unripe ripens in time), Dogen understands it in the opposite way: Time is always ripe. Buddha nature always manifests in time, because time is always impermanence.

Of course, time is impermanence and impermanence is time! Time is change, development, and loss. Present time is ungraspable. As soon as it occurs, it immediately falls into the past. As soon as I am here, I am gone. If this were not so, how could the me of this moment ever give way to the me of the following moment? Unless the first me disappears, clearing the way, the second me cannot appear. So my being here is thanks to my not being here. If I were not not here, I couldn't be here!

In other words, this becomes very quickly paradoxical and absurd, but in living, it seems to be exactly the case. Logically it must be so, and once in a while (especially in a long meditation retreat) you can actually, viscerally, feel it. Nothing appears unless it appears in time. And whatever appears in time appears and vanishes at once, just as the Buddha said on his deathbed. Time is existence, impermanence, change, loss, growth, and development—the best and the worst news at once. Dogen calls this strange immense process buddha nature. "Buddha Nature is no other than all are, because all are is Buddha Nature," he writes.[3] The phrase "all are" is important. Are: existence, being, time, impermanence, and change. All are: existence, being, time, impermanence, and change is never lonely; it is always all-inclusive. We're all always in this together.

The other day I was talking to an old friend, an experienced Zen practitioner, about her practice. She told me she was beginning to notice that the persistent feeling of dissatisfaction she always felt in relation to others, the world, and the circumstances of her inner and outer life was probably not about others, the world, or inner and outer circumstances, but instead was about her deepest inmost self. Dissatisfaction, she said, seems in some way to be herself, to be fundamentally ingrained in her. Before realizing this, she went on, she'd assumed her dissatisfaction was due in some way to a personal failing on her part—a failing that she had hoped to correct with her Zen practice. But now she could see that it was far worse than that! The dissatisfaction was not about her, and therefore correctable; it was built into her, it was essential to her self!

This seems to be exactly what the Buddha meant when he spoke of the basic shakiness of our sense of subjectivity in the famous doctrine of *anatta*, or nonself. Though we all need healthy egos to operate normally in the world, the essential grounding of ego is the false notion of permanence, a notion that we unthinkingly subscribe to, even though, deep in our hearts, we know it's untrue. I am me, I have been me, and I will be me. I can change, and I want to change, but I am always here, always me, and have never known any other experience. But this ignores the reality that "all conditioned things have the nature of vanishing," and are vanishing constantly, as a condition of their existing in time, whose nature is vanishing.

No wonder we feel, as my friend felt, a constant nagging sense of dissatisfaction and disjunction that we might well interpret as coming from a chronic personal failing (that is, once we'd gotten over the even more faulty belief that others were responsible for it). On the other hand, as Dogen writes, "all are is Buddha Nature." This means that the self is not, as we imagine, an improvable permanent isolated entity we and we alone are responsible for; instead it is impermanence itself, which is never alone, never isolated, constantly flowing, and immense. It is buddha nature itself.

Dogen writes, "Impermanence itself is Buddha Nature." And adds, "Permanence is the mind that discriminates the wholesomeness and unwholesomeness of all things."[4] Permanence!? Impermanence seems to be (as Dogen himself writes elsewhere) an "unshakable teaching" in buddhadharma. How does "permanence" manage to worm its way into Dogen's discourse?

———— ▶◀ ————

I come back to my dream of being stuck in the doorway between life and death with my mother-in-law. Which side is which, and who is going where? Impermanence and permanence may simply be balancing concepts—words, feelings, and thoughts that support one another in helping us grope toward an understanding (and a misunderstanding) of our lives. For Dogen, "permanence" is practice. It is having the wisdom and the commitment to see the difference between what we commit ourselves to pursuing in this human lifetime and what we commit ourselves to letting go of. The good news in "impermanence is buddha nature" is that we can finally let ourselves off the hook. We can let go of the great and endless chore of improving ourselves, of being stellar accomplished people, inwardly or in our external lives. This is no small thing, because we are all subject to this kind of brutal inner pressure to be and do more today than we have been and done yesterday—and more than someone else has been and done today and tomorrow.

The bad news in "impermanence is buddha nature" is that it's so big there isn't much we can do with it. It can't be enough simply to repeat the phrase to ourselves. And if we are not striving to accomplish the Great Awakening, the Ultimate Improvement, what would we do, and why would we do it? Dogen asserts a way and a motivation. If impermanence is the worm at the heart of the apple of self, making suffering a built-in factor of human life, then permanence is the petal emerging from the sepal of the flower of impermanence. It makes happiness possible. Impermanence is permanent, the ongoing process of living and dying and time. Permanence is nirvana, bliss, cessation, relief—the never-ending, ever-changing, and growing field of practice.

In the Buddha's final scene, as told in the *Mahaparinibbana Sutta*, the contrast between the monastics who tore their hair, raised their arms, and threw themselves down in their grief and those who received the Buddha's passing with equanimity couldn't be greater. The sutra seems to imply disapproval of the former and approval of the latter. Or perhaps the approval and disapproval are in our reading. For if impermanence is permanence is buddha nature, then loss is loss is also happiness, and both sets of monastics are to be approved. Impermanence is not only to be overcome and conquered. It is also to be lived and appreciated, because it reflects the "all are" side of our human nature. The weeping and wailing monastics were expressing not only their attachment; they were also expressing their immersion in this human life, and their love for someone they revered.

I have experienced this more than once at times of great loss. While I may not tear my hair and throw myself down in my grieving, I have experienced extreme sadness and loss, feeling the whole world weeping and dark with the fresh absence of someone I love. At the same time, I have felt some appreciation and equanimity, because loss, searing as it can be, is also beautiful—sad and beautiful. My tears, my sadness, are beautiful because they are the consequence of love, and my grieving makes me love the world and life all the more. Every loss I have ever experienced, every personal and emotional teaching of impermanence that life has been kind enough to offer me, has deepened my ability to love.

The happiness that spiritual practice promises is not endless bliss, endless joy, and soaring transcendence. Who would want that in a world in which there is so much injustice, so much tragedy, so much unhappiness, illness, and death? To feel the scourge of impermanence and loss and to appreciate it at the same time profoundly as the beautiful essence of what it means to be at all—this is the deep truth I hear reverberating in the Buddha's last words. Everything vanishes. Practice goes on.

12

Suffering Opens the Real Path

2011

O N JANUARY 12, 2009, my dear friend of forty years, my best friend who was more than a brother to me, Rabbi Alan Lew, died without any warning or any known illness. I won't go on about our long friendship. Suffice it to say, we were as close as people can be; we were spiritually linked. We knew each other before either of us had started on our religious paths, and we began practicing Zen at the same time. We studied for many years together at the Zen center in Berkeley and went to Tassajara Zen Mountain Center where we were monks together. As time went on, we created our own version of Jewish meditation and together we founded Makor Or, a Jewish meditation center in San Francisco. We practiced there together, side by side, for more than a decade.

So when Alan died all of a sudden, it was hard to take. I'm guessing that I will not get over it, that his death probably holds a permanent place of sadness in me. I'm not so sure that I want to get over it. The sadness is OK. It's not so bad.

About a week before he died, we led a retreat together. At that retreat he gave me what turned out to be his last teaching, although we didn't know it at the time. Alan was really a great person and a great rabbi, and his teachings were often humorous. He would present very profound things in a silly way. It would take you a while to realize how profound his teaching actually was.

For some years Alan had been collecting fountain pens, which he liked to tell me about. I like fountain pens myself. I didn't think much of it until I went over to his house one day, and he showed me his collection. It was an astonishing thing. There were hundreds and hundreds, maybe five hundred fountain pens that he kept neatly in special binders that are made for such collections. These were rare antiques that were worth quite a bit of money. Apparently, there's a whole world of fountain pen collectors out there. There are fountain pen conventions and fountain pen websites. There's even a whole kind of stock market of fountain pens; you buy and sell and the prices go up and down. I didn't know this, but it's a huge deal.

A few months before his death, Alan decided he would sell off some of his fountain pens. He brokered the transaction online and sent thousands of dollars' worth of pens to some person he found online. While he was waiting for the check to come in the mail, the guy who had purchased the pens from him died suddenly. His widow hired a lawyer to clear the estate, but the lawyer didn't find a convincing paper trail for these fountain pens, so he informed Alan that he was not going to get paid for them.

Alan thought, "Well, I could get a lawyer, and no doubt I would win the case, but by the time I pay the lawyer, it's probably not worth it. So the heck with it." He never pursued it. He said, "You know, I don't mind losing that money, because I learned something that's worth every penny of it." I asked him what he had learned.

"I learned that when you're dead, you can't do anything," he said. "This guy was a very decent person and he would certainly have paid the money, but he was dead, and he couldn't do anything. You'd think that I would have already known this. And in a way I suppose I did. But I didn't really know it. Now, with the loss of all this money, I really know it. When you're dead, you can't do anything."

This is a really profound teaching. When someone you love is gone, that person can't do anything anymore. This means that you have to do something, or that you have to do something differently. Somehow, you, who are connected to that person, have to do what they can no longer do. You have to ask yourself, "Now that this has happened, what will I do, what will I do in place of my friend?" There is always something to be done. This was Alan's last teaching to me.

Alan was really concerned about others. He would get agitated and upset if the people he loved weren't doing well. If his family members were having troubles, he would tell me about it with anguish in his voice. His death made me want to care more for other people. It's not something that comes naturally to me. When my friends are ill or in need of help, I have to put a real intention into thinking about them, calling them, and doing something, instead of just going about my business. I have far to go, but I think of Alan and I keep working at it.

We think we're trying to get rid of suffering. I want more suffering. I want to feel more suffering of the people who are suffering everywhere. I want to feel that suffering more, care about it more, and do something about it more. That's my commitment to Alan and to myself.

The other thing I learned from Alan's death is that love will naturally rush into the vacuum that loss creates. Alan knew a lot of people, and we knew many people in common. Many people loved him, and when he was gone, I felt so much closer to those people. Even though we had been close before, the vacuum caused by the loss created much more love. Love creates love. That feeling wasn't something that came and went in a month or two. With loss, difficulty, and the total overturning of the plan you had for your life comes more love and more depth if you turn your heart in that direction.

Loss, disappointment, and difficulty can be really devastating. They can damage us permanently; they can even destroy our lives. But if we yield to our sadness and turn toward our difficult feelings, we can remember these lessons that I learned from Alan: there is always something to be done and there is always more love. I don't know if you believe this already, but it is certainly true.

———— ▶◀ ————

These are tough times, full of objective difficulties and anxieties. But times are always tough, and even when times in general aren't tough, your time might be tough at any given period in your life. Nobody escapes tough times. Nobody escapes suffering.

By suffering, I mean pain, whether physical or mental. I suppose a small minority of us might say, "I like suffering; I want more suffering." But most of us don't. When I'm in the presence of something I really don't want, then I'm suffering. Suffering seems to be the opposite of happiness. If there's happiness, there is no suffering. If there's suffering, there is no happiness.

The most astonishing fact of human life is that most of us think it's possible to minimize and even eliminate suffering. We actually think this, which is one reason it's so difficult for us when we're suffering. We think, "This shouldn't be this way" or "I'm going to get rid of this somehow." I think many of us believe that since suffering is so bad and so unpleasant, if we were really good and really smart, it wouldn't arise in the first place. Somehow suffering is our own fault. If it's not our fault, then it's definitely someone else's fault. But when suffering arises, we think we should surely be able to avoid it. We should be able to set it to one side and not dwell on it. We should "move on," as they say, go on to positive things, do a little Buddhism, meditate, get around the suffering, and go forward. We shouldn't allow the suffering to stop us, not allow it to mess us up. We believe that if only we play our cards right, we could have a positive life without much suffering. We constantly come back to that way of thinking.

It's incredible that we would think such a thing. The more we look around us, the more we pay attention to what we're feeling and what others around us are feeling, the more suffering we see. There is more suffering than we know. Anxiety is suffering, isn't it? There is a lot of anxiety. Not getting what you want is suffering. How many of us don't get what we want? Irritation is suffering. Anger is suffering. Having to put up with things you don't like is suffering. Knowing that you're going to have to die, and you really don't want to—that's suffering. Sickness is suffering. Old age is suffering. Not having enough money is suffering. Losing your job is suffering. Having a bad marriage is suffering. Having no marriage can be suffering if you want to have a marriage. Fear is suffering. Knowing you could lose what you think you have is suffering. Being ashamed is suffering. Feeling disrespected is suffering. Feeling unloved is suffering. Feeling loved, but not loved enough, is suffering. Feeling lonely is suffering. Feeling bewildered is suffering. Being too cold, being too hot, being stuck in traffic, getting in the wrong line and the guy in the front is very, very slow, and the other line that you could have gotten into is going much faster, and you could have been in the front of that line by now, but if you joined it now, you'd be at the end—all this is suffering. Even without talking about the earthquakes, the wars, the deprivation, the oppression, the illness, and the hunger that is happening all over our world, suffering is really common. It's not a special condition. Suffering is a daily experience.

Even if we try to ignore it, we really don't escape the suffering. It registers in our psyche and becomes a conditioning factor in our lives. We may find that we're living in reaction to the suffering that we're unwilling to see and think about. So the idea that suffering is some sort of mistake and a minor problem that we could overcome with a little bit of meditation and a positive attitude is the towering pinnacle of human self-deception.

Part of the problem might be that "suffering" is such a drastic word; it sounds like a rare thing. The idea of suffering is a central thought in Buddhist practice. The original word in Pali is *dukkha*, which is most often translated as "suffering," but is sometimes translated simply as "unsatisfactoriness" or "stress." Dukkha refers to the psychological experience—sometimes conscious, sometimes not conscious—of the profound fact that everything is impermanent, ungraspable, and not really knowable. On some level, we all understand this. All the things we have, we know we don't really have. All the things we see, we're not entirely seeing. This is the nature of things, yet we think the opposite. We think that we can know and possess our lives, our loves, our identities, and even our possessions. We can't. The gap between the reality and the basic human approach to life is dukkha, an experience of basic anxiety or frustration.

Seen in this way, dukkha could actually be another name for human consciousness itself. Dukkha is not a mistake. It is not a correctable situation; it is human consciousness. Dukkha is every moment, every experience of our lives, not just the things that obviously seem to be dukkha, like pain, suffering, and loss. Pain, suffering, and loss are built into every moment of consciousness, even if they don't appear on the surface to be pain, suffering, and loss.

The great and beautiful secret of meditation practice is this: you can experience dukkha with equanimity. Isn't equanimity the secret of happiness? If you tried to eliminate dukkha, it would be like trying to eliminate life. But if you can receive dukkha with equanimity, then, in a way, it's no longer dukkha. Impermanence could be the most devastating fact of life, and often it is. But impermanence could also be incredibly beautiful, if you receive it with equanimity. It could be peace itself.

If we stop, perhaps for a moment we can see the beauty in this impermanence. But then we go back into our lives in the world of activity and desire. We go back to grasping things that aren't really there and to operating in the world that we want, rather than the world as it is. Beneath our daily consciousness will be this anxiety and fear and this immense longing. Dukkha is this basic fact of our lives. When we are dying, our whole lifetime habit of denying dukkha will end, and dukkha will become inescapable. One way or the other, we're going to have to grapple with it. So it's good to get a head start.

▶◀

Our culture is so focused on consumerism and youth that we don't have a good model for what aging and dying could be like. All we feel is the lack of things: we're not as youthful as we were, we're not as limber as we were, we're not as this, we're not as that. Almost everything that we hear and see in the media is about how to maintain your youth as long as possible. All this focus on stopping aging implies somebody made a big mistake in the universe. It's as if we should be getting younger instead of older.

But we're missing a very important point. There's something beautiful about quiet and peace. There's something beautiful about not trying to do anything, but simply, in some way, your heart joining the whole world. There's a time in life when we should be running around doing things. We should go out dancing; there's a time in life for that. There's a time in life for building something up in this world, a family, an institution, a business, a creative life; there's a time for that. There's also a time for becoming quiet, a time for slow conversations with people that we love, and a time for reflecting on all the things that we've seen in many years of living. When the time for those things comes, it's beautiful. It's not a terrible thing, it's sweet. There's also a time for letting go of our life, not "Damn, somebody's snatching this away from me," but "Yes, it's beautiful to exhale after you inhale." At the right time, when the chest is full, breathe out and let go.

In Buddhist cosmology, there are six realms: the god realm, the demigod realm, the human realm, the animal realm, the hungry ghost realm, all defined by constant desire, and the hell realm, defined by constant pain and suffering. In the god realm, everything is perfect. There's no pain because there's no solid body. Everything is ethereal, floaty. Sounds nice. But this is not the best realm to be born into because in this realm one becomes addicted to pleasure. The best realm is the human realm because in the human realm, there's just enough suffering to give us the incentive to seek liberation, but not so much suffering that we are consumed by it and cannot focus on a spiritual path.

So suffering, if we can relate to it properly, is an advantage for the spiritual path. If we imagine somehow that our suffering will dissolve if we only do such and such, or if we are crushed by the weight of it, then we don't have the energy or resources to understand it as a tool for greater consciousness. This is an improper response to suffering. The question then is not: Can we ameliorate or eliminate suffering? The question is: How will we receive and make use of the suffering in our lives?

Suffering is not a mistake. It's not a problem. It's not your fault; it's not my fault. It's not the government's fault. You and I and the government may make plenty of mistakes, but the question of suffering is much bigger than that. Suffering is pivotal for human life. It's what gives us the incentive, the vision, and the strength to really take hold of our lives spiritually.

Whether or not you have a spiritual or religious point of view, if you're human and if you have language, you know that life could either be meaningful or meaningless. The difference between these two perspectives matters to all of us. None of us can bear a meaningless life. We all need to find some way for life to have meaning. This is part of being human. If we don't have meaning, we become brittle, brutal, and numb. Suffering can reduce us to meaninglessness. So much of the overt suffering in this world is caused by people who have themselves suffered and been crushed by the weight of that suffering. But suffering can also bring us to the deepest possible sense of meaning for human life. We can all likely recall a story of someone who, due to tremendous suffering, found a beauty and meaning in life that they never would have seen without that experience.

In difficult times, the key thing is to turn toward the suffering instead of trying to figure out how to get rid of it or paper it over with all kinds of positive things. We need to learn how to turn toward suffering, really take it in, find the meaning in it, and let it open a path for us to a new life. There's nothing more beneficial than being able to be present with the breath and with the body to what's happening when we are suffering, without flailing all around in resistance. That's the beginning of a new path.

———— ▶◀ ————

Rabbi Lew wrote a great book called *Be Still and Get Going*. In it he discusses the Garden of Eden story, which is essentially about people who have everything that they could want, but want the one thing they can't have. The result, no surprise, is suffering. He writes, "Is the universe essentially deficient and in need of improvement? Is God flawed? Why was this desire, which would prove to be our undoing, implanted in our souls in the first place? Is God a screwup?"

Rabbi Lew writes in terms of God, but if that's not your way of looking at things, you could rephrase it as, "Is there a screwup in the nature of things? This is a horrible mess—what's going on here?" He continues: "Or is there something about the process of healing, of working through suffering and death, of mending a broken world, that is both necessary and good?"

I have a friend who was going through a period of tremendous suffering, a complete breakdown in his life; he couldn't work or do anything. I've known him well over many years, and he was very discouraged and ashamed of himself for his suffering. I said to him, "You know, I guess this is just your way of digesting a new phase in your life. The last time this happened to you, you were about to enter a new phase. Perhaps this is just what you do: you go all to pieces, then you pick yourself up and you go forward." He was going through a big reorganization, which is always painful. But then when he was done, he was able to move ahead in a way he hadn't before.

Rabbi Lew is saying that often suffering is needed for reorganization. We're stronger after we reorganize. This raises more questions. Suffering may very well be inevitable, but can it also be useful in this way? Is the history we were thrust into after our fall from Eden not only inevitable but also something we needed to go through, something that benefited us more than remaining in a static paradise? We're all looking to get rid of suffering. We're looking for a way to be consistently happy. But maybe that's not actually so good.

Accepting suffering as part of our lives doesn't mean we give up hope or stop wanting some things to be different. For example, if someone you love is diagnosed with cancer, of course you will hope for and search for a cure. You can accept the fact of the diagnosis at the same time that you do everything possible to ameliorate it. There is no contradiction between acceptance and hope. In fact, acceptance and hope are connected. Acceptance is not resignation. Acceptance is a lively engagement with conditions as they are.

Of course, there is a kind of hope that is really more like desperation: the sense that if something bad happens, you'll be ruined forever, and so you hope desperately that there will be a good outcome. That's the less effective kind of hope because there is only one outcome that is acceptable to you. So you mightily focus on it, shutting out everything else, including all fear and all sorrow. Then there's the kind of hope built on acceptance, with some uplifted spirit, of conditions as they are. Acceptance strengthens this kind of hope. You still do everything you can, including all kinds of objective things such as looking at different treatments and making that person comfortable. You hope and pray for a good outcome. If you do this with the awareness and acceptance of suffering, you strengthen your ability to face with love whatever happens next.

———— ▶◀ ————

There is suffering that is necessary, and there is a lot of suffering that is absolutely unnecessary. All of us cause ourselves unnecessary suffering. A huge percentage of the suffering that we feel on a daily basis is extra. We don't need it. There's plenty of suffering built into human life; we can just wait for it. We don't need to add more by unintentionally making choices that cause more suffering. We don't need to add more by getting trapped in our mind's attachment to past or future problems and potential pitfalls.

We complicate our lives and we have a lot of desires. In this way we make more suffering than we need to. If I decide I'm going to accomplish fifteen important things today, and I only accomplish thirteen of them, then I am suffering—I am dissatisfied. But I made this up myself! Why not only ten? Or seven? If I have an idea about how my day is supposed to go, or my life, and my day or my life doesn't go that way, I have a reason, it seems, to be unhappy. But I have created that reason myself. There are plenty of reasons to be unhappy without my creating more reasons. Maybe I could just pay attention to the basic and actual suffering that comes, rather than making more suffering than I need. The basic suffering, the actual suffering, is difficult, but it is useful. The extra suffering is usually trivial: it doesn't illuminate my life; it only makes me crabby.

In Zen we have koans to practice with, stories of the old masters that are sometimes hard to fathom. We can suffer over these stories; we can become miserable if we think we don't understand. But we don't need these stories to give us artificial problems. There are enough real problems to get our attention, like sickness, aging, and death; like loss. When real suffering comes, it gets our attention. We're forced to go beyond crabbiness. If, in the face of suffering, we take up our spiritual practice and use the suffering to strengthen our motivation, then we can find some real benefit in the suffering.

Meditation can help. The more we practice, the more awareness we have. The more awareness we have, the more we can notice when we're creating the needless suffering, and we can decide to do something else. You can see all this quite clearly on your meditation cushion. Let's say a pain comes into your back. There it is—it hurts! And then you begin to squirm, and you begin to complain, maybe about someone else whose fault it is that you are trapped in this body in this moment, or maybe about yourself. Your mind is raging all over the place. And this makes the pain much worse. If you are just willing to sit still and experience the pain, you see that it's not so bad. You can endure it. It can even sometimes disappear. But even if it doesn't, at least it's real. There's a dignity in bearing pain that must be borne. It is much better than squirming and complaining and making matters worse. You actually find that the more you squirm and try to improve things that cannot be improved, the worse it gets. The more you are willing to endure something that cannot be changed, the easier it is.

When we stop creating the unnecessary suffering, we can notice all the real suffering around us. All the fake, unnecessary suffering is actually distracting us, protecting us in a way, from the real suffering around us. The real suffering is much more intractable. It's horribly painful. But it connects us to everyone else in the world, and so in that sense, the real suffering is OK. We become numb and isolated because we want to avoid the suffering, but it's the numbness and isolation that feel the worst. When we break through the unnecessary suffering and connect with others, it's hard and it's painful, but it's also better. When we open up to the real pain of caring for others, we do feel better.

13

Everything Is Made of Mind

2019

THE TEACHINGS about mind are perhaps the most precious, profound, and foundational in Buddhism. Without some understanding of the expansive concept of mind described in these teachings, it's hard to appreciate the full context of Buddhist meditation practice and the enlightenment promised as its ultimate goal.

The Awakening of Faith in the Mahayana, an important text in East Asian Buddhism, begins by saying that mind—not only mind in the abstract but the actual minds of sentient beings—"includes within itself all states of being of the phenomenal world and the transcendent world."[1]

In other words, mind isn't just mental. It isn't, as we understand it in the West, exclusively intellectual and psychological. Mind includes all the material world. It also includes the "transcendent world," which sounds odd. Isn't it commonplace to think of Buddhism as having, refreshingly, no idea of the transcendent, which sounds like God? We are told that Buddhism is practical and down-to-earth, a human teaching for human beings. It's about calming and understanding the mind in order to put an end to suffering.

This is certainly true, and is a prominent theme of early Buddhism. But in contemplating what mind is, later Mahayana Buddhist pundits teased out huge and astounding implications embedded in the early teachings.

They began by distinguishing two aspects of mind—an absolute aspect and a relative, phenomenal aspect. These, they said, are both identical and not identical. So mind (not only in the abstract, but also my mind, your mind, the mind of all sentient beings) is at the same time both transcendent and not.

This means that the transcendence isn't a place or state of being elsewhere or otherwise: it is here and now. Mind and matter, space and time, animate and inanimate, imaginative and real—all are mind. Mind can be both absolute and phenomenal because it is empty of any hard-and-fast characteristics that could distinguish one thing from another. It is fluid. It neither exists nor doesn't exist. So, strictly speaking, it isn't impermanent. It is eternal.

In effect, mind equals reality equals impermanence equals eternity. All of which is contained in the workings of my own mind and that of all sentient beings. So this little human life of mine, with all its petty dramas, as well as this seemingly limited and painful world, is in reality the playing-out of something ineffably larger and grander. As Vasubandhu, the Indian Yogachara (Mind Only) sage, writes in his famous *Thirty Verses*, reality is simply the transformations of mind.

This is staggering, baffling, and heady. What does it have to do with the inescapable fact that I definitely feel as if I am suffering? My mind may be empty, eternal, transcendent, and vast, but I still experience my life unhappily. What to do?

We could pose the question like this: If my mind is mind, and mind is reality, what is the relationship of my unenlightened mind, the cause of my suffering, to the enlightened mind that puts suffering to an end?

From a psychological and logical point of view, enlightenment and unenlightenment are opposites. I am either enlightened and not suffering or unenlightened and suffering, and these certainly feel to me like vastly different states. But the teachings on mind assert that enlightenment and unenlightenment are in actuality not different. They are fundamentally suchness (and the word *fundamentally*—meaning "at bottom, at their core"—is important here). *Suchness* is a word coined in the Mahayana to connote the mind's perfect appearance as phenomena. When we receive phenomena as suchness, we don't experience what we call suffering—even if we suffer!

What we call suffering, and experience as suffering, isn't actually suffering. It is confusion, illusion, misperception, like seeing a snake that turns out to be merely a crooked stick. Suchness is the only thing we ever really experience. But since we mistake it for something painful and dangerous, we stand apart from it. We see ourselves as its victim, and so are pushed around by it, although in truth there is nothing that pushes, nothing that can be pushed, and no reason in the first place to feel pushed. Reality is not, as we imagine it to be, difficult and painful. It is always only just as it is: suchness.

But lest we project suchness to be something we can reach for or depend on, something other than what we are and see all the time in front of us, we are reminded that suchness isn't anything. It is a mere word, and the limit, so to speak, of verbalization. It is a word proposed for the purpose of putting an end to words and concepts whose mesmerizing effect on us is the real source of our initial mistaken perception. Since all things are equally and fundamentally suchness, there is literally nothing to be said. Even calling it suchness is too much!

So my suffering, as real as it seems to me, is delusional. But it's a powerful delusion! Its very structure is built into mind, and therefore my personal consciousness. Since its shape and location (these words are metaphorical: mind has no shape or location) is the same as that of enlightenment, to which it is identical, and since both are empty of any grounding reality, my delusion can't be gotten rid of. How can you get rid of something that doesn't exist? Trying to get rid of it will only make matters worse. Besides, to get rid of my delusion is to get rid of my enlightenment, which is my only hope!

In a famous metaphor, Mahayana teachings liken the relationship of delusion and enlightenment to that of a wave and the ocean.

The wave is delusion, full of motion and drama. It rises up, crests, breaks, dissipates, and gathers strength to drive again. With my eyes on the wave, I see it as real.

But the wave isn't anything. There is no such entity as "wave." There is only water, in motion or not. Wind acts on water to make what we call a wave. If the wind stops, the movement ceases and the water remains quiet. Whether there are waves or no waves, water remains always water, salty and wet. Without wind, the water is quiet and deep. But even when wind activity is strong on the surface, deep below water remains quiet.

Mind is like this. It is deep, pure, and silent. But when the winds of delusion blow, its surface stirs and what we call suffering results. But the waves of my suffering are nothing more or less than mind. And even as I rage, the depths below remain quiet. Life is the wind. Life is the water. As long as life appears as phenomena there will be the stirrings of delusion. Delusion is in fact the movement, the stirring, of awakening. My ocean mind is inherently pure and serene, always. When I know this, I can navigate the waves with grace.

───── ▶◀ ─────

The Awakening of Faith, the text I referred to above, offers an even better analogy. A man is lost. He is confused about which way is north and which way south. He has a place he is trying to go, but because of his confusion he can't get there. He feels disoriented and deeply uncomfortable. He has that sinking feeling of being lost, of not being in the place he wants and ought to be. But then he suddenly realizes there actually is no north or south—that these are just names people give to this way or that way, and that, no matter where he is, he is in fact here, where he has always been and will always be. Immediately, that man no longer has a feeling of being lost.

Likewise we are lost when we don't settle our lives in suchness. Misperceiving the wholeness of our mind, we see confusion and lack, which naturally gives rise to desire. We desire a destination, a state, that will bring us peace. But we don't know how to get there. We feel lost, ungrounded, desperate for road signs.

"Delusion" is the place we are fleeing. "Enlightenment" is the destination we seek. But it is a false destination. The path and all its teachings are like north and south, names for various directions that have some provisional value but in the end only confuse us if we take them as real in a way they are not.

Since people need maps and directions when they feel lost, enlightenment is proposed as a destination some distance from delusion. The teachings are serviceable, if provisional, navigation aids to point us in what we believe to be the right direction. But after we have gone on long enough to have calmed down a bit, we see the truth: there is nowhere to go and no way to get there. We have been there all along. In Mahayana Buddhism this is called original enlightenment, or *tathagatagarbha*—the Womb of Suchness.

This same point is made in a famous parable in the *Lotus Sutra*, an Indian Mahayana text that became profoundly influential in Chinese Buddhism. People are lost. They hire a caravan leader who takes them to what turns out to be an illusory city, where they find some respite. Somewhat refreshed, they are then told by the caravan leader that this is not and has never really been their destination. The destination is endlessly far ahead. In effect there is no destination; they have always been where they wanted to go. But if the caravan leader had told them this at the outset, they would never have believed him.

Now let's get practical. Given all this, what does what we think of as enlightenment actually amount to? Are these teachings proposing, as they seem to be, that we give up practice altogether and somehow suddenly leap out of what we experience as suffering, by some kind of mental magic trick? That we somehow will or think ourselves into enlightenment?

No. The entire culture of practice (including meditation but also study, dharma relationships, ritual, and much more) is necessary. But not in the way we thought it was, not as a way to make things different. Rather, we practice to shift our understanding of our lives. In effect, as *The Awakening of Faith* puts it, "The process of actualization of enlightenment is none other than the process of integrating the identity with the original enlightenment."[2]

Practice, then, is both a sudden (we have flashes of insight) and a gradual (it develops over a lifetime) identity shift. We stop seeing ourselves as the child of our parents, a poor lonely soul in a difficult world, with various conditioned imperfections, drawbacks, desires, and hopes, most of which remain unfulfilled. Instead we have confidence in our original enlightenment, which is and has always been at the center of our lives, despite our limitations and pain. *The Awakening of Faith*: "The state of enlightenment is not something that is to be acquired by practice or to be created. In the end, it is unobtainable, because it has been there from the very beginning."[3] This teaching about mind reminds me of a conversation I had with my mother toward the end of her life. She was dying. I knew it, everyone in our family knew it, but we didn't talk about it because my mother didn't like to think about it. But once, when we were having bagels and lox at a little deli near where she lived, she said to me, casually, as if it were a matter of mere curiosity, "What do Buddhists think happens after you die?"

"Well," I said to her, "it depends on who you think you are. If you think you are just this body and mind, just these memories and experiences and relationships and thoughts, then death is very bad news. Because when you die you will lose all that. But if you think you are also more than this, something you don't understand but somehow feel and have confidence in, then when you die that something—which was never born and so can't die—never goes away. And that would make it easier and happier to die."

I am not sure my mother got any comfort from those words. As I recall now, she looked more bewildered than comforted. But perhaps what I said did help toward the end, when her consciousness faded and her mind was quiet.

Certainly, the intention of the great Buddhist teachers who over the centuries have detailed these teachings on mind is not only to comfort us. They offer us these teachings on what mind really is to give us a sound basis for a way of practice that can transform our lives, and the world.

14

On Looking at Landscape

1993

THE LANDSCAPE is talking to me. I am hearing voices. They are not speaking words in the usual sense; they are speaking words of another order, impressions more powerful and moving than ordinary words, a singular, symbolic, terribly precise communication, as if a dream, that is rearranging my internal apparatus. My intentions are changed. My motivations are completely altered. My perspective is, literally, changed. The history that I thought I had is not now my actual history; an identity wholly other than the one called up by my name is insinuating itself into my most subtle feelings.

I hardly understand, consciously, as it happens. But underneath the play of my ceaseless thinking, which gradually becomes less compelling, and then finally stops altogether, I can sense it. Because I don't really know it is happening, I do nothing about it. I don't evaluate it or wonder about it. Consequently, I am open to the landscape; I do not grapple with it; rather, my mind and heart receive it in an empty condition. It is a liberating and a calming experience. I am renewed, magnified.

I am walking up the steep hillside behind my house. Ahead of me I can see layer on layer of hills, gray-brown and green, covered with scrub. Above that the sky is full of dense, slate-colored clouds over the ocean, with open patches blazing sunlight on the water. It is winter. The fallen stalks of hemlock slash against the earth-colored hills. Mostly I don't understand the landscape, don't know the names of the plants or the natural history of what surrounds me. I used to know more but I've forgotten. Knowing the names of things, I relate to them more closely and they appear to me more as individuals. My relationship is warmer. But after a while, my desire to know more about them, the feeling that I know them because I know their names and something of their histories, blunts my relationship to them. I want to protect them or love them, and I have less ability to be unknowingly influenced by them. Maybe that is why whatever I have known or now know about them so easily falls from my mind and I walk around in the weather like an idiot or an animal.

A sense of place escapes me. I do not know what that would feel like. I am not a regionalist, if that means using a place, belonging to its specifics, identifying with that place as though it were my own, affecting it, being affected by it in ways that I can understand.

Every place on earth has a long geological history. These hills were at one time at the bottom of the ocean. I say "these hills," but when they were at the bottom of the ocean they were not these hills. Their shape, the earth and rock that form them, the vegetation that grows on them were at one time all completely otherwise. And this coastline is drifting slowly north, a few inches a year. So when I think of this place, what of all that do I mean? All of it shifting, past and future present now.

I am nowhere when I am here, or I am everywhere. Hard to name any of it. But I can sense something about which I cannot speak.

In the High Sierra, a place I like to go and that has influenced me as much as any place on earth, you can stand in a completely silent place, a place that feels ancient, eternal, and you can know that a devastating event happened in an instant a long time ago. A tree suddenly uprooted by lightning or the weight of snow. A burst of lava shooting out of the earth. The rocks speak of it.

I first came to California driving west from Iowa City. I remember the journey as if it were a dream, mile after mile of prairie, then mountains, desert, mountains again. I had never seen such vistas of open space, where you could look at the skeleton of the earth, where you could feel the past so graphically, where the human was so dwarfed and irrelevant. This landscape exposed you on all sides. There was no shelter. It was at once frightening, exhilarating, and comforting.

Looking at a river flowing by is a particular kind of communication. There's a sense of urgency, of restlessness. The sunlight sparkles on the rippling water. If you throw something in, it vanishes downstream right away; in this way you can feel the speed and the power of the river that otherwise seems motionless in its constant motion. Night and day it never stops; sometimes muddy, sometimes clear; powerfully destructive in winter, inviting and cool in summer.

I grew up on a river. I crossed it by bridge almost every day and looked down on the wide expanse of moving water. The river received the force of all my moods and purged me of them. Walking across the bridge, I imagined that unexpected things were possible. That between the west side of the river and the east, some ultimate, life-changing event might happen, and might happen today. I have never gotten over this. Sometimes I think it is a childish notion, one that only a lonesome boy in a very small town would dream up. Other times I know it is really true, and that my experience has proven it. The river is not stupid.

To be a regionalist, to be too tied to a place, seems narrow-minded. There are many places, each with its charms and influence, and we need to be open to them all. To be too tied to one place is to neglect the relativity of things, to be closed to the unexpected. Humankind grew up, advanced and changed in places that allow great commerce with other people, the great seaports or river ports, the crossroads. Maybe we are or can be citizens of the earth.

And yet, do we ever escape our region? Is this a possibility?

Intellectuals from New York, the Bay Area, China, Germany are all different in their points of view. What influences that? Though the landscape is covered with asphalt and the sky obscured by tall buildings, what is it that gives rise to all the words that are uttered in parlors and cafes, written down in books and periodicals? We imagine that we have ruined or will destroy or save the earth, as if we possessed a consciousness that had a view of the earth. I sometimes imagine that the reverse is the case: that we are, in fact, products of the specific regions we inhabit, expressions of the stones, the waterways, the soil and air of our regions, for the amusement and curiosity of all. No region can be defined or exactly located.

Seeing mountains from a distance. Approaching the foothills from the plain. Looking at a lake in the early morning. Surveying the lowlands from the top of a mountain. Viewing the ocean at sunset, at twilight, at noon.

---- ▶◀ ----

When I first moved to California, I had two ambitions: to live in a redwood forest and to spend a lot of time looking at the ocean. I was fortunate to be able to do both. I wanted to do these things because I felt that the world and myself were broken. I had been involved in politics and had come to a kind of inner and outer chasm over which there was no passing. I felt, unconsciously, that the redwoods and the ocean would heal me. This more or less worked. I went to live first in an abandoned sawmill in the middle of a redwood forest. It was cold and damp. Every day I went out to walk in the forest. I spent a long time looking up at the sky, sighted along the trunks of the tall trees. A redwood forest is very quiet, cathedral-like. Now and then a shaft of sunlight shines through a gap between the tall trees onto the thick carpet of needles underneath. Only a few plants grow, and not much wildlife.

At the ocean, later, I watched the powerful movement of the water, restless, unsettling. Here was something foreign. You can walk up and down the beach for a long time, your thoughts seeming to roll and repeat themselves like the water. The ocean mirrored my inner confusion; it increased it, stirred it up, I think. Through the living room window of my friends' house we could see the expanse of ocean as we talked. The water's movement dwarfed our words and our emotions. When there was a storm over the ocean, it was impossible to talk at all. There was just the storm.

It is the imagination, not the intellect or the emotions, that responds to the landscape. Intellect and emotions react to what is present or to what is desired, what is possible but not present. Hand and mind define and alter things, and heart loves it or hates it and complicates it in the loving and hating. But we have unrealizable goals, impossible, undefinable, even shocking desires. And it is to these desires that the imagination responds, as if the imagination were a *supraphysical* sense of which our ordinary self can't be entirely aware. Imagination doesn't proceed from us directly; it seems to come as a song or as speech emanating from someone else. It's as if we overhear its communication from a distance. Imagination makes something out of us and out of the immediately present world that releases the tension produced by these unrealizable goals. Imagination, play, receptivity, the power of the unknown. That is why the encounter with landscape is a personal encounter. Landscape doesn't exist outside our mind; it is the shape of the mind, the shape of the imagination.

Suppose that human development proceeded in a spiral, passing through the same point at each higher revolution. At first the personal, the individual—what are these hands and feet, these eyes and ears; then the interpersonal, out of which comes our language and a deeper, more perplexing sense of who we are: knots and snarls, wishes and dreams. And perhaps a further quite natural development—the healing development, beyond which there can be no other—is into the *suprapersonal*, the undefinable, the realm touched only by the imagination, into which ordinary language, senses, and emotions are powerless to travel. Landscape. Our relationship to the nonhuman.

White bark pine at mountain's top
Dead manzanita tortured arms in moonlight
Quiet evening lake, vapors and trout rising
Coast Live Oaks dotting straw-colored hills
Quick white stream at the bottom of the canyon
First view of the ocean
Nighttime sky

15

Beyond Language

2011

A SEEMINGLY INESCAPABLE FACT of my life is that I write poems. Why would I feel the need to do this? I don't think of poetry as self-expression or making something beautiful with words. So these ideas furnish me with no motivation. And I don't get paid. But I seem to be convinced that there's a point to poetry: to clarify language through a process of ongoing exploration, so that I can more and more find out how to live within language as joy and liberation, rather than as bondage, which it can be and is when I am constricting myself and the world in language, without knowing I am doing this. Think about political discourse and how hopelessly entrapped within itself it is, and we are when we are talking and talking within a narrow, conflictual framework. This happens in our inner lives. We are our own CNN and Fox News. It's terrible.

So I am interested in and fascinated with language and its grip on us; language is a vital social and personal force that cries out for clarification—or exorcism. I realize that not many people see language this way. But whether or not you do, language is important to you because language describes and creates the world you live in; language describes and creates you. If the world is difficult and life is difficult, it is not so much that there is something wrong with you or the world (though there may be something wrong with you and the world—but what does this mean outside language?), it is rather that there is something wrong with the way you employ your various descriptions of self and world.

We usually think there is something and then there is talking about something and that the something is substantial and real and the talking about it is secondary. But in fact, there's no way to separate something from talking about something. Even perception is in part (the greatest part) a process of talking about something. As in phenomenology from Husserl to Heidegger; as in Wallace Stevens's "Description without Place":

> Thus the theory of description matters most.
> It is the theory of the word for those
> For whom the word is the making of the world,
> The buzzing world and lisping firmament.[1]

Language is humanness; human consciousness is language consciousness. We are so close to language (it is us; we are it), we can't understand it. We are in language as a fish is in water: for the fish there's no such thing as water; water is just the way things are; it's the medium for being. Language is that for us. I have been wondering about language and I cannot understand it and I cannot get used to it. I have been trying to understand language and yet I am no closer to understanding it now, after all these years of exploration, than I have ever been. Still, I am always writing about this effort to become familiar with language. It seems to be my chief topic: can we get friendly with language; can we know what we are? In "The Meridian," the poet Paul Celan writes, "Whenever we speak with things in this way [in poetry] we dwell on the question of their where-from and where-to, an open question without resolution."[2]

So language is, on the one hand, a prison: we're locked inside it, created by, defined by it, and can see only as far as we can say. On the other hand, language frees us: it unlocks our imagination, allowing us to reach out to the world, and to fly beyond it. This is what poets try to do. Of course, they always fail. The point is not to succeed but to make the attempt; in this there is already some freedom and some delight.

In Zen practice you are always trying to stand within language as an amazement, to open up the hand of thought and gawk at language, let language gawk at you. This means coming to understand and dwell within language in many ways. A word means something and not something else. But also a word is gone even as we speak or write it and so it isn't anything. When we speak or write something, we think we are understanding or communicating, but actually that is not so. When we are speaking or writing, we are speaking about nothing. Primarily what we are doing when we are speaking or writing is articulating humanness. Speaking or writing is just being ourselves, expressing that. When we get tangled up in something we think we are speaking about, we suffer. All language is music. Music doesn't mean anything, but this doesn't diminish its importance. We need music. Air and water don't mean anything either. And yet the paradox of language is that meaning is part of the medium; words have meanings assigned to them, but meaning doesn't mean anything, it's just part of the procedure.

This is a simple point, but mostly we don't appreciate it. We grip objects we have created with language, objects that don't exist as we imagine that they do, and we suffer for it. If we could experience language as it really is for us, and truly abide within that experience, no need to change it, probably we can't change it—we could be free from the suffering language creates. This doesn't mean that we'd be free from pain or sorrow. Only that we'd be free from the special sort of anguish that human beings feel when they are lonely and estranged from themselves, others, and the living world.

This thought lies at the heart of Buddhism and has from the beginning. The first three members of the eightfold path—right view, right intention, right speech—all hinge on language. These make right conduct (fourth) and right livelihood (fifth), conduct's extension, possible, and when there is right conduct there can be right effort, mindfulness, and meditation (six, seven, eight), which will deepen and reinforce right view—and round and round the path turns, making liberation possible. So from the first, Buddhist thought recognized language as pivotal to human conditioning— that views, intentions, and uttered words need to be examined and revolutionized. In later Buddhist thought this insight was strengthened and made more explicit with the teachings on emptiness, which understood the nature of human experience to be "mere designation," language, empty of any fixed definable reality.

───── ▶◀ ─────

As a spiritual teacher operating in the real world with real students, the historical Buddha was sophisticated and quite practical in these matters. He knew that getting caught up in language was a trap. He saw that nothing was more fundamental than right view—out of right view everything good unfolds—but he also saw that right view isn't some specific propositional truth. People sometimes ask me what is the Buddhist view of this or that. But there is no Buddhist view of this or that. The Buddhist view is a nonview, but not a nonview that is the opposite of a view, a wishy-washy noncommittalism. Nonview includes various views that arise in response to conditions. Nonview is an attitude, a spirit of openness, kindness, and flexibility with regard to language. Nonview is a way to stand within language, to make use of language so as to connect, without being caught by and separated from the world and others by language.

Buddha spent his life talking to people. Like Socrates, he was one of the greatest masters of talking to people in recorded history. One gets the sense in the sutras that the Buddha talked not because he was particularly loquacious, or because he was given to elaborate explanations, but in order to help people see through the smokescreen of their own language and views. Once someone asked him for his secret in answering questions as effectively as he did. He said that he had four ways of answering questions: One way was categorically—simply to say yes or no without ambiguity.

The second way was to examine the question analytically, clarifying definitions of terms, trying to determine what was actually being asked, usually by deconstructing the question. Most of the time when the Buddha employed this method, there was no need to answer the question: under analysis the question proved meaningless. The third way was by posing a counterquestion, whose purpose was to bring the questioner back to his or her own mind, redirecting attention away from the entanglement of the language of the question to something real that stood behind it. The fourth way was simply by putting the question aside, because some questions are so hopelessly entangled that to take them up on any terms at all would be to get stuck in them like flypaper—which doesn't help. Trying to answer these questions is like trying to get through a wall by beating your head against it—it is ineffective and you get a sore head. To put the question aside is to walk around the wall without beating your head bloody. This way you do get to the other side, which is, after all, the important thing. So sometimes the Buddha's response to a question was silence.

In his discussion of right speech, the Buddha similarly evidenced the subtle and nuanced understanding that words do not have fixed meanings and ought never to be taken at face value. The meanings of words depend on context: who is speaking and listening, the tone of voice employed, the underlying attitude, the situation in which the words are spoken. The very fact that the Buddha did not recommend that his words be written down—that he allowed others to explain the teachings in their own words, and did not designate a special sacred language for religious discourse but insisted that ordinary common language be used—shows that he understood language to be a process, essentially a dialogue, a dynamic experience, rather than a tool of exact description or explanation. Far from being a neutral conduit for the conveying of preexisting meanings, the Buddha saw that language is an ever-shifting vehicle for the self, and that the way to clarify the self, and the world, is to hold language in an accurate and sensitive way.

Of all the teachings of Buddhism they inherited from India, the Zen masters of ancient China emphasized most this point about language:

> A monk asked Zhaozhou, "What is the Great Perfection of Wisdom?"
> Zhaozhou replied, "The Great Perfection of Wisdom."[3]

> Another monk asked him, "What is meditation?"
> Zhaozhou replied, "Nonmeditation."
> Monk: "How can meditation be nonmeditation?"
> Zhaozhou: "It's alive."

> Another monk: "What is one word?"
> Zhaozhou: "Two words."

> A monk asked Feng Hsueh, "How can I go beyond speech and silence?"
> In response, Feng Hsueh quoted lines from a famous poem.[4]

What makes us miserable, what causes us to be in conflict with one another? It's our insistence on our particular view of things. Our view of what we deserve or want, our view of right and wrong, our view of self, of other, of life, of death. But views are just views. They're not ultimate truth. There's no way to eliminate views, nor would we want to. As long as we are alive and aware there are always views. Views are colorful and interesting and life-enhancing—as long as we know they are views. These Zen masters are just pointing out to us that views are views. They are asking us to know a view as a view, and not to mistake it for something else. If you know a view as a view, you can be free of that view, beyond views through views. If you know a thought as a thought, you can be free of that thought, free of thought through thought. Views are language, thoughts are language. To train ourselves in language, to open language up, is a practice that cuts to the heart of Buddhist liberation. It is why the Buddha never engaged in metaphysical debate and kept silence in the face of language-trapping questions.

Going beyond language through language is something we can actually practice and develop through meditation, study, awareness in our daily life acts, and through a practice of writing. In meditation we can learn to pay attention not only to sensation, but also to emotion and thinking. Learning to let thinking come and go, we can eventually understand a thought as a thought and a word as a word, and with this understanding we can find a measure of freedom from thoughts and words. With study, we can begin to appreciate Buddhist thought not as a new set of correct concepts, but as mental yoga, counterweight to the concepts we already, unconsciously, hold, and that hold us locked into small atomized selves. When in daily living we learn to return again and again to where we are, in body, emotion, and mind, we are learning to hold our language and views lightly, to see that they are ever-evolving currents of being, which are ours and everyone else's. Playing close attention to the way we talk to ourselves, we won't fool ourselves too much. Another old Zen master used to call out to himself and answer himself. He'd say, "Don't be fooled by anything." And he'd answer, "I won't be!"

16

Phrases and Spaces

2008

THE TECHNIQUE of working with phrases is the special genius of Zen practice. This technique consists of living with, penetrating, being penetrated by, phrases, until they become large and strange, revealing themselves to us. That is to say, through them we are revealed to ourselves.

By *phrases*, I mean literally phrases—clusters of meaningful words, identifiable, explainable, conceptual. But *phrases* also means the silence, the expansive, ineffable space that you will find in the middle of and surrounding all words and concepts if you meditate on them long and deeply enough.

In Zen meditation this is accomplished by practicing zazen—meditation—with phrases, breathing them, inquiring of them, casting off usual notions of linguistic comprehension. Practicing, as Zen master Dogen puts it, "thinking not-thinking." That is, allowing thought to arise and disappear, without grasping, without entanglement, without driving thought through fear, desire, smallness, stupid unrecognized circular habits, as we usually do. So that instead of going out toward the phrases, as if they weren't alive, interpreting or explaining them, gaining mastery over them, you allow the phrases to come forward toward you, until you feel them on their terms, free of the usual aggressive activity of the conceptual mind. Feeling them in the gut; letting them work on you.

In Zen there are various specific traditions and methodologies for working with phrases. In contemporary Western Zen, there are several koan traditions, all influenced by Rinzai Zen. Some of these traditions are very well organized, with koan curricula and prescribed ways of responding to koans in a fairly regimented format; others, though based on this kind of system, are more free-form and various, with a curriculum of stories used according to need, and with more flexibility in responding. In the Soto Zen that I practice, working with phrases is practiced in a fuzzy and disorganized way. There is no curriculum and no particular format. This has suited me, because I find I resist things that are too well organized; real life is fuzzy, and spiritual approaches that seem organized (they never really are organized; they just seem to be) and therefore suggest progress and reasonable development strike me as less honest than disorganized approaches that admit progress is a problematic concept to begin with. Though I have always been fascinated with religious systems, organized or not, I have a hard time taking them literally. But I realize that for many people, maybe most, organized approaches are good. They provide a map and a way of checking yourself.

I have said that the Zen practice of phrases involves actual phrases—word clusters—but also the silence that's always inside and all around words. Like the vast spaces inside atoms, without which what we call the "solid" world could not exist, silence makes words possible. In Soto Zen there's a way of practicing with phrases without any words. This is Zen mindfulness, which is not mindfulness of something, but mindfulness of silence, spaciousness, or emptiness or—another way to say it—of presence, of being itself. This is practiced using the breath or whatever is in front of you—a person, a task, a physical object—as the phrase. Life becomes the phrase, not in the abstract but as it appears uniquely, wherever and whenever you are. You pay close attention to it, avoid pegging it down to an explanation or an evaluation, and you wait with intense inquiry. The hope is that everything will illuminate you. Everything will open you up. Everything will surprise you. Although in real practice this doesn't always happen; it is a direction, an aspiration. In any case, the main point is to keep up a continuity of practice.

It doesn't make much difference whether you are practicing with what's in front of you or whether you are using a literal phrase like "Who is this?" or "What is love?" that may have arisen from the issues of your life; or whether you are using a classical Zen koan phrase like Zhaozhou's "Mu" or "the cypress tree in the courtyard." The more you meditate with the phrase and maintain your meditating with it through your activity (because, like phrases, which are more than phrases, meditation is more than literal sitting meditation), the more your practice can be continuous and the more will be revealed.

———— ►◄ ————

In the mid-1980s I was living in a Zen center led by Bernie Glassman. We practiced phrases in the Greyston Bakery, which was at that time the main project of the center. The bakery was a crazy place; we had more business than we could handle, and it was always a special time for breakneck effort: Halloween cookies, Christmas cakes, Thanksgiving pies, Valentine's Day heart-shaped tarts. It was always something. We were working very hard from morning till night. Bernie was tireless and expected everyone else to be tireless, too. And we were not professional bakers; in fact, we didn't know how to bake; we were learning as we went along. So it was exhausting work, going very quickly all the time, trying to fill rush orders, to get things right, and, of course, making many mistakes and constantly having to do things over again. In the middle of all this, Bernie would open up shop for *dokusan* (in his tradition it is called *daisan*), the traditional Zen interview in which the teacher examines the student's understanding of his or her koan phrase. He'd sit in his manager's office at his desk while you— in your baker's whites, covered with flour—sat in the outer room on a chair taking a few moments to quickly come back into touch with your phrase, which was right there at your fingertips, easily brought back into full consciousness. When Bernie rang the bell, you'd go in and respond and he would respond back and then he'd ring the bell and you'd go back downstairs to the assembly line as the next person came in. Such things are possible.

One of my favorite phrases—"Who is sick?"—comes from a koan collection, *The Book of Serenity*:

> Guishan asked Daowu, "Where are you coming from?"
> Daowu said, "I've come from tending the sick."
> Shan said, "How many people were sick?"
> Wu said, "There were the sick and the not sick."
> Guishan said, "Isn't the one not sick you . . . ?"
> Daowu said, "Being sick and not being sick have nothing to do with him at all. Speak quickly! Speak quickly!"
> Guishan said, "Even if I could say anything, it wouldn't relate."[1]

Later Tiantong commented on this, saying, "Say something anyway!"

It seems as though Daowu had the practice of visiting the sick, a marvelous spiritual practice. I do this practice, but not nearly as much as I would like. Walt Whitman spent the greater part of the Civil War visiting the sick.

It is also possible that Daowu was not visiting the sick. "Where are you coming from?" is a Zen question meant to evoke a response perhaps different from the mundane facts. When Daowu said he had come from tending the sick, he could have meant anything or everything by it. This is an answer we could give on any occasion: What are you doing? I am tending the sick. What else are we ever doing? This is the first noble truth of Buddhism: sentient beings are by their nature sick. To be alive is to have a terminal illness. The whole world is a hospital ward.

But then Daowu says, "There are the sick and the not sick." Who are the sick? The ones who think they can escape the pain and loss, who think they aren't sick. Who are the not sick? The ones who know we all are sick together, and have sympathy. They know the world is a hospital ward and we are always tending the sick, ourselves included. When we know this intimately, we are not sick. Ultimately, as Daowu says, the True Person is beyond sick and not sick. The True Person simply "is," and in this "is" is living and dying, sickness and health. In the face of this, Daowu asks Guishan to speak, and he does. Guishan was a great Zen master. He understood Daowu perfectly. Saying something won't explain anything, he says in so many words. Which is surely true. It's like asking someone, "Explain your life to me, I want to understand it." It's not possible to explain even a moment of life. But as Tiantong chimes in, "That may be true, but still you have to say something." That's right. Not saying anything is not an option. We tell our stories. We try to help.

PART THREE
East/West

NOTES ON CULTURAL ENCOUNTER

THE QUESTION OF cultural influence is complicated and, these days, a point of bitter contention. Who owns what? Who gets to speak? Who speaks for whom? Colonialism and historical dominance of one culture by another mean that cultures have often encountered each other on unequal terms. Sometimes the very survival or ongoing development of a culture is at stake in the encounter. What we call Buddhism is a case in point; it has traveled from India through the many cultures of Central, Southeast, and East Asia, and now to the multiple cultures of the West.

Cultures, of course, have always communicated, they can't help doing this, and the taking on by one culture of a form or idea from another changes both. The receiving culture, necessarily bound by its own way of looking at things, is guaranteed to misunderstand and twist what it is taking in. And it goes both ways: the transmitting culture will be influenced in a feedback loop by that very misunderstanding (or perhaps a different understanding) to see itself in a new light. There isn't and has never been any unitary or coherent culture, pure and distinct, no matter how much anyone claims this; and though it's the job of historians and cultural critics to parse shapes and processes of cultures, no one can have anything to say about this that isn't tentative and itself culturally biased. We are all culturally myopic, as we have been discovering and acknowledging for some time now.

When it was introduced to the modern West several hundred years ago (taking under advisement dubious terms like West and East), Buddhism was naturally considered an exotic and quite strange Eastern religion. When I first began to practice, Zen possessed a distinctly Japanese aura. Of course we assumed that our Japanese teachers understood Zen—we did not, so we ought to take their word for it. These powerful men (they were all men) were charming, charismatic, and dedicated. We asked them lively questions, of course, but we did not question their authority or the religion they were bringing. My first encounter with a Japanese Zen master (the great Shibayama Roshi of Nansenji Monastery) was at a month-long retreat in upstate New York in the late 1960s. At the end of each day, our retreat cohort would discuss whether Shibayama Roshi appeared special and impressive to us because he was enlightened or because he was Japanese. We could never decide.

Fifty years on, Zen and Buddhism are almost completely acculturated into Europe, Australia, and Latin America, and, because of this, although Zen is essentially the same religion it has always been in Japan, it is understood differently there. (I have written about this in my poetry diary *Escape This Crazy Life of Tears: Japan 2010*.) Now young Japanese monastics come to the United States or Europe to study Zen because they imagine something there more authentic and more lively than the time-encrusted tradition that stifles them at home. At the same time, there are, of course, traditionalists in Japan (and elsewhere in Asia), and there are American and European Zen priests who go to Japan seeking what they consider authentic Zen. So who owns Zen? Whose Zen is authentic? Is the very idea of authentic Zen suspect? Is there or was there ever, really, East or West?

The basic thrust of human character formation as Sigmund Freud conceived it in Vienna in the late nineteenth century doesn't necessarily compute if you are born and raised in Beijing, Tokyo, Mumbai, or Lhasa. There's the famous story of the Dalai Lama being baffled by the concept of "low self-esteem," since as far as he was concerned (and Buddhist teaching states) all human beings love themselves much more than they love others. In Tibetan Buddhist practices for the development of compassion and love, students are instructed to visualize their mothers, the assumed paragons of caring and kindness. Tibetans at first did a double take when they heard that Westerners did not always view their mothers as loving individuals and that "mother issues" were not uncommon.

———— ▶◀ ————

When I was doing a reading at a bookstore in Vancouver, British Columbia, a young Chinese woman in the audience said that when she was growing up in China she thought of Buddhism as very silly stuff, relevant only to superstitious grandmothers. As far as she knew, Buddhist temples were dusty dark places where people burned paper money to provide economic sustenance for their relatives in heaven. When she emigrated to Canada, and noticed to her surprise that educated and aware white people were practicing Buddhism, she decided to investigate. She discovered something completely different from what she had seen at home: a practical psychological practice that would help you in your life. When I repeated this story some months later at a public dharma talk, I was castigated by a white American woman who told me that I sounded like a cultural imperialist, implying that old Chinese people were stupid and backward, and that only we educated modern Westerners really knew what Buddhism was or was supposed to be.

She had a point! It took Western convert Buddhists of the 1960s only a decade or so to move from unquestioning respect for Asian teachers to an unconsciously arrogant sense that they were casting aside the "cultural baggage" of Asian Buddhism to find its "true essence." Some of the British and German scholars who first translated Buddhism for the West in the early nineteenth century (and who were representatives of colonizing cultures) proceeded on this assumption from the start. They assumed that the pure and true Buddhism they were finding in the original texts had been corrupted by years of tradition and was only now being refurbished—by them! According to this way of looking at it, Buddhism (or any religion or philosophy or praxis) is an eternal essence to be extracted from ancient sacred texts, which essence is bound to be corrupted over the centuries by ignorant practitioners.

Contemporary scholars of religion have a very different point of view. They are uncovering the biases of the early scholars, who were studying a Buddhism they did not realize they themselves were constructing. Today's scholars say that religion isn't what texts seem to say it is. Texts can be read in many ways—especially across cultures and languages. Rather, religion is what the people who practice it feel and think, do and believe, as they interpret (or ignore) those texts. Religions don't become corrupted over time, they simply change, for better or worse, according to the uses people need to make of them.

In the early days when we American Zen students were earnestly trying to do things the way the Japanese did, we always failed. No matter how hard we tried, we inevitably did things our own way, because, like anyone, we were products of our conditioning; we simply couldn't escape being who we were. On the one hand, you might say we were botching up our project of trying to understand and practice Zen. On the other, you could say that without really knowing what we were doing we were practicing the religion that we, in our world, needed to practice, so as to eventually make it available to others like us who also needed to practice it in this way.

And this adaptive Western Buddhism has taken many forms. Throughout what we call the developed world, employee training programs are a huge business; training of all sorts is mandatory for people in almost all walks of life, from workers in manufacturing corporations to service employees in both public and private sectors. Much of what is offered in these programs is influenced, usually indirectly, by Buddhist practices and concepts, through programs created by people who have practiced Buddhism and have adapted it to a business setting. Psychotherapy is enormously influenced by Buddhist ideas and practices. It is not unusual now for therapists to recommend meditation to their clients, and there are therapeutic methods (like cognitive behavioral therapy) that are outgrowths of Buddhist practices. Mindfulness is now so ubiquitous in the therapeutic and corporate training communities that some Western Buddhist practitioners have begun to complain about "McMindfulness" (mindfulness as a form of fast food), which they consider a capitalist plot to trick workers into being more productive. Though this may be going a bit far, there are other more nuanced critiques of mindfulness in the corporate world. Yet I have no doubt (since I know many mindfulness teachers) that those who offer mindfulness in business and other secular settings do so with a sincere desire to help.

———— ►◄ ————

For better and worse, Buddhism easily lends itself to this morphing and adaptation because it is maximally flexible in form and doctrine. In fact, "pliancy of mind" is prominently mentioned in Buddhist lists as a desirable mental factor conducive to spiritual advancement. And Buddhism is famous for not insisting on belief, instead advancing a "try it and see if it works" attitude. Most contemporary Buddhists in the West, though enthusiastic about their practice, genuinely do not care whether someone becomes a Buddhist or not. They are completely open to the mixing and matching of religious practices and concepts wherever this would be beneficial. From a Western point of view, this may seem a refreshingly strange attitude for a religion to take. But actually I think it's Western (that is, Greek and Judeo-Christian) culture that is strange in its assumption—insistence is perhaps a better word—that there be one truth and one truth only. In general, most people in most times and places, when left to their own devices, have not been bothered by living with lots of contradictions.

Which gets personal with me, since I have been for some years seriously involved with both Zen Buddhist and Jewish practice. This came about by chance: my good friend Alan Lew, whom I'd met at the University of Iowa Writers' Workshop on the first day of classes, and with whom I had practiced Zen, became a rabbi and moved to San Francisco to lead a congregation. He asked me if we could do some meditation events together, and I happily said yes. These events were great fun for me, but torture for him. He soon found himself in the position of defending the faith, in response to the many Jews who had a respectful feeling for peaceful Buddhism and a lot of animus against the judgmental Judaism of their childhood. Eventually we suspended those early Jewish-Buddhist retreats and started, at the turn of the millennium, a Jewish meditation center, Makor Or (Source of Light). As codirector of a Jewish center, I had to study Judaism (though I grew up in the tradition, I was not knowledgeable) and have been doing that with great delight ever since.

People ask me sometimes how I can practice both Judaism and Buddhism at the same time. Don't I get confused? I respond in a typically Jewish way, with a question: Why not? Where's the confusion? Buddhism seems to have no problems with this, and so far as I know, my Buddhist colleagues do not complain. At first it looked like the Jewish community was going to be a bit nervous about this mixing, but now there is a thriving international Jewish meditation movement that has influenced several of the more liberal denominations, and even some of the conservative ones. I've also had experience meditating with Christians, who, like many Jews, practice meditation as a way to gain deeper access to the teachings of their own tradition.

This seems important. We live in an age when religion is both deeply contested and at the same time desperately needed to give comfort and guidance to a challenged humanity. It would be hopeful to imagine (as I do) that meditation—simple silent sitting that doesn't require doctrine or belief—could help humanize and soften our great religious traditions, making them more friendly and flexible.

It's even possible that this friendly and flexible spirit could be extended beyond silence to teachings. Since Buddhist teachings do not require metaphysical commitment or passionate faith—they are to a great extent psychologically oriented—they can be used side by side with traditional teachings of other religions. These days there are lots of "Jubus," committed Jews who also practice Buddhism and even teach it. I work with several rabbis who do this seriously, and who are good at it. There are Christians who do the same. (I am less connected to the Muslim community but would be surprised not to find this there as well.)

I write in this section about Dogen, whose writings are, to me, the strongest expression of this flexibility and openness that enables Buddhism to be so useful. Dogen expresses the nondual teaching that is essential in Zen and all of Mahayana Buddhism and is, I believe, basic, at core, to all generous spiritualities. I have been studying Dogen all my adult life; I am sure that his teachings have entirely colored my point of view. *Nondual* is a fancy word that means more or less that opposites are not really opposites. God and humanity, heaven and earth, the world of passion and the cool world of serene nirvana, society and the monastery, even good and evil, right and wrong, true and false, life and death—these dichotomies are not at war with each other, they are in balance, they depend on each other, and are even, at the deepest levels of understanding and experience, identical. To read and fully appreciate Dogen's teaching is to fully accept this sad world, including one's sad self, as it and you really are, and, at the same time, to see transcendence and bright possibility right in the middle of it. I first found this in Dogen, and since then, have found it everywhere else, certainly in all the art and spirituality that has moved me over a lifetime's contemplation.

17

On Dogen's *Shobogenzo*

2011

Shambhala Publications' publication of Kazuaki Tanahashi's translation of the complete text of *Shobogenzo* (*Treasury of the True Dharma Eye*) marks a watershed moment for Western Buddhism. The masterwork of the founder of Japanese Soto Zen, Dogen Kigen (1200–1254), *Shobogenzo* has been legendary for centuries. At first known only to adepts and disciples, the text was later brought to light and venerated, but for centuries almost never read. During the Tokugawa period the text was unearthed, edited and published, and used as the basis for a radical reformation of Soto Zen. In twentieth-century Japan, secular Japanese philosophers touted it as their answer to the great philosophies of the Occident. In the West, *Shobogenzo* stands almost alone among Buddhist writings as a work that philosophers and intellectuals with or without Buddhist affiliations take seriously. Its notorious difficulty and startlingly modern themes (like language, being, and time) have caused it to be compared in scholarly essays and books to the work of Heidegger, Wittgenstein, and others. Naturally, contemporary Soto Zen practitioners, both here and in Japan, have embraced *Shobogenzo* as the basis for their practice.

With all this, it is no surprise that *Shobogenzo* has been amply translated into English. In addition to many volumes of selections, there have been three complete translations of the text (which runs usually to several volumes) into English: one by Nishiyama and Stevens, one by Nishijima and Cross, and one by Rev. Hubert Nearing, a monk from Shasta Abbey. All three of these works, impressive though they are (translating *Shobogenzo* is justly considered the feat of a lifetime), have remained fairly obscure, published in small editions and generally only studied by specialists. With the Tanahashi version, we now have an edition that will receive the sort of attention this great work deserves.

———— ►◄ ————

Tanahashi has been at work on this project for fifty years. In 1960 he began a translation into modern Japanese of Dogen's difficult medieval Japanese text, and within a few years had produced (with the late American Zen teacher Robert Aitken) the first English translation of what is probably Dogen's best-known essay, "Genjokoan" ("Actualizing the Fundamental Point"). Since then he has been translating steadily, working with dozens of Zen teacher-collaborators from around the country, from several Soto Zen lineages, and producing several volumes of selected works, the first of which, *Moon in a Dewdrop* (published in 1985), has become a contemporary Zen classic in its own right. The present full version draws together all the previous work and adds considerable material that had not been included before.

Tanahashi's version, compared to the others, has two key advantages: first, the long time frame and the sheer number of collaborators, almost all of whom have been practicing and/or teaching Zen in America for decades, make for a deeply considered and deeply relevant text; and second, Tanahashi's insistence on emphasizing the poetic flavor of Dogen's prose—combined with the excellent work of poet and Zen teacher Peter Levitt, overall associate editor of the present volumes—brings to the text a beauty of tone, diction, and style the other versions lack. I have been studying *Shobogenzo* for almost forty years (though only in English versions), and to my eye and ear, the Tanahashi-Levitt version seems not only most accurate but also—and especially—truest to what I imagine to be Dogen's potent expression in Japanese. To put it most simply:

Dogen writes profoundly, and Tanahashi, Levitt, and their collaborators have paid more attention to the quality of expression in
English than any of the other translators. (Disclosure: I am one of
the collaborators, so can make no claim to objectivity.)

Japanese Zen was the first of the Buddhist traditions to make
big waves in the West. In the 1950s, the Japanese Zen scholar-
practitioner D. T. Suzuki taught at Columbia University in New
York, where his lectures were attended by many of the leading cultural players and avant-garde artists of the day. Through them his
influence spread to the Beat writers, who popularized Zen as a form
of aesthetic improvisation and passionate present-moment awareness. With the cultural space for Buddhism opened by Zen and the
arts, many other forms of Buddhism rushed in. By the 1970s, what
we now call Vipassana, as well as Tibetan Buddhism, were becoming well established. Western Buddhism moved beyond its original
Japanese basis, with a strong emphasis on the aesthetic, to a more
psychologized perspective, in which personal transformation and
"the science of mind" became most important. From today's van-
tage point, it is easy to forget how important Japanese Zen and
Japanese culture were to the original establishment of Buddhism
here.

Contemplating this new translation, I find *Shobogenzo* inspiring
and important exactly because of the Japanese spirit that Dogen
brings to his rereading of Chinese Chan. Two Japanese cultural
concepts that seem to me to be major influences on the general
mood and tone of *Shobogenzo* are *yugen* and *aware*. *Yugen* means,
roughly, "mystery." It refers to the fact that this human world that
we see and hear and take completely for granted is, in fact, deeper
and more mysterious than we can ever know. Yugen was an aspect
of Japanese court poetry even before Buddhism arrived, but in
Dogen's hands it becomes conflated with the East Asian Buddhist
doctrine of tathagatagarbha, or original buddha nature, as taught in
the *Lotus Sutra*. In this text, of signal importance in China, though
noncanonical in Theravadin countries and barely read in Tibet, the

Buddha reveals that his practice, enlightenment, and parinirvana, as taught in the Pali suttas, were an illusion, a tale told for effect, because human beings were not capable of grasping the shocking and more mysterious truth. But now, in the *Lotus Sutra*, this truth at last is revealed: the true Buddha was in reality not born, did not attain enlightenment and enter nirvana; in fact, he has existed, exists, and will exist everywhere and in everything, and all practice is nothing other than the manifestation of his True Illumination, all pervading and everlasting. Like a phantom city that is produced by a magician to encourage weary travelers far from their destination, the earlier teachings of a historical Buddha were given to aid practitioners who needed them. In truth, reality itself is Buddha, and even our suffering has its buddha nature. Dogen couldn't help receiving this teaching as profound confirmation of the mystery of human life that is a deeply embedded value of Japanese culture.

The second Japanese cultural concept that Dogen brings to Chinese Chan is *aware* (pronounced "a-wah-ray"), "impermanence." *Aware* appears as a form of nostalgia and sadness, love for a fleeting world we can never grasp. Of course, impermanence is also a cardinal principle of Buddhism. In Dogen's hands the two conceptions collapse into one, so that the fleeting world and its human sadness and sense of beauty are one with the three marks of Buddhism, suffering, not self, and impermanence.

Because of these cultural roots and combinations, *Shobogenzo* presents a radically unique view of Buddhism and of Zen as being not so much a retreat from or a transcendence of ordinary reality, which is essentially *dukkha*, suffering, a vale of tears to be overcome, as "instead" the full embrace of the human world as the world of nirvana. To be sure, this radically nondualistic approach to Buddhism is not Dogen's invention; it is a clear doctrine of Mahayana and Vajrayana Buddhism. But in combining this doctrine with his Japanese cultural sensibility, Dogen brings a poignancy and an appreciation for humanity that other Buddhisms lack. This sensibility is everywhere in *Shobogenzo*, but perhaps nowhere better expressed than in "Genjokoan," where, after delineating the dialectic between enlightenment and delusion, Dogen concludes, "Yet in attachment blossoms fall; in aversion weeds spread."[1] In other words, for Dogen the ultimate standpoint of dharma is simply the full affirmation of our ordinary human world of attachment and aversion and their consequences. It is precisely through full appreciation of this vale of tears that Buddha's illumination shines in us.

I remember, as a young Zen student, being enormously moved by these words when I first read them. It made sense to me then, and still does, that the point of my practice was not to overcome my humanity, to transcend it in becoming enlightened, but rather to settle into it with ultimate depth and appreciation. This is the overwhelming point of *Shobogenzo*.

There's little doubt that Dogen did not intend to reread Buddhism in the light of his own culture. He apparently felt, as he often wrote, that what he was transmitting was not Soto Zen, and not Zen—it was simply dharma itself, as originally taught by the Buddha. He felt that in his teaching and practice he was returning to the root of the Original Teaching, as he had received it from his own Chinese teacher, Rujing.

Nevertheless, his reenvisioning of the Zen tradition is clear throughout the text of *Shobogenzo*. Quite often he will comment on a traditional Zen story in a way that seems quite blatantly to turn upside down the typical way the story is understood. Usually the key to this reinterpretation has to do with the fact that whereas in the usual view of the story someone is enlightened and someone else is not, in Dogen's version everyone in the story is equally enlightened from the start, no matter how much this would seem not to be the case. For example, there is the famous story of the First Zen Ancestor in China, Bodhidharma, who calls his four disciples together for a contest, to see which of them has the best understanding. He poses a question and they each answer. To the first he says, "You have my skin," to the second, "You have my flesh." The third has his bone, and the fourth, Huike—clearly

the winner and in Zen's sacred history the Second Chinese Ancestor—has his marrow. But Dogen reads the story as if all four equally
possess the full measure of Bodhidharma's truth, using expressions
like "the skin contains the skin, flesh, bones, and marrow."[2]

Such a rereading of the tradition, on such radical principles,
connects to the perspective that *Shobogenzo* is most famous for,
and that becomes almost a fixed doctrine in Japanese Soto Zen:
that practice and enlightenment are one phenomenon. This runs
completely counter to the normative Buddhist view (which dove-
tails fully with our conventional materialistic and psychological
view) that one practices in order to achieve nirvana or enlightenment, which comes after the practice has been accomplished, as a
consequence of it. After all, what would be the point of practice
if it weren't a process leading to a positive result? This is what we
all want, and it seems to be exactly what the Buddha's teaching
promises. The Four Noble Truths seem to point to this: suffering,
cause of suffering, end of suffering, path to bring this about. To
explode this conventional view in as many ways as he can, Dogen
takes on many fundamental questions in *Shobogenzo*: Time (Uji),
Space (Koku), Practice (Gyoji), Compassion (Kannon), Meditation
(Jisho Zammai), Language (Mitsugo), Enlightenment (Daigo). In
essay after essay he is at pains to show that the way we conventionally understand the teachings is not in accord with what the
Buddha actually taught. The view that time is sequential, yesterday coming before today and tomorrow coming after, is incorrect,
Dogen tells us. Time is nonexistent, and simultaneously eternal: so
the thought that practice leads to enlightenment is wrong; it is a
superficial view. Practice doesn't lead to enlightenment: a moment
of practice is a moment of enlightenment. And enlightenment,
to begin with, is not a state in contrast to delusion; it is "delusion
throughout delusion."[3]

Given this, one might wonder, why practice at all? For Dogen
this is a question that could only come from ignorance. To ask

why one should practice if practice doesn't have a payoff in enlightenment is for Dogen to completely miss what practice, enlightenment, and human life actually are. We practice because of enlightenment, which is the key to our essential human nature. *Shobogenzo* is a powerful argument, made in many ways—from the deeply conservative to the wildly radical—that the only thing that counts for dharma, and for human life in general, is continuity of practice. Ongoing practice that is inspired by and is a manifestation of Original All-Pervading Enlightenment.

For Dogen, this radical fact of life pervades everything. Because of it, we can't talk or write about practice as if practice and enlightenment were objects or states we could examine and comment on: our talking and writing are necessarily a form of practice. This understanding accounts for both the beauty and the famous difficulty of *Shobogenzo*. It's not that Dogen is obscure for the fun of confounding his readers. It's simply that we do not find in Dogen's writing what we expect to find. His insight is that explanatory teachings will always be misleading because they will reinforce delusional concepts of cause and effect, time and space, enlightenment and ignorance, and so on. Therefore, speaking and writing about dharma must avoid explanation in the ordinary sense and tend toward the poetic, suggestive, and all-inclusive statement. Thomas Cleary once collected a group of his Dogen translations under the title *Rational Zen*, to make the point that, unlike almost all other Zen masters, Dogen did not consider Zen to be a mystical teaching "beyond words and letters," but rather something that could and should be discussed. But the word *rational* is misleading. Dogen's painstaking discussions of koans and other traditional Zen and Buddhist material are not rational in the usual sense. They are essentially poetic. *Shobogenzo* has been prized over the centuries and especially now as a text whose religious and philosophical insights are perfectly matched by its form of expression. Dogen's literary mastery is impossible to bring over into English.

No translation will do justice to it; all translations will be essentially incorrect. But as far as I can tell, no better attempt in English for a general audience has been made than this present version.

18

The Place Where Your Heart Is Kept

2014

This piece appears as the introduction to Mitsu Suzuki's book of haiku *A White Tea Bowl: 100 Haiku from 100 Years of Life,* translated by Kate McCandless.

IN THE SUMMER of 2010, I went with a group of close students and friends on pilgrimage to Japan. We spent a week at Rin-so-in, the original temple of Shunryu Suzuki Roshi, founder of San Francisco Zen Center and of our Zen practice lineage in America. Author of the most widely read of all Zen books, *Zen Mind, Beginner's Mind,* Suzuki Roshi was a beloved spiritual master. He was also Mitsu Suzuki's husband. Her years with him, and all that they brought to her life, certainly fed the silent depths whose waters gave rise to the exquisite poems featured here.

Rinso-in is a relatively small temple in Yaizu, formerly a fishing village, now a port city on the Pacific Ocean. In style and feeling, it is a far cry from the large Japanese Zen training monasteries, famous (if not legendary) for their tough practice. The students and friends I brought—many of whom were Zen priests—had all practiced Zen with me for many years in the United States. I myself have never trained in Japan and do not emphasize Japanese ways in my teaching. But I wanted my closest students to experience the feeling and flavor of the Zen that Suzuki Roshi expressed, the simple life of caring for a temple and its members that he had lived at Rinso-in, and that his son and successor, Hoitsu Suzuki, still lived.

We spent the week sitting in Rinso-in's small zendo, chanting in its Buddha hall, cleaning around the temple, and watching Chitose, Hoitsu Roshi's wife; their son Shungo, who is also a priest; and his wife Kumi take care of the many tasks necessary to serve a local community of farmers and small-business people. The busy, if also essentially peaceful, life flowed all around us as we foreigners sat zazen, talked, drank tea, cooked our meals, and cleaned around the temple.

Mitsu Suzuki lives with her daughter a fifteen-minute drive from Rinso-in. We phoned to wish her well, not expecting to see her. At ninety-six (her age in 2010) she deserved by now some peace and quiet, and we had been told that she was no longer receiving visitors, especially people from her San Francisco days, because the effort to speak and listen in English was becoming too difficult. But when one of our group who had been a close tea ceremony student spoke to her on the phone, she said she wanted to come to meet us. We were surprised and delighted.

Okusan, as we had been used to calling her, arrived at the temple with a burst of energy. She bustled straight past us into the Buddha hall, where she immediately made prostrations and said quiet, concentrated prayers, her head bowed, her prayer beads in her hand. She then got up without assistance and, beaming, said loudly in English, "Welcome home!" We were touched by this, thinking she referred to us—that, as students inspired by Suzuki Roshi, his temple was in some way our real home. But later we realized she was saying this to herself—"Welcome home, Mitsu, to the place where your heart is kept."

We sat for a long while having tea and cookies. She spoke English astonishingly well, as we sat on the tatami floor, she on a little chair, to preserve her knees, she said. She was like a queen holding court, self-contained and dignified, still able to hold her trim, tiny body as she had always done, energetically upright, with elegant hand gestures accompanying her words. She had brought photo albums of Suzuki Roshi in the old days. "Here," she showed us, "is Suzuki

Roshi at the moment of leaving Rinso-in for the last time." Hoitsu was behind him: the two priests, father and son, were enjoying a private joke long gone by now.

She had also brought a copy of *Love Haiku,* an anthology edited and translated by Patricia Donegan, in which two of her haiku appeared. Then she recited another haiku in Japanese, which had recently won a prize.

No limit
to kindness—
winter violets.

After a while, when she tired of English, she went on energetically in Japanese, with one of our group translating. When asked how she kept so fit in body and mind, she replied, "I walk around the neighborhood every day for an hour. I make sure to say hello to those who live alone." She mentioned in particular the school next door for children who "can't go to school"—she visits them every day, bringing small gifts and good cheer—and the businessmen's boardinghouse on the other side, where many men come and go, staying only for a day or two.

At the end of her visit, a traditional children's song about spring bubbled up from her memory. She continued to sing as she strode out of our sight to her waiting car and driver, her crisp white *hippari* and matching white pants hardly making a sound as she glided away. Her sudden absence left the room somehow sadly empty, though the group of us filled it well enough. For years in America, teaching tea ceremony and Japanese ways was her practice. Now, apparently, it was kindness.

———— ►◄ ————

The long life of Mitsu Suzuki (she turned one hundred on April 23, 2014) is an unrepeatable marvel. As it spans the changes and disasters of one of the most spectacular centuries in history—

one in which East and West have been struggling to meet and understand one another—the winds of time have blown her back and forth across the ocean. Beneath her sweetness, one senses the stoic toughness she possesses not so much because she was raised to it but because it was required of her.

She was born in Shizuoka City in 1914, amid growing Japanese militarism and competition with the West. Her mother died when she was eleven, leaving Mitsu the woman of the household. At nine-teen, dissatisfied with the conventionality and coldness she found in Japanese Buddhism, she converted to Christianity, becoming a member of the local Methodist Church. In 1936, at twenty-two, she married Masaharu Matsuno, a naval pilot. When war broke out in 1937 between China and Japan, Masaharu went off, with Mitsu seven months pregnant. He was killed just two weeks after seeing the first photographs of his daughter.

After the war, Mitsu trained as a schoolteacher and, when her daughter was three, began teaching at a local kindergarten. When the Pacific War—the war Americans know as World War II—began, and American pilots began flying their interminable and devastat-ing raids over Japan, Mitsu and the other teachers would take their students into bunkers every day as bombs rained down on the city. On the night of June 16, 1945, less than three months before Japan surrendered, the entire city of Shizuoka was burned to the ground.

Mitsu, like almost all Japanese of her generation, had been brought up to believe—and had experienced as a fact—that Ameri-cans wanted to kill her and her countrymen. How strange, marvel-ous, and probably disturbing then that by the early 1960s she would find herself living in the United States, the new wife of a Soto Zen priest stationed in San Francisco. A working Japanese Christian single mother would not have been able to imagine such a thing in 1940. Yet it happened.

After the war, the schools of Japan were in terrible shape, most of them closed, their facilities destroyed. Civic leaders everywhere rushed to take care of this problem as fast as they could. In Yaizu,

Shunryu Suzuki was keen to reopen the historically important kindergarten attached to Rinso-in. He had been told of Mitsu by a mutual friend and was determined to hire her to run the school, though she insisted she would not leave Shizuoka, and that, in any case, how could a Christian woman run a Buddhist school? But Shunryu was extremely persistent. He kept reappearing in Shizuoka again and again to ask Mitsu to simply come visit the school. Finally she agreed. One visit was enough to convince her to take the job. As for the Christian problem? "Well, at least you have some religion," he told her.

Shunryu visited the school daily, leading the children in chanting and Buddhist lessons. He and Mitsu became close colleagues and friends—two strong, opinionated, and charismatic people, with lively senses of humor. Then tragedy befell the Suzuki family: Shunryu's wife was killed by a mentally ill priest whom he'd allowed to stay at the temple during one of his absences. He was left with three young children. He needed a wife. The Rinso-in community (including Shunryu's mother-in-law) quickly agreed that Mitsu was the only possible choice.

The two were married in the fall of 1958. He was fifty-four, she was forty-four. Within the year, he had been invited to become abbot of Sokoji temple in San Francisco, fulfilling his lifelong dream of going to America to teach Zen to Westerners. His short-term appointments to Sokoji kept being renewed, and the longer he remained in America, the more young Western students began to come to practice zazen—not necessarily what the Japanese-American temple members were interested in. Eventually Shunryu turned over Rinso-in to Hoitsu, resigned his post at Sokoji, and threw in his lot entirely with the young Western students. By 1961 Mitsu had come to join him. She remained for thirty-two years—returning home in 1994, twenty-three years after Shunryu's death. During those years Mitsu Suzuki became—by the account of the many American students who studied tea and, yes, in an informal way, Zen with her—an accomplished spiritual master. She inspired affection and respect and was a second mother to many. In her quiet yet forceful and definite way, she expressed and embodied Zen spirit and continuity with the founder. She continued to live in the small apartment in the temple building, where she taught tea, cooked, cleaned, tended altars, and received guests. She was an anchor. As long as Okusan remained, as long as she went on day by day quietly expressing her life in engagement and sympathy with the community, things would be OK.

———— ▶◀ ————

Suzuki Roshi died too soon. Even the most developed students he left behind were young and green, full of idealism and Zen theory and moxie but not enough maturity. They had not lived through the sorts of challenges that Okusan and her husband had experienced during their years in Japan and so had no basis for appreciating Zen as the religion it actually is—a powerful consolation and source of strength in times of suffering and instability. Okusan's presence expressed this strength and depth during the long years of Zen Center's rocky coming of age. She held down the fort, shored up the foundations. When that work was done, the maturity of the center established, she went home.

More than anything else, what Okusan taught in America was what Japan lacked after the war and perhaps still lacks—confidence in the depth of the Japanese way as formed by the culture's long encounter with the Buddhist teachings. Although she had studied tea casually as a child, it wasn't until she came to America that she began to study in earnest. Her practice of writing haiku also began in America, during the time when Suzuki Roshi first fell ill. How strange then that the powerful expression of her life, her essential Japaneseness—that elusive and almost ineffable feeling that unites tragedy, toughness, delicacy, beauty, and simplicity—was oddly never fully expressed in her until it came out in America, possibly as a way of coping with the strangeness, or maybe the pain, of living so many years among the people who had burned her country nearly to the ground—incomprehensible people, in many ways completely oblivious to who she was and what she had lived through—yet who, at the same time, perhaps understood and appreciated her more than anyone else ever had. Only in America did Mitsu Suzuki finally find and express her Japanese heart.

> I bow to my ballpoint pen
> and throw it out—
> year's end

19

Why Do We Bow?

1997

MANY PEOPLE have this question the minute they walk into the zendo and are told to make full prostrations to the Buddha image on the altar. They come with an idea that Zen is beyond words and letters, beyond religion, beyond rules, beyond piety, and so the idea of such a thoroughgoing and outrageous display of what seems like religious fervor seems quite disturbing to them.

So why do we bow? I had this same question myself in the beginning of my practice. My teacher took me up to the altar and let me look closely at the tiny Buddha there. He pointed out to me that the little Buddha was also bowing. So I was bowing to the Buddha and the Buddha was bowing to me. "If he can do it, you can do it," he said. I thought that was fair enough.

Bowing is just bowing. You do it mindfully, in a particular way, aware of the body and mind in the doing of it. The so-called meaning of it is extra. It's not a symbolic or conceptual act. It's just another form of sitting practice. You sit, you walk, the bell rings, you get up and bow. To just do what you do with full attention and without much worry is an important part of the method in Zen.

And there's another way of looking at it: We are bowing to an image that suggests something to us. The image feels like compassion, peace, maybe transcendent wisdom when we gaze at it. So the bowing is a training method. We offer our whole body and mind to wisdom or to compassion, opening ourselves, in the act of the bow, to that quality, letting go of everything else in our life but that quality, bringing it out, making it big, fashioning it day by day, bow by bow.

When I bow to the Buddha on the main altar at Green Gulch, I train my mind deeply, creating a powerful predisposition in myself toward the development of love and appreciation for the buddha nature that is my own nature. When I bow to Tara, I am training my mind, creating a predisposition in myself toward the feminine and active in my own nature.

This kind of training is not something most of us are used to. Our sense of training has largely to do with will or skill, and this kind of training has to do with warmth and devotion. Yes, piety. But after all, piety is all right, devotion is all right. In fact, they are very tender and splendid emotions if you can cultivate them without getting hysterical about it. It's OK to respect Buddha and make offerings to Tara. We can appreciate Buddha and Tara and all the other figures that we practice with as "other" when we really appreciate that they aren't really other. The more familiar we are with ourselves as we actually are, the more comfortable we are with Tara and Manjushri and everyone else. As my first teacher said, the bowing is always mutual; there is one bow back and forth. Buddha bowing to Buddha, Tara bowing to Tara.

A long time ago, when I was serving as his attendant, I noticed that Katagiri Roshi always mumbled something as he bowed. I asked him what it was, but he couldn't tell me since it was in Japanese. Later on, I received in the mail a translation of the bowing verse, which I have used ever since.

"Bower and what is bowed to are empty by nature," it goes. "The bodies of oneself and others are not two / I bow with all beings to attain liberation / To manifest the unsurpassable mind and return to boundless truth."

20

Applied Dharma

2009

HAD MY FIRST experience with "applied dharma"—using Buddhist practices to try to help people in need, whether they are Buddhists or not—watching a video. It was a tape of a PBS show called *Healing and the Mind* that featured Jon Kabat-Zinn teaching a Mindfulness-Based Stress Reduction class at the University of Massachusetts Medical Center. As everyone knows by now, Jon had invented this vocabulary and technique, an adaptation of Buddhist mindfulness practice, to help patients at the hospital whose cases had been pronounced hopeless.

Since there seemed to be nothing the doctors could do to alleviate their chronic pain and illness, the hospital decided to give Jon, then a medical school faculty member, a shot. His six-week course turned out to be wildly successful. Over many years it brought not only relief but also wisdom and happiness to thousands of patients with previously intractable conditions.

As a Zen priest who'd spent my whole adult life in monasteries and temples, I was initially skeptical as I watched that video. For me, Buddhism was a radical religion, whose goals and practices were at odds with what people were normally looking for in life. I had been trained to view enlightenment as the goal of Buddhism— total liberation that went far beyond worldly aspirations like health and well-being. In my Soto Zen tradition, the desire to derive any benefit at all from the practice, "a gaining idea," as Suzuki Roshi, our founder in America had called it, was really bad. Gaining ideas would blunt your sincerity, and sincere effort was the most important thing.

Yet as a religious person I was sympathetic to the idea of helping people in need. It also thrilled me to think that the esoteric practice I was engaged in might be serving larger numbers of them. So it took almost no time for Jon's compassion—his sheer love for the people he was working with and his passion to try to help them—to win me over. All doctrines and notions about what the practice was supposed to be or not be were swept aside by the depth of caring I saw in action in that video. Jon was not trying to sell anybody anything. The claims he made for the practice were honest and encouraging. "Try this—I think it will help—but you have to be patient, you can't hate your illness and be desperate to make it disappear. Be patient and work with your condition, not against it. Then maybe something will change." A different way of speaking about Buddhist practice than I was used to, but one that was clearly authentic. Later I went to the clinic at UMass to witness classes. I met and spent time with Jon, and we quickly became friends. I learned from him that what I'd read in the sutras was true: the path is available to everyone and must be shared, and to guide others effectively you must be willing to use whatever comes to hand ("skillful means," as it's called in Mahayana Buddhism).

Since news of Jon's work has spread, a host of ways have developed to apply dharma. Mostly these efforts have used, as Jon has used, the language of mindfulness to describe the method of practice. The Buddhist word for "mindfulness," which means basic awareness, is *sati* in Pali, *smrti* in Sanskrit, which includes the idea of remembering, holding in mind. That is, remembering to come back to awareness when the mind has strayed from it. Although what we call meditation includes many forms and techniques, basically meditation is mindfulness. Sitting quietly, you establish awareness of the body and of the breathing. When your mind wanders, you bring it back. Once basic awareness of body and breath is established, you can also be aware of bodily sensations, thoughts, feelings, and so on—whatever arises in the field of awareness can be appreciated as long as you let it arise and pass away without too much identification, judgment, or entanglement. In fact, one definition of mindfulness is "nonjudgmental awareness." Just seeing what's there.

In the *Mindfulness Sutra*, the primary pan-Buddhist text on mindfulness practice, the Buddha says that mindfulness is "the only way to deliverance." This is very counterintuitive to our can-do Western mentality. Mindfulness proposes that the more we try to fix or improve things, the more we get stuck in them. But that if we are willing to simply be aware, without entanglement, things will slowly come naturally to wise equilibrium.

What we call meditation—sitting quietly without moving—is a particularly focused form of mindfulness. But mindfulness practice goes beyond conventional meditation. Once we have some training in mindfulness meditation, we can extend mindfulness to any other activity, until eventually mindfulness becomes a way of life. We become much more aware of what is going on, within and without. When we're angry we know we're angry, when afraid we know we're afraid. With awareness of our state, we don't react wildly compelled by unconscious impulses; instead we respond with much more accuracy and kindness. This movement from reactivity to response is the key shift that mindfulness practice aims for. But it comes about organically, with training, without forcing anything.

Mindfulness is easy to explain, but the actual practice is subtle. Since we arc always to some extent aware, unless we are asleep, it can be hard to grasp the difference between normal awareness and the more subtle, eyes-wide-open, nonjudgmental awareness of mindfulness practice. But with some training you do get the hang of it. In the last decade or two there has been an enormous amount of research corroborating the efficacy of mindfulness in healing and mind training of all sorts. At this point there is not much doubt that mindfulness practice brings benefit on many fronts—it reduces stress and so promotes basic health; it provides methods to bring healing to difficult illnesses; it improves personal effectiveness in work and personal relationships; it can be a basis for the cultivation of all sorts of positive emotional and attitudinal states, like compassion, loving-kindness, equanimity.

Jon had found himself at UMass Hospital, had seen a local problem, and had the intuitive sense that the basic Buddhist mindfulness practice he knew might help. I have tried to do the same. Whenever someone has appeared asking me to help with an issue that mindfulness practice might address, I have always said yes.

———— ▶◀ ————

In the 1980s, even before I saw the video of Jon's program, colleagues and I at San Francisco Zen Center began the Zen Hospice Project. We had noticed that the simple act of mindfully caring for the dying—simply offering a damp towel, a cup of tea, and a smile, with a spirit of acceptance of rather than resistance to impermanence (a hallmark of mindfulness)—was powerfully healing. Our community had cared for Alan Chadwick, our gardening teacher; for the Buddhist writer Lama Govinda; for the philosopher and anthropologist Gregory Bateson; for our friend and Native American teacher Harry Roberts; and for our own Zen teacher, Suzuki Roshi, when he died in 1971.

It seemed natural, then, for us to apply dharma in this simple way, especially at the height of the AIDS crisis in San Francisco, when so many of our friends and fellow practitioners were in need. Today the Zen Hospice Project continues to do its caregiving work and has spun off another organization, the Metta Institute, that aspires to have an impact on how end-of-life care is delivered in America through training health care professionals who work with the dying in the kind of mindful care we have developed over the years.

I am on the faculty of Metta and have found it interesting to figure out how to teach mindfulness practice in the professional context. Professionals have a lot of knowledge about medical and psychological issues relating to the care of the dying and their families. But what they are not necessarily good at, and where mindfulness practice can help, is in the development of a compassionate presence—the ability to evoke an atmosphere of love, forgiveness, and acceptance, so that whatever healing is possible in those last days or weeks can be encouraged to take place. Any time death is imminent, this atmosphere is potentially present. But where there's too much fear and denial, or too much pressing for a particular result, things don't go well. Sometimes professional knowledge and experience not only don't help with this but can get in the way. Thinking you know what to do, having experienced past cases, can blind you to what is uniquely present now. With careful attention to what is going on deep inside, mindfulness practice can bring you to more awareness of your basic confusion about death, your possibly exaggerated need to help heroically, all your unconscious stumbling blocks. If you can learn to be aware of such things with acceptance and forgiveness, if you can also receive some training in becoming comfortable with silence through intensive meditation training, you will have a deeper capacity to be with dying in a healing way.

I have two old friends, Gary Friedman and Jack Himmelstein, who train professionals in conflict resolution and mediation. After years of talking about how mindfulness meditation could be used in their work, we began to include it in the training. Gary and Jack practice what they call "understanding-based conflict resolution." The goal is to help people in conflict understand one another as a basis for resolution of issues, rather than to simply act as a broker to bring about a compromise solution, which is generally the method used in mediation. One of Gary and Jack's key concepts is the notion that no conflict is about what it seems to be about. Impasses over money or property are really about deeper concerns that usually do not surface. Any solution that does not address these deeper concerns won't really hold.

For years they have taught a method of dialogue that will help mediators guide parties to a discovery of what lurks beneath the surface of conflict, and they have been successful. But the introduction of ongoing mindfulness practice has taken the work to a new level. When mediators learn to see more deeply into their own motivations and prejudices with a sense of acceptance and curiosity, rather than with judgment, they are able to make use of their own emotions—and to come to understand others better. The conventional wisdom in mediation work is that the mediator must keep his or her emotions out of the equation and be a neutral, dispassionate observer. But anyone who has practiced mindfulness knows that there's no way to keep your emotions out of anything, and that imagining you are doing so only means you are prey to your emotions rather than guided by them with some wisdom. I remember the aha moment in one of our training sessions, when a mediator realized that she didn't have to pretend to herself she wasn't angry at one of the parties—that mindfulness practice had given her the capacity to be aware of her anger without expressing it inappropriately, so that she could admit it to herself, learn from it, and make use of it to help the parties find a solution.

I have also for some years worked with lawyers under the auspices of Contemplative Mind in Society, a nonprofit with a mission well described by its name. Here the issue is, "How can mindfulness practice help to humanize what has become a very stressful and difficult profession?" Contemplative Mind's Law Project sponsors a group of lawyers who meet with me regularly to meditate and engage in dialogue and experimentation about this. Each year we offer national mindfulness retreats for lawyers on both coasts to share our explorations with others.

Over a number of years these lawyers have revolutionized the way they view and carry out their work, moving from what some of them have called "the gladiator" model of zealous advocacy to one in which they see themselves as wise counsel and ally to their clients, trying to bring healing to very difficult human situations rather than simply to win cases. The lawyers have often noted that sometimes winning the case with maximum aggression does not actually serve the needs of the client.

──────── ►◄ ────────

Probably the clearest way to understand mindfulness work with lawyers, mediators, and end-of-life-care professionals is as training in emotional intelligence. EI is a concept popularized by journalist Daniel Goleman, another Buddhist practitioner motivated by a desire to usefully apply dharma. While it is clear from many studies that emotional intelligence is a key factor in effectiveness in all sorts of spheres, it is not so clear how or if one can develop it. It turns out that—as I have found—mindfulness practice is the most effective way to improve emotional intelligence. At Google, the enthusiastic and idealistic young engineers are not looking for calmness or healing, but they are interested in developing emotional intelligence, for work and for their personal lives. Our six-week course there, called "Search Inside Yourself," uses meditation, journaling, mindful dialogue, and a host of other techniques to improve EI.

Many of the practices I use there, and in the other trainings I do, are simple extensions of mindfulness practice. They are readily adaptable by anyone who would like to use them to develop more mindfulness in everyday life. We're using an e-mailing practice, for instance, that incorporates mindfulness. You can try it. Instead of shooting off a hurried e-mail, and dealing with the consequences later, take an extra moment. Write the e-mail, then close your eyes and visualize the person who is going to receive it. Remember that he or she is alive, a feeling human being. Now go back and reread the e-mail, changing anything you now feel you want to change before sending.

We also train in a communication practice called "looping": when listening to someone, intentionally try to pay close attention to what is being said, rather than entertaining your own similar or dissimilar thoughts. When the person is finished talking say, "Let me make sure I understand what you are saying. I think you said . . ." and then feed back what you heard. This way the person feels truly heard and respected, and has a chance to correct whatever distortions in your hearing there may have been. Looping saves a lot of trouble and misunderstanding, especially when the communication is sensitive or difficult.

There are many more practices like this, simple but powerful techniques to maintain mindfulness throughout the day:

- Taking three conscious breaths—just three!—from time to time to interrupt your busy activity with a moment or two of calm awareness.
- Keeping mindfulness slogan cards around your office or home to remind you to "Breathe" or "Pay Attention" or "Think Again."
- Training yourself through repetition to apply a phrase like "Is that really true?" to develop the habit of questioning your assumptions before you run with them.
- Practicing mindful walking whenever you get up to walk somewhere during the day.
- Instituting the habit of starting your day by returning to your best intention.

My mediation training partner Gary Friedman practices returning to his best intention by pausing before he sits down to meet his first clients of the day. He silently reminds himself as he places his hands on the back of his chair that he is about to participate in a sacred act—the effort to bring peace to conflict. In these and many other ways you can invent, mindfulness can be extended to practically any situation in daily life. And it will make a difference.

I believe the Buddha never intended to create a specialized sphere of life called "religion." In his time, there was no question of secular or sacred, church on Sunday and work during the week. There was only life and life's difficulties, and the possibility that with cultivation one could live with less trouble and strife.

Although many of his teachings were given in the context of the monastic community in which he lived, many more were given to laypeople to make their lives more peaceful and successful. The contemporary application of dharma to so many spheres of contemporary life would not, I think, seem strange to the Buddha.

Philip Snyder, executive director of Contemplative Mind in Society, and an anthropologist, is fond of saying that a thousand years ago our civilization was profoundly altered by the spreading of literacy to the general public from the monasteries where it had been exclusively practiced. Could it now be the case, he wonders, that the practice of mindfulness developed for millennia in monasteries and temples will similarly be released and spread throughout the world, with just as large an impact?

21

Putting Away the Stick

1998

I REMEMBER my first time inside a zendo. I loved the feeling.
The atmosphere—profoundly quiet, but supercharged with
energy. The way everyone sat absolutely straight and motionless, dressed in black, in the very precise, dim room. The ambience
was much enhanced by the use of the "encouragement stick" that
was carried during almost every period of zazen.

A long, thin, flat hardwood stick, the *kyosaku* was marched up
and down the aisles with great ceremony by the experienced students. If anyone fell asleep during zazen (as happened more than
occasionally), the monitor would pounce: Whack! . . . whack! One
good hit on each shoulder and the wary offender was awake. The
sound, repeated unexpectedly but regularly throughout the period,
made the feeling in the zendo electric.

The kyosaku, the older students would be quick to tell you, did
not actually hurt, despite its dramatic sound. If the monitor hit you
properly, the experience was invigorating. I frequently requested
the service and found this to be true. Later on, I carried it myself.

Occasionally, of course, monitors messed up. When their aim
or attention flagged, the results could be painful. There were also
now and again monitors whose intentions were not always good;
who, subject to minor fits of sadism, seemed to miss more often
than others.

In addition to this anomaly, there were two other important
downsides to kyosaku practice. Because the zendo was open, and

newcomers were constantly coming to sit, it was impossible to orient everyone to the kyosaku. I used to wonder what such first-timers thought—or felt—when they heard a gunshot-like report coming out of nowhere as they peacefully meditated.

It also became gradually apparent, quite oddly, that the kyosaku, and the samurai spirit it fostered, served to increase rather than decrease sleepiness in the zendo. It is difficult to say why this is so, but I suspect it has to do with the fact that externally imposed discipline has a deadening effect on the spirit, and the kyosaku, whatever its real purpose and intention, was understood by many people as external coercion.

The Gulf War of 1990–91 was a very upsetting time in our sangha. Several of our sangha members had relatives who were in the combat zones, and signs of the almost gleeful response to the war in the society at large were everywhere. Much was said and written in the press about how the war was in a sense an answer to Vietnam: this time, we were winning. In the midst of that time, our abbot, feeling that the kyosaku was a symbol of the violence that is never far away from any of us, and has certainly been a part of Zen history in Japan, put the stick away for good, as a gesture toward peace.

We no longer carry it, the zendo feels much more friendly and compassionate, and people rarely sleep in zazen anymore.

22

On God for Sue

2013

W HEN SUE MOON was guest editing "the God issue" for the Buddhist magazine *Inquiring Mind*, she asked me for a piece. I told her I had nothing to say on the subject, and she said, Well, suppose I ask you some questions, would you answer them? I said I would, and the piece below is the result. Some years later Shambhala Publications asked me to write an updated introductory Zen book, and I told them I had nothing to say. Then I remembered this essay and asked Sue to ask me some questions, which resulted in our coauthored book *What Is Zen? Plain Talk for a Beginner's Mind.*

Sue: When you were a child growing up in an observant Jewish home, how did you feel about God? Was God important to you?
Norman: My impression of belief in God in Judaism—at least the way I grew up Jewish—is that it isn't a question. It was never discussed because it wouldn't have made sense to discuss it. It was just assumed—deeply assumed. The ideas of "belief" and "faith" seem to be inherently Christian concepts—because Christianity does have a complicated and interesting doctrine of faith. And "belief" is an important word in Christianity. But growing up, we had no such idea. Judaism was identity and praxis—that is, you *were* Jewish whether you liked it or not: if you tried to escape being

Jewish, eventually you'd be found out, so there was no use denying it. It was for better or worse a fact of life. And then if you *were* Jewish, you *did* Jewish, that is, you went to synagogue, observed kashruth, and so on. So God wasn't an issue; God was just a basic assumption that had to do with being Jewish. You were you; ergo God was God. Something like that. To tell the truth, this still seems true to me.

As a child, the way it seemed true to me (and still does!) had to do with the strangeness of the experience of being alive: literally perceiving, feeling, thinking, and so on. The world just seemed strange. This must have to do with God—was the reasoning. So, for instance, walking to synagogue holding my dad's hand, seeing the sparkling substance, whatever it was, dazzling in the sidewalk as we glided by. How else would that be possible if not for God?

In Judaism as I knew it, there was no theology: there were just stories. You read the Torah every week in shul and you knew the stories. These were stories about God and about people trying to engage God—not because they believed but because God was involved in their lives as a fact: experientially. Clearly these were stories. Not exactly historically true: more true than that. There was no end to trying to understand what they meant. This was obvious. The stories assumed God. It all made sense to me at the time. I remember being very small and listening to a recording of Bible stories. God spoke in a booming baritone male voice—very intimidating, very frightening. I used to hide under the table. On the other hand, it was thrilling, and I listened to this record again and again.

Sue: How did your sense of God change when you were a young man?

Norman: As I grew up, my sense of God didn't particularly change. I studied religion and philosophy and, of course, became sophisticated in my way of thinking and speaking about God. I no longer believed (but I don't think I ever did) that God was watching over and protecting us in some spatial and anthropomorphic way. But somehow this increased sophistication did not touch my earliest ideas about religion, God, and so on. It just seemed like I was learning more and more developed ways of thinking about what I knew all along. Now I *do* believe in the benevolent protection of God. Not in the sense that good things will always come to good people whom God loves, but in the sense that something always happens, and that what happens is what it is and not something else—and that therefore there is a special virtue in it. Whether or not we discover the virtue is our problem. That seems to me to be ample evidence of God's tremendous compassion and grace. We can absolutely depend on it!

Sue: When you began to practice Zen, did you think about God? Did you miss God? Were you glad to be done with God?

Norman: When I started to practice Zen, it was like when I stopped going to synagogue and began chasing girls and playing sports as my primary obsessions: that is, I didn't think, "Oh, this religion stuff is no good, I quit." I just went on to the next thing that naturally called to me, assuming that the religion stuff was still relevant and would still be there when I needed it. I guess I had an enormous confidence in my sense of Jewish identity, backed up by God. It seems I didn't think I needed to tend to it, that I could move on to whatever was next and it would all be OK. When I started to practice Zen, it was like that: my explorations had led me to Zen naturally, and this is what I was going to give myself to, with the same kind of full-on hysteria that I'd given myself to the great American triumvirate of baseball, football, basketball—and girls. Now it was Zen. But I didn't miss God or wonder whether I was abandoning God or God was abandoning me. I figured (or rather, I didn't figure, I just assumed without thinking about it) God would always be around. Because when you think about it, if God is, as I had assumed, simply embedded in the strange and uncanny fact of existence, then how could God *not* always be part of the equation?

The fact that God is officially not an issue in Buddhism—or is, in some forms of Buddhism, apparently denied, didn't trouble me at all. Different language game. No problem. Anyway, Zen seems not to be invested in denying the idea of God. Suzuki Roshi mentions God several times in *Zen Mind, Beginner's Mind*, with apparent approval.

Sue: Did you return to your Jewish practice after you were a Zen practitioner/teacher, or was it always there?

Norman: I didn't practice Judaism much when I began doing Zen. I was living in a Zen temple and it was a very full life, no time for it. But when our kids were old enough, we did seders and other stuff, and then when my mother died in 1985, I wanted to say Kaddish (the prayer for the dead said in synagogue for eleven months after a parent dies) for her so I went to a synagogue in Tiburon, the nearest place to where I lived at Green Gulch, and told the rabbi who I was (a Zen priest by then) and why I wanted to be there. He said OK; he was a very nice man. And I got involved with regular attendance there, with my mother in mind. Then in 1990, my dear and now departed friend Rabbi Alan Lew returned to the Bay Area, and from then on, I began doing a lot of Jewish practice with him. We started a Jewish meditation center, Makor Or, that I still direct and teach at. I learned a lot from him, a tremendous opportunity, and he got me to study a lot, which I still enjoy. Judaism is so great, so fascinating. So I actually have quite a lot to do with Judaism.

Sue: How does your Jewish meditation practice frame the idea of God? Is there any conflict with your Zen practice? Do you speak about God freely in the context of Jewish meditation and Makor Or?

Norman: Our Jewish meditation theory is that God is presence, presence both within and beyond your life (within and beyond turn out to be completely mutually implicated, when you look closely).

And that while Judaism knows this and Jewish practice is meant to foster it, in fact most contemporary Jews do not have access to the richness of God-encounter that Judaism contains—even often those who are observant. (Because a major motivation for Jewish observance is to strengthen the community—which is not only reasonable and salutary; it is also self-protective conditioning from a long history of oppression.) This is where the meditation comes in—it is easy access to God-encounter—through encountering your own body, breath, mind, and presence. I speak of God all the time at Makor Or—and sometimes at Everyday Zen, too.

Sue: What, if anything, did you tell your children about God?
Norman: I communicated to my children what my parents communicated to me—God is obvious, necessary, and ubiquitous. It is not a matter of belief or faith. And you don't need the word *God* if it seems to cause you problems. After all, does it make sense that God would be limited to positive feelings about a three-letter word in the English language, and that if you had a problem somehow with that word (because maybe where you live it is socially unacceptable) God ceased to exist for you? No, this makes no sense! There is no doubt there is more to life than meets the eye, more to being alive than the material world. In fact, there is more to the material world than the material world! What is this "more" if not God? It's also fine to call it something else. As to the question of God as personal: as the French Jewish philosopher Emmanuel Levinas once said, "Of course God is personal, because we are persons."

Sue: Do you pray? To whom do you pray?
Norman: I pray all the time. To God. I am asking God to help out with this and that, mostly friends who are ill, people who have died, the crazy messed-up sad and foolish world. Please help with all this, God, as I know you will. I am never disappointed with God's active

response. Because I know what to expect. And I am thanking God a lot for almost everything.

Sue: Have you had moments of feeling directly connected to God?
Norman: I usually feel directly connected to God. I'm alive and I can tell I am alive.

Sue: What is God like?
Norman: God is like being alive—like life, like being. Which of necessity involves death and not being—which is where the God part comes into it.

Sue: Do you think about God in connection with death? Do you think people go to God when they die?
Norman: I think that, yes, death is the mother of God—or vice versa. So of course when you die, there's nothing left but God—no more resistance.

Sue: What is your responsibility as a Zen teacher, in talking to students (like me) who yearn for God, or to other students who come to Zen relieved that at last they don't have to "believe in God"?
Norman: I try not to think too much about my responsibility as a Zen teacher. As you know, I resist the idea of myself as a Zen teacher. It seems like such a trap—for me and for anyone else who practices Zen with me. I always think of the old koan "There are no teachers of Zen; I don't say there is no Zen, just no teachers of Zen." There are roles to occupy, and I have mine; everyone has his or hers or theirs. I am interested in responding honestly to anyone I meet, as far as I can understand that person, and the life I have lived, in the practice. I hope it helps but I never really know. If it does help, the reason is not my wisdom and brilliance; it is the luck (you could also call it karma) that will produce some fruitful encounter between two people meeting in the middle of

a dazzlingly complicated world. Since I am sensitive to language because of my long-standing poetry habit, I usually do not get caught up in debating with someone about their choice of words. I think useful truth is in the meaning, not the words. The art is to find the words to indicate something to this person now. Speaking of which, I'll close with a poem from my 2004 collection, *Slowly but Dearly.*

How God Gets into It

God arrives in the transitions—
the times between before and after
the shatterings, bendings, breakings
moments of devilment and blasted pose—
The feeling then arises, a draft in the system
tiny shaft of light in the visual field
which, when noticed and affirmed,
opens out to an aura on the screen of eclectic ineffability—
One's arms open in quietude and perplexity
There's nothing to say, do, or think

23

Reencountering the Psalms

2002

This piece was written as the introduction to my book *Opening to You: Zen-Inspired Translations of the Psalms*.

SOME YEARS AGO I stayed for a week with the Trappist monks of the Abbey of Gethsemani. There I encountered for the first time the Christian monastic practice of choir, which consists, for the most part, of daily recitation of the Psalms. Although I had grown up chanting the Psalms in Hebrew (a language I can pronounce but not comprehend), it was at Gethsemani that I first paid attention to what these texts were saying.

There are many uplifting, inspiring, and soaring verses in the Psalms. But the passages that caught my ear during those early morning and evening hours in that Kentucky summer were not those. I was astonished at the violence, passion, and bitterness that was expressed. For me, whose lifelong spiritual practice has been silent sitting meditation, it seemed almost impossible to believe that intoning these disturbing and distancing words could be the basis for a satisfying religious practice. In all innocence I asked the monks about this and received many cogent and impassioned responses: that the anger and violence in the Psalms were human emotions that could find healing through expression; that these things are part of our human life and must not be left out of religious contemplation; that the suffering the Psalms express is holy suffering and that to enter into it is to become close to God; and much more. All of it made some sense to me, but I wasn't really satisfied. Nor could I dismiss the Psalms as irrelevant. I saw that these good brothers of Gethsemani were true treaders of the path, sincere practitioners, possessed of wisdom and knowledge. If the Psalms had meaning for them, clearly I was missing something. I felt I had to investigate for myself. These selected versions of the Psalms are the results of that investigation.

———— ▶◀ ————

I call them "Zen Songs" because I approach them the only way I can: as a Zen practitioner and teacher, with a Zen eye. Yet I have not tried to rewrite the Psalms as Zen philosophy; quite the opposite, my intention has been to learn from them, to expand my own understanding under their influence. Nevertheless, although my way of life and understanding has been thoroughly saturated by Zen, I am still a Westerner, and so I have found in the Psalms a very familiar music that seems to express my own approach to enlightenment: the passionate, prickly, and lively noise that naturally seems to rise up from the silent depths of my heart.

And I do not think I am unusual. Western Buddhists are Buddhists, yes, but also Westerners. This makes a big difference. It is why Buddhism in the West is and will continue to be very different from what it has been in Asia. No matter how much Westerners try to immerse themselves in the Buddhism presented to them by their Asian teachers (and expressed in the Asian texts), they will always inevitably see it colored by Western concepts and views and by a Western feeling for life. You could view this as a problem, a distortion of real Buddhism, and I know that many Asian Buddhist teachers feel that Westerners just don't "get" Buddhism, and that it will take several generations for them to get it. While this is a reasonable way to look at it, I prefer to see the problem as an advantage, and to view the inevitable mixing of Western and Asian Buddhist perspectives as something fresh and inspired, rather than somehow incorrect.

I have seen in myself and in my students just how deeply the Western feeling goes. It is simply not to be denied, not to be papered over with a veneer of Buddhism. There has been much written of and discussed about this in relation to Western psychology, and in many ways the Western Buddhist movement has been thoroughly, probably for good and for ill, psychologized. But I am sure our Westernness goes deeper than the personal. Our whole sense of what we think of as human, what we think of as the world, and how we are to stand in the world, is thoroughly Western, thoroughly Judeo-Christian. Certainly Buddhism will have a powerful effect on these deeply held views if we practice it for a lifetime; for many people the change has already happened. But even so, even as quite thorough Buddhists, we will continue to stand on Western ground and will continue to hold, in the depths of our hearts, some Judeo-Christian sensibility.

Once at a Jewish-Buddhist retreat we were leading at Tassajara monastery, my old friend and colleague Rabbi Alan Lew was asked to make the odious comparison: strengths and weaknesses, Judaism versus Buddhism. He said that the strength of Buddhism is that it really makes sense; it is clear and useful and will help your life. Judaism, on the other hand, doesn't make sense. But that is exactly its strength: that it doesn't make sense. Just like us, he said: we don't make sense. And the weakness of Buddhism is precisely that it makes too much sense.

Buddhism does make sense. It is full of practical, clear advice on how to work with anger, jealousy, confusion, and other painful emotional states, sound advice that supports in many ways the psychological-spiritual preconceptions that many of us hold. But the trouble is, our irrational and sometimes conflicted Western selves that persist somehow, even in advanced stages of Buddhist practice, waylay us now and again with deeply held emotions like longing, sorrow, loss, loneliness, unknowingness, despite all our good Buddhist practice. We find there is still sometimes a need to call out, to sing, to shout, to be heard and answered. These passions persist even though we have cleared up much of our confusion. All of this is the territory of the Psalms.

The Psalms are a fundamental text of Western Judeo-Christian spirituality, perhaps the most fundamental. They are chanted daily in Christian and Jewish services, and they contain all of the theology of both the Old and New Testaments. For three thousand years Western peoples have been contemplating these poems, resonating emotionally their deepest feeling for life through them.

Buddhism begins with suffering and the end of suffering and the path toward the ending of suffering. This is essential and useful for everyone, not just Buddhists. But this approach can easily lead to a grave spiritual error: the notion that suffering is something to be avoided, prevented, escaped, bypassed. I have seen many Western Buddhist students suffer a great deal because of this natural error, thinking and believing they could go beyond or had gone beyond their suffering, only to find that it was there all along, underneath their seeming calmness and insight, and that because they had tried not to see and accept it, they had made it far worse.

The Psalms make it clear that suffering is not to be escaped or bypassed: that, much to the contrary, suffering returns again and again, a path in itself, and that through the very suffering and admission of suffering, the letting go into suffering and the calling out from it, mercy and peace can come (this is most poignantly expressed, of course, in the example of Jesus).

There is a crucial corollary to this point: if suffering is a path, then those who suffer are to be honored. A key theme of the Psalms— and therefore of Judaism and Christianity—is the nobility of the oppressed, and the necessity of justice and righteousness, that the oppressed be cared for and uplifted, and that there ought to be social justice for all. These ideas have not been part of Buddhism in Asia, but they are becoming an indelible aspect of Western Buddhism. So here, too, the Psalms have something to show us.

In fact, I would go so far as to say that for Western Buddhist practitioners a sensitive and informed appreciation of the problematic themes included and so powerfully expressed in the Psalms is probably a necessity.

For many, however, the Psalms remain—as they did for me when I first encountered them in English at Gethsemani—hermetically sealed. This is because their language has become opaque after centuries of use and misuse. I am sure there are some (like the monks of Gethsemani and some Jewish practitioners I know) for whom the traditional language still sparkles, illuminated by their inner experience, and the words take on added dimension with repeated encounter. But for most of the rest of us, it is not so. For those who have not made a practice of the Psalms, the traditional language communicates little, and can even be quite off-putting; for others, who read the Psalms but without much contemplation, the traditional language may still have meaning and emotion, but not much meaning that is spiritually fruitful.

So I wanted to use my own spiritual experience as my guide in reading and living with these most ancient of all poems, to try to make them fresh and lively for myself and for readers like me.

And the Psalms are poems. They stand at the origin point of all of Western poetry, which is intimately connected with prayer.

I came to appreciate this about ten years ago when I went to Jerusalem and visited the Kotel, the Wailing Wall. I had never been there before and was moved by the power of the place, with all its history, with all the prayer and lamentation that had gone into it from the lips of so many people over the generations. Although prayer had never been a part of my spiritual practice, I found myself with my forehead pressed up against the cool stones, speaking heartfelt words, and then writing words on a piece of paper and shoving the paper scrap into a crack in the wall, as people customarily do.

The feeling I had quite clearly was: language is prayer. Utterance, whether silent or voiced, written or thought, is essentially prayer. To speak, to intone, to make words with mouth and heart: where does that come from? Debased as it so often is, language always sources in what's fundamental in the human heart. The imaginative source of language-making, that uniquely human process, is the need to reach out to the boundless, the unknown, the unnamable. Prayer is not some specialized religious exercise; it is just what comes out of our mouths if we truly pay attention. To pray is to form language, and to form language is to be human.

———— ▶◀ ————

If Buddhism makes sense, because it is strong on teachings that show us how to work with the mind and heart to relieve our suffering, it is at the same time perhaps weak on the question of relationships. And although our lives are located in our own hearts and minds, they are also located, perhaps most poignantly, in the space between us. Martin Buber's thought, his quintessentially Jewish outlook, emphasizes this with a fierce thoroughness. For Buber there is no God, there is no absolute, there is no present moment, outside the profound relationship that takes place between the I and the you, between the self and the other. Within the hallowed reaches of that ineffable experience (which is not an experience, Buber insists) our true life takes place.

Relationship is the theme of the Psalms: specifically that most difficult of all relationships, the relationship with God.

What or who is God? Clearly the word *God*, with all of its synonyms and substitutes as they appear in the Psalms, presents a serious problem for many. I find it meaningful, and use it freely in my teaching where it seems helpful (although it is absent in Zen language, and Zen is agnostic on the subject of God); but for many people the word *God* evokes parental and judgmental overtones, and even worse, false, meaningless, or even negative piety associated with what they have taken to be their less-than-perfect religious upbringing. In fact, the word *God* often seems to militate against exactly what it is supposed to connote: something immense and ineffable toward which one directs enormous feelings of awe, respect, gratitude, desire, anger, love, resentment, wonder, and so on.

For most of the religious seekers I encounter, the word *God* has been all but emptied of its spiritual power. Even where it is taken in a positive light, it seems often reduced and tamed, represent-ing some sort of assumed and circumscribed notion of holiness or morality. For me, what is challenging about "God" is exactly that it is so emotional, even metaphysically emotional. The relationship to God that is charted out in the Psalms is a stormy one, code-pendent, passionate, confusing, loyal, petulant, sometimes even manipulative. I wanted to find a way to approach these poems so as to emphasize this relational aspect, while avoiding the major distancing pitfalls that words like *God, King, Lord*, and so on create. My solution was a simple one. I decided to avoid whenever I could all of these words and instead use the one simple English word that evokes the whole notion of relationship: you.

There was a personal dimension to this choice. For some years I had been noticing that the inspiration for my own poetry comes from the fact that the audience I am writing for is not any usual sort of audience. When I write poems, I am not talking to ordi-nary persons. The hearer of my poems seems to be someone more silent and receptive than any ordinary human being could be. The person I am addressing isn't a person, real or abstract. It's no one, no thing. And the fact that this nothing or no one is the one being addressed, and is even, in a way, participating in the composition, is what makes the writing of poems important to me. Otherwise I am sure I would not write at all.

Because of this experience that I have persistently had, I have for many years explored in poems words like *me* and *you* or *I*. I have explored, in the light of this experience, the sounds of words, their shapes, the simple extraordinary fact of words simply being words. Many of my poems are, in fact, nothing more or less than such explorations, such flights into essential language. The whole idea of writing and speaking, what it might mean and what its purpose might be, to whom it is addressed and from where it arises, has been enormously important to me. Shakespeare's sonnets, whose power comes from the fact that they are passionately addressed to a "you" who is mysteriously never identified, have been very influential for me, and I believe the whole sense of the lyric in Western poetry (beginning with the Psalms) has its source in this notion of a writing addressed to an unspecified but somehow magnificent nonexistent or supraexistent listener.

The fact that the perfect silence of being is necessarily broken, with human consciousness, by language that calls out always to a you who is profoundly unspecified, even, strictly speaking, nonexistent, has always struck me as marvelous. If we can say that the heart of the world is silence, undifferentiated being, before the arising of a single thing (which both theistic and nontheistic traditions like Buddhism assert, more or less), then the impulse toward language is this calling-out of one seemingly separate being toward all that inconceivable immensity.

For me, the word *you* contains all that process, and includes all of its sadness and passion and power.

This single translation decision has made an enormous difference in how my versions read. God becomes not a distant figure carrying a received and, for some, unfriendly load of emotional attachments, but rather intimacy itself, the painful intimacy of reaching out for something (in the act of language itself, in the act of the Psalms as the Psalms) that is at once so close to you it is absolutely hidden, and so far away you can never hope to reach it.

There is certainly a theology implied in all this, and there are Buddhist roots to it. Although classical Buddhism emphasizes impermanence and nonself, clearly denies the existence of any abiding entity, and seems quite far from any feeling for a concept of a monotheistic God, with all its overtones of omnipotence and eternity, the later Mahayana schools come very close to introducing the theistic. The Mind Only or Consciousness Only schools describe consciousness itself, in its profound transpersonal aspect, as buddha nature or dharmakaya, ineffable, neither existent nor nonexistent, neither inside nor outside, neither different from nor the same as the world, inconceivable and indescribable. In the Chinese *Shurangama Sutra*, for instance, there are many passages exhorting practitioners to "turn the mind around" away from the world so that it can "revert" and realize its real nature as eternally perfect and ineffable. In the *Lotus Sutra* the Buddha reveals himself as an eternal principle, who only pretended to appear as a human being, teach the original doctrine, and die for the sake of beings who were not able to understand the higher singular doctrine.

In the history of Buddhist philosophy there is an ongoing dialogue about the nature of such expressions. Since a cardinal principle of Buddhist thought is precisely that it be nontheistic, there has been continuous criticism of such doctrines, contending that they are, in fact, subversive attempts to introduce the concept of God into the Buddhist system of thought. The Mind Only adherents defend themselves by replying that their conception of consciousness doesn't violate the principle of emptiness, which states that all things are mere designations, without substance, like a mirage, so consciousness cannot be said to be a God. I am surely not doing justice to this complex debate, but the point I am making is that such Buddhist speculations (the *Shurangama Sutra* even includes, quite un-Buddhistically, a detailed section on the creation of the mind and the physical world out of the original primordial nameless consciousness) are not so far removed from many Jewish and Christian discussions of the idea of God.

———— ►◄ ————

The Psalms are historical documents of a particular people whose sacred narrative stands behind every line. My dilemma in making versions that I considered useful to myself and to others like me was how to preserve the emotion of that peoplehood and historicity and yet, at the same time, widen it. Although the Jewish and Christian commentarial literature on the Psalms opens and expands them into a more universal application, still, translated versions I have seen do not attempt to fold those interpretations into the poems themselves. This is what I wanted to attempt. So: how to handle these historical and particular words?

I began with the obvious fact that words like Israel, Zion, Jerusalem, and so on, originally carried meanings beyond their limited later senses. In other words, if Israel became a nation, what was the original impulse or spiritual dynamic that made it a nation? If Jerusalem is a holy city existing in a particular location, what is the content of that holiness? More often than not, what I was looking for could be found in looking closely at the etymologies of the words themselves. So Israel is literally "one who struggles," which, for me, is the ideal of a certain type of spiritual seeker, one whose faithfulness is always full of doubt, one who is forever pressing on with the practice, for new and fresh insight, for deeper experience. So I rendered the word Israel usually as "the ones who question and struggle." Jerusalem is, literally, the place of wholeness, the place where the soul can feel whole and complete. Egypt is "the narrow place," in contrast to the place of freedom and wideness and opening.

With these ideas to start with, I looked at each Psalm I studied for the way a particular term functioned within it, and at a number of Psalms to see how that term was developed throughout the collection. As I worked on this, I began to have a feeling for the spiritual and literary movement and shape of the terms, and they took on a depth of meaning for me that they did not have before.

In my versions I sometimes retain the original words, sometimes replace them with what I feel are their spiritual analogues, and sometimes use both. My hope is that over the course of reading several Psalms, the reader will need finally nothing other than the word, say, Jerusalem, to hear the range and depth of meaning that the Psalmist no doubt intended. I am aware that for many readers familiar with the Psalms all of this and much more is already available in the traditional English versions. But I wanted to make versions for myself and for people like me, who have lost the thread of the meaning of the Psalms and need some fresh language to recapture it. Perhaps such readers will find my interpretations useful, and possibly even seasoned readers will find their innocence and enthusiasm reinvigorating.

Respiritualizing some of the political and geographical references in the Psalms brought up for me the wider question of what was behind these references. From a Buddhist perspective, Judeo-Christian spirituality is challenging indeed. As I have said, Buddhism teaches simply suffering and the end of suffering. This seems a far cry from the personal and political anguish and group catharsis that one sees throughout the Psalms. It made me wonder: what does all of this amount to? If I assume the spiritual path to be, more or less, general throughout the traditions, what could the drama of the Psalms be pointing toward?

The idea of sovereignty seems to me to be one of the key themes of the Psalms. God is the ultimate fountainhead of sovereignty. Through God, sovereignty is conferred on the kings and through them, in turn, to the people. With sovereignty, there is honor, reality, a secure place to be, the possibility of wholeness and salvation, a way to live. With sovereignty, exile in the world ends, and one comes home.

The most powerful Psalms seem to yearn for the sovereignty that only God can confer, to praise it where it is present, to lament it where it is gone, and to constantly evoke God's presence and praise God's name—all because of the potency of sovereignty. I have pondered this, investigated it for what I could begin to see of its spiritual content, and have finally formed a notion of sovereignty as spiritual authenticity—some deeply felt but almost indefinable quality of meaningfulness that is the highest potential of human experience. It is as if a human being exists but doesn't live, is physically present but spiritually dead, if this quality of sovereignty is absent.

This thinking personalized for me all of those passages in the

Psalms that deal with praise and gratefulness to God, or with king-
ship and political tragedy, and gave me a way to understand the
difficult passages, the so-called cursing Psalms. While I did not
want to make things too pretty, turning outward enemies into
internal demons and making curses into gentle reminders toward
self-improvement, I did feel in the end that the Psalms' historical
narrative and poetic drama of sovereignty was also a personal and
spiritual one.

As I considered the issue of sovereignty, I began to see a connection in the Psalms between it and the Buddhist notion of mindfulness. In the *Mindfulness Sutra*, the Buddha calls mindfulness "the
only way to liberation." As you read that sutra, with all of its careful
instructions for training, it is clear that what is pointed to differs
from the usual idea of mindfulness, which amounts, more or less,
to self-consciousness: I know that I am feeling this or sensing that;
I know that I am myself and not another. This is how we generally
understand mindfulness. But Buddhist mindfulness is, by contrast,
a resting in a level of consciousness that is antecedent to the experience of ego, or to any notion of separation from the world. It is an
appreciation of all that is arising within the field of consciousness,
without defining an inside or an outside.

I began to feel that the sovereignty of God referred to in the
Psalms was a species of consciousness, beyond the human and yet
not separate from it, a kind of settled and steady contemplation
of or union with the deity constantly evoked and longed for in
the poems. If that were so, I had a way of understanding concepts
like wickedness and punishment. Wickedness became heedless-
ness, unmindfulness, egotism, off-centeredness, crookedness. To
fall into such a state is to suffer alienation, to be off course and
terrified. Sin becomes a question of being off the mark, of being
a distance away from the unity that one finds within mindfulness,
and punishment for sin is natural and necessary if there is to be a
course correction. I came to feel that the enemies mentioned in
the Psalms were external but also internal. Praying for their defeat

could be seen to be akin to praying, as in Tibetan Buddhism, to fierce guardian deities to destroy the powerful inner passions that keep one in bondage. Certainly I do not want to claim the Psalms as Buddhist texts. But such reflections helped me to understand their passion in a new light.

———— ►◄ ————

Despite all of this, I do not think that the difficulty of the Psalms can in the end be entirely avoided or explained away. Earlier I mentioned that many of the brothers at Gethsemani offered good explanations as to why the difficulty was something necessary, and in the end positive and useful. There are, however, many other committed Christians and Jews who dispute this, and who feel that the Psalms need to be edited, that there are passages and whole poems that simply ought to be eliminated, or at least, in the case of Christian monasticism, eliminated from liturgical practice. In fact, there has been a lengthy debate about this for some years in the Catholic community.

The tragedy of this difficulty and its serious consequences came home to me recently when I was in Belfast, Northern Ireland, at a peace conference. We were listening to a group of speakers who were victims of the Troubles, as they are called. Among them were a woman who had been confined to a wheelchair for most of her adult life as a result of a drive-by political shooting, a man who had been blinded as a boy by a British bullet, even a man who had taken part in assassinations and whose spirit had been crushed by what he himself had done. I found all of these people to be inspiring and eloquent in their presentations. In each case, the personal suffering had purified them, forced them to find a way to transcend their handicaps, and so had in the end become a source of happiness for their lives. None of them was bitter, and all of them were living good lives, doing their best in various ways to try to benefit others. But there was one exception to this pattern. One man, a Protestant minister whose father had been senselessly gunned down at his own front gate in full view of his family, seemed to continue to harbor strong feelings of hatred and vengeance. He said that after many years he was now finally satisfied and had been able to put the matter to rest because he believed that the killers of his father had themselves finally been gunned down, and that this made him finally happy, to see that justice was done. His speech was the shortest of all, and consisted mainly of a quotation of Psalm 10, which includes a line about how God will "break the arms of the wicked." This strong expression of righteous vengeance, bolstered by the man's religious faith as developed through a lifetime reading of the Psalms, was chilling to me.

―――――― ▶◀ ――――――

I want to mention finally one further influence that stands behind the efforts I have been making with the Psalms. This is my reading of the German-language poet Paul Celan, a deeply spiritual and inward writer, a Holocaust survivor, whose works are an attempt to meet the tremendous challenge to the human spirit that that event (which Celan refers to only as "what happened") occasioned. Celan uses biblical material (including the Psalms) with all the traditional feeling it evokes, yet at the same time manages to make it personal, as if the ancient lines and their echoes were coming from his own mouth for the first time, expressing the depth of all he had seen and experienced. Writing in German, the language of the murderer and oppressor, he could not help recognizing with each word how easily language betrays us even as it provides us with the emotional and religious connection to that which we need most in our extremity. In time Celan's poems became more and more terse, more and more dense, until by the end of his short life (he committed suicide in Paris in 1970, in his forty-ninth year), they were all but incomprehensible, closely approaching the boundary of what can be said.

Celan's project as a writer is the desperate attempt to find meaning in a terrible situation, one in which a return to an innocent or traditional faith seems impossible. This is why it is so important for our time, in which it is the challenge of religious traditions to do something more than simply reassert and reinterpret their faiths, hoping for loyal adherents to what they perceive to be the true doctrine. Looking back at the last century, with its devastating wars and holocausts and the shock of ecological vulnerability, I have the sense that religious traditions must now take on a wider mission, and it is in recognition of this mission, I believe, that interreligious dialogue becomes something not only polite and interesting but essential. I have come to think, after working intimately for many years with people along the course of their heartfelt spiritual journeys, that traditions now need to listen to the human heart before them as much as and more than they listen to their various doctrines and beliefs. In recognition of this I offer these tentative versions of the Psalms.

24

The Two Worlds

2007

M Y WIFE, KATHIE, and I were in Fuji Kawaguchiko, a lakeside resort town at the foot of Japan's Mount Fuji. We had come to see, and perhaps climb, Mount Fuji, but we couldn't see it at all, only roiling silver-gray clouds. We'd expected as much—it was July, and the humid Japanese summers are often cloudy and rainy. Fuji is almost as famous for its absence as for its presence. Besides, I'm used to the idea that the more you count on the arrival of an important experience or accomplishment, the greater the likelihood that it won't arrive and that instead you will get to enjoy something completely different.

Studying such normal human experiences is one of the pleasures of Zen Buddhist practice. When I was abbot of Green Gulch Farm Zen Center near San Francisco, we celebrated the Buddha's enlightenment every year by going outside in the predawn hours to see the morning star, as the Buddha had seen it on the day of his awakening. Most years, however, we saw no star, only fog. So Kathie and I weren't much fazed by not being able to sit in our hotel room's soaking tub while looking at the crown of Mount Fuji, as the travel brochure had promised. Instead we went for a stroll around Lake Kawaguchi, and then we decided to explore the town.

Though a resort town, Fuji Kawaguchiko is not fancy. In fact, it's a rather dull, ordinary spot. Its little shops reminded me of the small town in which I grew up. On our walk we noticed—as one can notice almost anywhere in Japan—the distinctive shape of a torii gate, signaling the entrance to a temple. The gate was open, as they usually are, so we went inside.

Walking into the temple compound, we walked into another world: quiet, serene, holy. Irregular stepping-stones led us through a mossy garden to a steadily dripping little waterfall. Off to one side was a standing figure of Kwan Yin, bodhisattva of compassion, standing on a lotus pedestal. She gazed down at us with a modest knowing smile that conveyed the ancient Buddhist feeling that all would be well in the midst of a world of inevitable suffering. The temple building, like the garden, was beautiful and well maintained. Its heavy wooden door was locked, but you could walk around on the veranda or sit on the steps and look out into the garden. We felt at home there, slowed down and refreshed.

When I began studying Zen in 1970, I was attracted to Japanese Zen's dynamic relationship to the arts—all the Japanese traditional arts have been heavily influenced by Zen—and to the Japanese sensibility in general. I was a young poet, part of a generation in revolt against American values, and all things Japanese struck me as superior in every way to the crude violence of the West.

But years of Zen practice in America changed my attitude drastically. After seeing the raw spiritual needs of the people I was practicing with, I came to realize that arranging flowers, sipping tea, and viewing raked-gravel gardens were not going to help them much. And the complicated bureaucracy and stifling traditionalism of Japanese Zen—which at first were invisible to me but later became an intimate part of my experience—weren't going to help either. People needed meditation practice, communities of support, teachings to relieve suffering—which is what, little by little, American Zen was coming to offer them. I was also disturbed by new scholarship that revealed how Japanese Zen teachers had supported Japanese aggression and blind obedience to the emperor during World War II. So I was developing an antipathy toward Japanese Zen. Which was an odd attitude for a senior Zen priest and abbot in a Japanese lineage.

Preparatory to our trip to Japan (Kathie's idea, not mine), we went to the Japanese tourist office in San Francisco to buy Japan Rail passes. The place was quiet and stacked with clutter, like a typical Japanese office or home, and everyone who worked in it was Japanese; not Japanese American, but Japanese. As soon as I entered, I felt the pervasive aura of tranquil courtesy that one feels in Japan. (Arrogance and aggression may also be Japanese characteristics, but these qualities were not on display in the Japanese tourist office.) The terribly sweet people there reminded me of the tender feelings toward Japan and Japanese people that I still had.

So when we entered that temple compound in Fuji Kawaguchiko I was reminded that there is more to Japanese Zen than formality, bureaucracy, and aesthetics.

In the West, especially in the United States, what we might call the sacred has been reduced to the "inner life," something private, personal, and in the end not very important or shareable. Our scientific materialistic outlook has domesticated the world, denaturing it of its uncharted mystery, and conditioning us to feel that anything we can't see or touch or reasonably explain is nonexistent and if not nonexistent certainly irrelevant. Japanese culture is now no less saturated with the scientific materialist outlook, and yet it seems to have preserved, in its primordial layers, a Buddhist sensibility which includes a vague and dark (if also beautiful and serene) sense of an alternate order of reality. That sensibility may be obscure to most Japanese people, but it lives within and around them. When most Japanese people enter a temple compound, they are experiencing much more than aesthetic enjoyment. They feel a sense of connection to their ancestors, to the mystery of life and death, and to the deep saving truths that the Buddha taught. This Buddhist feeling (which is both more and less than a belief) lies at the heart of what it means to be Japanese, regardless of what religion you happen to follow. There's great comfort and consolation in such a feeling; a palpable sense of shared meaning and belonging, of knowing that one's busy, frustrating, bewildering life somehow makes sense and has purpose. There's a basic human need for such a feeling, for a sense of the sacred that grounds us and gives our small lives meaning. Without it, we go a little crazy.

On another hot and humid July day in Japan, Kathie and I went to Toji, Kyoto's oldest Buddhist temple. It was full of people crowded into small shrine areas, where memorial rituals were in progress. Golden-robed priests rang bells, offered incense, chanted sutras. Temple-goers stood with palms together, some of them crying. When the priests filed out of the shrine rooms, everyone bowed low with respect.

Outside the temple gate we saw an old Buddhist nun shaking a *vajra*, a ritual implement that symbolizes the destruction of ignorance, ringing a ceremonial bell, and, with eyes closed, chanting sutras, her face ravaged but serene. A bent old woman passing by stopped to bow to the nun, who broke into a wide warm grin. The two women began to talk. It looked to us like the old woman was telling the nun her woes, pouring out her sadness and complaint, and the nun was listening with great sympathy and understanding, because it was her practice, her role, and her obligation to do so. After the recitation was over, the nun chanted blessings for the woman, then turned her around to give her a brief but vigorous back massage. Then they embraced, and the old woman put some alms into the nun's bag and went on her way.

When we got home from Japan, we watched Kenji Mizoguchi's classic film *Ugetsu*, in which ghosts figure prominently, as they often do in Japanese stories. Almost all traditional Japanese religion and storytelling assumes that there are two worlds, the tragic yet ordinary world of daily living, in which people are constantly victimized by their passions and by karmic forces beyond their control, and the world of mystery, of death, ghosts, darkness, and night. This second, liminal, world is the world of the Buddha, which is why it is not ultimately terrifying: for once the Buddha enters this world he will subdue the darkness and things will be put to rights.

The liminal world is larger, more mysterious, and more powerful than the everyday world, and from time to time it bleeds into the everyday world. So it can never be ignored. In Japanese literature the figure of the Buddhist monastic always evokes the liminal world. The purpose of the monastic's life is to tend to the liminal world so as to secure its benevolence.

In Japan, Kathie and I visited Eiheiji, the main training monastery for Soto Zen priests, and the largest and probably most storied functioning Zen monastery in the country. Kuroyanagi-san, the monastery's international director, knew who we were and rolled out the red carpet. We were given a formal tatami room and served a sumptuous vegetarian feast in our room by Domyo, a young priest who seemed quite nervous to be waiting on an American Zen abbot—and in English! Domyo was our "assistant," but also our keeper: he gave us strict instructions never to leave our room without him.

The following day, we attended Eiheiji's elaborate morning service in the great Buddha hall. On a high altar, accessible by steep stairs, and decorated with curtains and hanging gold-lacquered chandeliers, a golden Buddha was enshrined. The screens enclosing the Buddha figure were opened, and the altar was lit by two massive lanterns, one on either side, but the image still seemed distant and mysterious.

The most spectacular part of the service was the passing-out of the sutra books by graceful acolytes, who moved as precisely and delicately as ballet dancers. Balancing the books on red lacquered trays, they slid down the neat aisles on white-clad feet. When they reached the end of a row, they swiveled dramatically to face the person seated there, swooped down to offer the books, straightened up smoothly, and swooped again to the next row—several of them on several rows doing all this in perfect unison. The service also included a traditional food offering, one of the attendants climbing the narrow steep stairs to the high altar with the food vessels,

where another attendant received them and put them on the plat-
form where the Buddha sat. All of this was done with meticulous,
elegant choreography.

Such is the training of an Eiheiji priest in precise ritual and
deportment, necessary to convincingly occupy the archetypal role
of priest-mediator between the worlds, so as to help parishioners
safely feel the protection and comfort they expect and need from
Buddhism. Like many other lively young Japanese Soto Zen priests,
Kuroyanagi-san was somewhat embarrassed by Eiheiji's formality
and traditionalism, especially when compared to the rough-and-
ready practice of American Zen. But I could appreciate that from
very different perspectives and historical contexts we were both
trying to do the same thing: to express Buddhism and offer it to
people for whatever good it might do.

———— ▶◀ ————

Home from Japan, I reflected that Buddhism's cultural import
there is almost the opposite of what it is in America. In Japan,
Buddhism expresses the national character; Japanese culture
begins with the self-conscious adoption of Buddhism as an ideology.
It's no surprise then that the Japanese Buddhist establishment
has always been a staunch supporter of the state, even in times
of militarism and war. In America, Buddhism is an outlier, the
province of nonconformists and renegades, however mild their
rebellion may be. To practice Buddhism in America is to take on
views and behaviors that contradict the American spirit of rugged
individualism and can-do materialism.

In Japan almost all serious Zen practitioners are priests who live
in temples or otherwise work as priests. In America most serious
American Zen practitioners are laypeople who live ordinary secular lives. A minority become priests, but there is no social role
in America for Zen priests so it is not easy to earn one's living in
that profession. Being a Zen priest in Japan is a reasonable career
choice; it's also a hereditary one: the typical Japanese Zen priest is

ordained by his father and inherits his father's temple (almost all Zen temple priests are male).

Like all old cultures, Japan is rooted in religion. But America's young culture was founded on the opposite premise: "no established religion," a principle that seems an obvious prerequisite for freedom, democracy, and modernity. We understand the advantages of not having an established religion (inclusion, fairness, social and economic openness) but don't see the disadvantages. Without an established religion a culture has a shallow taproot; it lacks a unifying sense of shared reality.

In place of a foundational religion, with its myths and rituals, America has its deified abstractions: freedom, democracy, and capitalism, about which we understand even less than the Japanese do about their Buddhism. Since Americans can't justifiably depend on religion as a source of national coherence, we are perhaps more confused about religion than we otherwise would be. In general, American religion tends to go one of two ways: it is either a polite social club that stands simply for generic goodness, or it is a semifanatic and overarching ideology that insists on its identification with the nation, exactly because it cannot justly claim such identity. And then, in reaction to this, an often aggressive secularism that implicitly and sometimes explicitly denigrates all forms of faith. The American relationship to religion is strangely paradoxical: no country as fiercely secular as we are is also as hysterically religious.

Religious fundamentalism can be a scary phenomenon, especially in its more recent manifestations, which are reactions to the confusions of modernity. At the end of the Middle Ages, Islam was the most broad-minded and tolerant major religion in the world. But in the twentieth century Islam began responding to its historic humiliation by Western colonial powers with exaggerated forms of expression that have by now succeeded in commanding the world's attention. Jewish and Christian fundamentalisms are equally dangerous and equally reactive to the arrogance of modernity.

To be sure, there is more to the American religious scene than this stark and perhaps exaggerated dichotomy. There are many positive, inspiring and nonfanatic spiritualities here. Think of the black church, or various other Christian, Jewish, Muslim, and Buddhist communities (many of which are populated with immigrants) that are spiritually lively and socially conscious. But the point remains that we are religiously diverse—which makes us fragmented and perhaps incoherent. This lack of coherence is a feature of our politics now, with red states and blue states that seem divided by fierce religious commitment or the lack of it.

A few decades ago, few would have denied the great benefits of modern technology and free trade. Now a consensus is building in the opposite direction: that there is something basically alienating, unfair, and unsustainable about our unbridled buying and selling, the ever-accelerating speed of our lives, and, especially and most urgently, the effects of our activity on the planet. Climate change is rapidly becoming the inescapable fact of our lives.

I am convinced that in the present emergency we need religion more than ever. We need to know that we live not only in the material world, with its enormous challenges that we are responsible to deal with, but also in the liminal, imaginative world of the spirit that can give us support, vision, and strength. America is not Japan; it doesn't and won't ever have an ancient and shared sense of that liminal world. We are too diverse. We need a postreligious religion: one that is deeply engaging, experiential, tolerant, and shareable, and that emphasizes above all loving-kindness and compassion. I am no fan of fundamentalism, but we may need to consider the possibility that the fundamentalists are right in their belief that religion needs to be not only at the center of individual lives, a personal private matter, but also at the center of our social lives as well. What would that mean in a country—and now, more and more, in a world—so multicultural that it's not unusual for several religions (or no religion at all) to be represented in a single nuclear family? It would mean a way of understanding our religious life that references our feeling and behavior more than it references God, doctrine, identity, or belief. It would mean we'd need much more interreligious dialogue and education, and new forms of religious practice, including practices that could be shared by people of different religions. And it would mean we would have to do something that is as difficult as it is crucial to our survival: talk to one another peacefully and honestly about what matters to us most.

PART FOUR

Difference and Dharma

NOTES ON SOCIAL ENGAGEMENT

THERE'S NO AVOIDING the world and its craziness. As a 1960s person, I was formed by my chaotic and desperate political moment. Though we thought of our political activism as moral, in fact it was personal: all of us young men were going to be killed in an unjust war that was brutal and confusing, without heroes, so we were marching in the streets, fighting with the police, going to jail, because our lives and the lives of those we loved were on the line. By 1970 we knew that you don't win political wars (as we thought we had on March 31, 1968, when Lyndon Johnson partially halted bombing in Vietnam and announced that he would not seek reelection); that the battles—their underlying causes never challenged in any serious way—go on and on. What to do?

My practicing Zen was fueled by this anguish, so long ago now that I can barely remember it. Am I the same person?

Although it may seem as if the silence and simplicity of contemplative practice, with its aura of timelessness, is the opposite of engagement in the loud and jostling world, this really isn't so. Mahayana Buddhism certainly teaches that contemplative wisdom and compassionate action imply and require each other, and religious life in all traditions is full of examples of this: from the radical politics of the French Catholic mystic Simone Weil to the passionate outspokenness of Thomas Merton and the marching of Rabbi Abraham Joshua Heschel side by side with the Rev. Dr. Martin Luther King, Jr.; from the dramatic antiwar activities of the Berrigan brothers, Catholic priests who were fugitives and eventually imprisoned, to the liberation theology and passionate advocacy for the poor among Catholic clerics in Latin America, many of whom lost their lives; from the anticolonialism of Mahatma Gandhi to the peace activism of the amazing young Muslim woman Malala Yousafzai (who won the Nobel Peace Prize in 2014)—there's a long tradition of full immersion in spirituality that can't but lead to concern for the world so thorough that action must flow from it.

Though I have never given up my early political concerns (or point of view) and pay close attention to what goes on in the world, speaking out when it seems right to do so, I don't consider myself an activist. There are a lot of strong Buddhist activists who do a better job than I could do, and somehow my writing and reading and sitting practices have drawn me more to my desk than to the streets and, more than this, have given me a greater sense of not knowing and acceptance of what happens than a good activist ought to have. But I am in the streets sometimes. And, as the following essays show, I have had plenty to say over the decades about the confusion and brutality of this world.

Some of these essays surprise me; I don't remember writing them and am impressed by what I had to say ten or fifteen or more years ago. In some cases, it seems that I knew more then than I know now. In others, I am too brash, riffing on big sweeps of history as if I knew what I was talking about; I am now far more doubtful about everything and regret that clear understandable writing requires oversimplification (if you try to tell the truth whole as far as you know it, you will confuse the reader with contradictory information—unless you are writing a poem, in which case confusion is allowed).

I wonder how capable anyone is of having worthwhile and effective opinions about the range of important topics—racism, climate change, political violence, sexism and the #MeToo movement, forgiveness and reconciliation—that I take up in these pieces. And yet I attempted it, inspired by my sense that the Buddhist teachings do not exist in a quiet corner, that they provide guidance in the middle of troubled times. If not, what good are they for anything other than comfort? Comfort is important! But it is not enough.

A lot of these pieces are quite old, and it is interesting to read them now, against the backdrop of a present that didn't exist when I wrote them. Buddha taught the contingency and ultimate unreliability of all fixed positions. Certainly opinion is contingent and unreliable, the product of a particular personal perspective at a particular moment. Among the many astonishing things about writing is the fact that a text remains forever as it was written, even though everything around it changes. With computers it is very easy to redraft texts (and, in fact, I have redrafted some of what you read below, for updating, smoothness, and so that I could agree with myself enough to feel comfortable), but still, a text written at a particular time retains the flavor of that time, though read in a new time. Oddly, this doubleness in time changes the text, much like the color of a painting is changed by the background against which it is viewed. Recently I was reading a memoir by Henry James, *A Small Boy and Others*, and was struck by how differently James's ponderous sentences read now, a hundred years after they were written. The sentences are the same; the language of the world around them has changed, which makes the same sentences different. So I wonder how some of these essays read now.

For instance, in the era of George W. Bush I could talk about the possibility (however much a stretch it may have been) of taking his sincerity at face value, as a way to understand his policies and argue against them. In the age of Trump, statements from the highest reaches of power have become so outrageous and sometimes preposterous that it is difficult to even use the words *sincerity* or *seriousness* anymore or, at least, to think such words could have the meanings we used to assign to them. We have entered an almost unthinkable world of political discourse that is so over the top that the very concepts of fact or truth seem moot. When, after the 2016 election, I tried, out of a sense of responsibility, to post short political thoughts on Facebook to calm things down, I soon saw this was impossible: that we had somehow gone beyond public discourse as we had known it, and entered a world in which spin, irony, and polemic were so thorough and so instantaneous that saying anything at all was counterproductive; it fed the beast you were trying, with your words, to starve. This present fact now serves as background for all the essays you are about to read, which makes them all different.

———— ▶◀ ————

Every issue I have discussed here persists, all these years later, as a social problem, in most cases a worse social problem than when I first wrote about it. With the great national wound of racism, a lot has happened. Unlikely as it would have seemed when I wrote these pieces, we have had a much loved (but not, as it turned out, by everyone) two-term African American president, which has given us, in reaction, an insistently white president who is fixated on erasing every accomplishment of the black president. Before any of this, most of us (if we were white) would have expected racial progress to take place in the normal course of things—not the virulent stirring-up of racial hatred that we have seen instead. And yet, by the logic of history, which goes forward and backward at the same time, this very backlash has had good effects. It's caused many white people, finally, to actually become educated on the question of race (something I was calling for in my 1993 essay, which is one of the pieces I felt compelled to redo, with help from Cynthia and my Shambhala editor Matt Zepelin; thanks to them, the worst of my 1993 ignorance about race has been corrected, but the spirit of the original piece remains). This education has been very humbling for me and most white people I know—and it is shocking to consider our previous self-satisfied and unknowing ignorance. To notice, as we had not noticed, the national, state, and local housing laws that for decades prevented black people from owning property that could appreciate, thus mandating poverty and ghettos that were not, as white people had falsely believed, creations of happenstance. Or the catastrophe of the inherently racist prison system, almost a re-creation of slavery, in the name of "tough on crime" or "war against drugs." Or the routine killings of innocent black youth by the police that Black Lives Matter has finally highlighted (and that President Obama grieved over, as no other president before him could, and as he would later grieve over the mass shooting of black congregants in a church in Charleston). Or the intentionally suppressed history of the Reconstruction era and the subsequent cooperation of the entire nation in preserving the Confederacy long past the Civil War, in the form of terrorism against black people, segregation, unjust laws, and voter suppression.

Like a lot of white people, I have, since writing the essays that reference race, learned a great deal. Not only about jazz (as I write) but also about history, and about black arts in general, reading great works by writers like Frederick Douglass, W. E. B. Du Bois, Toni Morrison, James Baldwin, Claude McKay, Langston Hughes, Gwendolyn Brooks, Amiri Baraka, Ta-Nehisi Coates, and others. As a poet, I've woken up to the fact that I had not paid attention (I wonder why!) to the robust tradition of African American poetry, nor had I really taken in that among my contemporaries there are great black avant-garde poets like Kamau Brathwaite, Nathaniel Mackey, Fred Moten, Ed Roberson, Will Alexander, Dawn Lundy Martin, Claudia Rankine, Harryette Mullen, Julie Ezelle-Patton, and many, many others, whose works ought to have been essential to my education. (So far rap and hip-hop still remain not part of my vocabulary.)

The question of gender identity is also far more contested and confusing than it was when these essays were first written. Possibly it's the question of our current moment. Gender studies as an academic discipline and a social concern is far more developed, and contentious, than it was then, and the #MeToo movement has stirred up long-ignored issues about male privilege and dominance that were always invisibly in plain sight.

How is the Buddhist world doing with all this now? Better, I think. Not perfect. There are still instances of sexual misconduct, and sometimes of predation, but now in most cases these are handled effectively, if painfully: we have learned from our mistakes. Buddhist organizations typically have ethics policies that take on the question of safety for sangha members and, specifically, teacher misconduct, and there are many women connected to Buddhist centers who have expertise in this area, and strength to handle what comes up, so no woman who is approached is without forceful and effective help, if she wants to access it. And there are plenty of empowered women teachers, which makes gender imbalance less common. (I believe all this is less the case in the Tibetan Buddhist sanghas, which must deal with the cultural dynamics of the Tibetan community in exile in India, complicating matters for them. The Western Zen and Vipassana sanghas are led by Westerners.) We have done less well with racial inclusion. Since by and large the Western-convert Buddhist community is white, it is less attractive to people of color. But there are increasing numbers of teachers of color, which means that this will change gradually, and there is certainly a desire for it to change.

I write in several of the pieces about my Jewish identity. It is a bit of a shock to have "Jewish identity," let alone identity as a white person. Until recently, such designations didn't really occur to me, I simply took them for granted, they seemed anodyne and invisible. (I now know that white males, no matter what their ethnic or religious identity, have always had the luxury of not needing to notice identity; nonwhites and women have not.) When I was growing up, my Jewishness was an obvious and ubiquitous fact. It was just who I was, who I was happy to be; I didn't notice that anyone else particularly noticed—I was never the victim of anti-Semitism, or, if I was, I either didn't notice or don't remember. I had the impression then—however false it now seems—that America really was a great melting pot (as they used to tell us) in which we could all be who we were, one happy family. Like in the World War II movies I grew up watching, where the Jew and the Italian and the Irishman fought side by side (no African Americans, probably, but as a white boy I didn't notice). The current understanding of identity is so much more informed and sophisticated. No more invisible identities. Now you know who you are and where your identities (you usually have more than one) stand in the social hierarchy of identities. By a sort of reverse logic, it seems to me, this new almost hyper self-consciousness about identity makes everyone feel less secure; the more you know where you stand in relation to others, who may or may not resent or misunderstand you for your presumed identity, the more you feel the necessity to define, defend, and assert yourself. Which makes us all uncomfortable and even embattled.

When I was a boy in the 1950s, people thought of Jews (along with Italians and other southern Europeans) as nonwhite. When I looked in the mirror, I actually saw my olive complexion (possible my skin is actually more white now than it was then). Along with other non-WASPs, I became white in 1963, after the assassination of John F. Kennedy. Kennedy's Irish Catholicism was an issue during the 1960 election campaign. Many thought it would be impossible to have an Irish Catholic president, who in their view would be loyal to the pope rather than the country. Kennedy assured people that he was not an Irish Catholic, he was an American. After he was shot and canonized as an American saint, some ethnic identities became obsolete—there were no more Irish, Italians, Jews, Swedes, Germans—there were only Americans, which meant white people. Yes, there were also nonwhite people in the nation, of course, African Americans and others, but since social and cultural power was entirely in the hands of white people—who took their position of dominance completely for granted—that fact was not particularly noted.

Now I am classified as a heterosexual white male, which means I occupy a position of privilege in American society. This is a social fact that has conferred great benefit on me, however much I may not have noticed it growing up, or been paying attention to it when

I wrote these essays. So not only has the historical background of these essays changed in the intervening years, as I've said—so has the identity of their author. He is not the person he thought he was. This also changes the essays. In 2020 the meaning of a piece of writing depends on the identity of its author. A sentence reads differently depending on whether you know it to have been written by a young cisgender African American woman or an older gay white male. Soon after the 2016 presidential election, I wrote a piece for the Buddhist magazine *Lion's Roar* saying, OK, this is bad, but we will survive. I was sharply criticized by a younger gay Buddhist teacher who said, Maybe you will be OK, but I won't. He was upset by the sense of confidence I was thoughtlessly expressing, because yes, he was right, I had been conditioned all my life to feel confident in a way that he could not.

In the light of this contemporary emphasis on identity and its social and psychological complexities, it is funny and odd to consider (as I write about below) the fact that the Buddha considered the fictitious creation of a self-identity as the basic cause of human suffering. The Buddha was not an identitarian. He might have agreed with Emily Dickinson (a single, possibly lesbian, white woman of privilege), who wrote: "I'm Nobody! Who are you?" But then again, I think the Buddha would have appreciated our contemporary efforts to figure out who we are socially so that there can be more respect and justice for everyone, because compassion, and mindfulness, in the fullest sense, demand this. But the Buddha would have also held identity lightly. He would have taught that behind and within our difference is our unity, our humanness, our basic existence. Each of us is a unique expression of the same phenomenon—life, which is precious, lovely, and entirely empty of identity.

———— ▶◀ ————

I mention climate change in these essays. I forgot that I have been concerned about it since the early 1970s because now, in 2020, my concern is so strong it is almost of a different order. How have we succeeded all these years in being so casual about an emergency whose consequences are so drastic? As of this moment it seems that we have the know-how and the economic capacity to completely eliminate the burning of fossil fuels on our planet within a matter of decades—which it seems we must do if we are going to avoid the worst and most nightmarish scenarios of climate dystopia. Our rhetoric is heating up quickly, which is a good thing, but so far serious action is not following—not to anything like the extent and the speed needed. I have hope, however, that this will change.

The Buddhist teaching of karma tells us, with great and I do not think misplaced confidence, that good actions bring good results, bad actions bad results, and that the network of good-bad causality is so vast, no one (and no computer model) can encompass it. So we do not and cannot know what will happen in the future. But we can have confidence that good is good, and that, as Buddhist practitioners who follow a teaching that emphasizes compassion, we must do good and avoid doing bad, for good brings benefit to others, and bad causes them harm.

In this sense, Buddhist teaching proposes political and social activism as a total life project; it is the heart of the practice. If you believe, as I do, that climate change is an urgent issue, and if you can take to the streets to stop a new pipeline or coal- or gas-burning plant, you should do that or support people who do. You should write letters, picket politicians and business owners, exerting pressure but with love, not bitterness. And yes, whatever your position, you should vote vote vote and make sure candidates and officeholders do the right thing. But the category of good political and social action is larger than such specifically political acts. Good political and social action is also a smile, a word of encouragement, a moment of gratitude and appreciation. It is promoting kindness and fairness among people in any and all ways. It is prayer, meditation, a moment of peace. There is no one who is not capable of practicing, and obligated to practice, political and social action in this widest sense. And if, as may well be the case, we are in for hard times, politically, socially, environmentally, we will need such good action more than ever to ensure that humanity will be able to meet the challenges ahead with a good spirit rather than hatred and strife.

25

Quick! Who Can Save This Cat?

2003

THE CASE (MUMONKAN CASE 14, NANCHUAN'S CAT)

Nanchuan saw the monks of the eastern and western halls fighting over a cat. Seizing the cat, he told the monks: "If any of you can say a word of Zen, you will save the cat." No one answered. Nanchuan cut the cat in two. That evening Zhaozhou returned to the monastery and Nanchuan told him what had happened. Zhaozhou removed his sandals, placed them on his head, and walked out. Nanchuan said: "If you had been there, you would have saved the cat."

MUMON'S COMMENT

Why did Zhaozhou put his sandals on his head? If you can answer this question, you will understand exactly that Nanchuan's action was not in vain. If not, danger!

MUMON'S POEM

Had Zhaozhou been there
He would have taken charge.
Zhaozhou snatches the sword
And Nanchuan begs for his life.

──────── ▶◀ ────────

This story involves Nanchuan (Japanese: Nansen) and Zhaozhou (Joshu), two of the most important figures in Zen history. Zhaozhou came to Nanchuan when he was only about twenty years old. Nanchuan was lying down taking a nap when the young man approached. Sitting up in bed, he asked the Zen question (a wonderful question for anyone at any time), "Where have you come from?" Zhaozhou replied, "I come from Standing Buddha Temple." "Are there any standing Buddhas there?" asked Nanchuan. Zhaozhou replied, "Here I see a reclining Buddha." Zhaozhou was a sincere, steady practitioner, devoted to his teacher, with whom he remained for forty years. They were very close, as this story shows, and they worked together to create a good learning environment for the monks.

Both Nanchuan and Zhaozhou figure in many stories in the koan collections. The present case is probably the best-known—and most disturbing—case in all of Zen. We could compare it to a similar story that appears in the Bible, involving the wise king Solomon and a baby. As the tale goes, two women are arguing over a baby, both claiming to be the mother. Like Nanchuan, Solomon proposes to solve the dispute by cutting the baby in two. He intends to give half to each of the women, an eminently fair solution. One of the women speaks up immediately and says, "No, don't do it. I am not the mother. Give the child to her!" And so Solomon discovers that she is the real mother, the one who cares most for the child's welfare.

The Solomon story is tidier and nicer than the story of Nanchuan and the cat. We can easily discern its point, whereas Zen stories seem harder to appreciate. People get confused when you say to them, "Say a word of Zen!" They can't help thinking there is something to this that they don't understand. It paralyzes them. They can't say anything. They think about it in a panic, and the more they think, the more baffled they become. A Zen monk is not half as smart as a mother. A mother knows about love and devotion, so she is never speechless when it comes to the welfare of her child. If the mother in the Solomon story had been there, she would have said to Nanchuan, "What's the matter with you? How can you even think of killing that cat? You are a Zen priest who has taken a precept against killing!" Surely these words would have saved the cat. If the monks had been reasonable ordinary feeling human beings instead of stupid monks with Zen gold dust in their eyes, they would have spoken up like that or simply grabbed the cat and run away. But they couldn't do it. Maybe they were too intimidated by the prestige of the teacher.

In commenting on the case, Dogen said, "If I were Nanchuan, I would have said, 'If you cannot say a true word of Zen I will cut the cat, and if you can say a true word of Zen I will also cut the cat.'" This would have been a much less misleading challenge than the one posed by Nanchuan. If I were one of the monks, I would have said, "We can't answer. Please, Master, cut the cat in two if you can." Or, "Nanchuan, you know how to cut the cat in two, but can you show us how to cut the cat in one?" And again Dogen says, "If I were Nanchuan and the monks could not answer, I would say, 'Too bad you cannot answer,' and then I would release the cat."[1]

We are all cut in two, of course. That's living in this world of discrimination and difference. I am me; therefore, I am not you. But we are also cut in one, only we don't know it. Being cut in one is "I am me and all is included in that, you and everything else." We practice zazen to remember that we are cut in one, as well as two. When we are dead, we'll all be cut in one and only one. But we are dying all the time. If we are Zen monks, we devote ourselves to sitting on our cushions so that we can see this and integrate it into our everyday living. When Zhaozhou comes back later and puts his sandals on his head, this is what he is saying. Putting a sandal on the head was a sign of mourning in ancient China. Zhaozhou is expressing, "Teacher, do not fool me with your pantomime. You and I both know that the cat is already dead. You and I are already dead. All disputes are already settled. All things are beyond coming and going, vast and wide, at peace."

This same story appears in the two other major koan collections, the *Blue Cliff Record* and the *Book of Serenity*, and the commentaries there say that Nanchuan did not cut the cat in two but only pantomimed doing it. Zen teachers do not commit murder, the commentaries say, even to make an important point.

In Zen precepts study it is always noted that there are three levels of precept practice—the literal, the compassionate, and the ultimate. On the literal level we follow the precepts according to their explicit meanings—not to kill means not to kill, not even a bug. But on the compassionate level we recognize the complexity of living—sometimes not to kill one thing is to kill something else. The network of causality is endlessly complex; our human ideas cannot encompass it. We recognize that precepts will be broken sometimes, and we affirm that our guide for precept practice will not be literality but compassion. We will follow precepts with a heart of love for beings. That motivation may sometimes cause us to break precepts in order to help someone.

On the third level of precept study, the ultimate level, we recognize that there is no breaking precepts. Precepts can neither be broken nor kept, for they—like everything—are empty of any identifiable self. When we understand this deep truth, we naturally want to follow precepts with a wide and flexible heart. And with humility and a constant sadness.

This case involves the ultimate level of precept practice: the recognition that there is no killing, that life can never be killed—or to put it another way, that life is already dead. When we know life at this level, we can really appreciate its preciousness. It is this recognition that Nanchuan and Zhaozhou have, but that the monks lack.

This is not just Zen talk. It's really true. We think death is later, but death is not later. It's now, as each moment passes irrevocably. No wonder we can't see this. It's too terrifying! Our death doesn't happen all of a sudden; it happens gradually—and always. But it is also true that our death never comes. When we enter what is conventionally called "death," the "I" we have always thought we were melts away, but the "I" we always actually were and always will be remains, as ever, unmoving. Although this may sound paradoxical, it's a plain truth, probably the most basic of all human truths: we are always dying, and there is no such thing as death. Seen in this light, the precepts are ultimately not simply rules of ethical conduct, a list of dos and don'ts. They are possibilities for us to understand life's profundity through our conduct in the ordinary world. Practice of the precepts takes us to the root of what it means to be alive, to the center of the human problem of meaning. We are always faced with the question whose depths we will never be able to fathom: what do I do with this life now? This is precepts practice.

---- ►◄ ----

We should back up a little bit, though: the monks in the east and west halls were arguing about a cat. In most monasteries in ancient China, the community was divided. Some monks lived in the meditation hall, devoting full time to formal meditation practice, while others were working monks who did the necessary support work for the monastery: cooking, farming, fixing, chopping firewood, and so on. These two kinds of monks were probably housed in different halls, the east hall and the west hall.

As soon as there are two halls and two functions, there are different viewpoints and inevitably there are disputes over which viewpoint should take priority. In our Zen center exactly this thing used to happen all the time. It probably still does. The monks who specialize in work think the monks who meditate a lot are indulging their taste for peace and quiet and are unrealistic about the world; meanwhile, the meditators think the workers are too worldly and are not really interested in doing the practice. This clash of perspectives happens in all monasteries and there is sometimes great strife. The Catholics had conflicts between the choir monks (the formal prayer people) and the lay brothers (support workers) that went on for centuries until Vatican II, a sweeping program of reform instituted in the 1960s, abolished the tradition of lay brothers.

The same thing happens, of course, and much more tragically, in the world at large. Jews—to take one drastic example among many—think Israel is their place, and that their customs and traditions should prevail there, while Palestinians think it is their place, and therefore their customs and traditions should prevail. Neither side considers its view to be merely a preference, an option among options. It is the truth. In Nanchuan's monastery maybe the working monks thought the cat would do very well in the kitchen as a mouser. The meditating monks, whose minds were very subtle, tender, and compassionate, could not bear the thought of a cat killing mice. This was, after all, murder! So the monks fought over the cat.

When there is difference and the underlying essence of difference —which is oneness—is not understood and appreciated, there will always be fighting. None of us is free from being blinded by our own view. So how do you handle this kind of situation? Which side are you on? Do you have to take sides? Can you take both sides? What do you do? Nanchuan demonstrates.

In Zen a knife always suggests Manjushri's sword of wisdom that cuts through duality. Manjushri's sword opens up the emptiness and identity of life and death, good and bad, Israelis and Palestinians. All oppositions are empty of real difference; all elements of all oppositions depend on each other. Manjushri's sword slices through views, showing that all views are empty of reality, depend on one another, and arise from an underlying unity that is beyond all views. That's life: unexplainable.

So Nanchuan uses Manjushri's sword in a little piece of street theater designed to take the monks' dispute to another level. Never mind the cat—what is life, what is death? What are we doing here in this monastery? You monks—and all humans—are arguing over the inarguable while the world is burning up in front of your eyes! Wake up! Don't waste time!

The problems of the world are actually fairly easy to solve. But people can't get along, can't work together, can't harmonize their views, so nothing gets done. Things only get worse. Technical and social solutions are at hand, but political problems block them at every turn—and that's the worst problem in the world.

I think this case strikes to the heart of what it means to be a monk in the world, which is our challenge as dharma students: to be fully committed to our practice, to make it the only thing in our lives, and yet to honor our daily activity in the world as the expression of our practice. How do we do that? We are all monks of the east hall—and of the west hall. We are all activists and quietists. How do we manage this?

Thomas Merton wrote about the special function of the monk for the world. The monk, he felt, lives life radically in holiness, apart from the world. Monks are unusual people. They are and must be outsiders. This means they are not on any one side. They are committed to truth, which means love, so they can't be attached to one side or another. Monks can't hate. They can't justify their views as right. They must always come back to the center, to zero, to the present moment, the in-between moment, beyond views.

So although monks may live harmoniously in the midst of society, they are always subversives—working internally and externally against the dominant modes of greed, hate, and delusion that make the world go round. Monks are living examples of an alternative to the self-centered world. They are secret agents of a foreign power—the power of selfless love. But they don't have a superior attitude about this, because humility is their most important practice. Humility is the practice of being aware of the selfishness that is a constant feature of our mind, while remaining committed to the usually imperfect effort to go beyond selfishness—and to encourage others to do the same.

I know a Christian hermit whose lifetime has been devoted to the study of the writings of Simone Weil. Weil was an extraordinary person, a French Jew who became a Catholic mystic. Her life was a testament to this union of the opposites of activism and quietism. She was a mystic through and through, and yet most of her life was spent in extreme political activism. She was a witness for peace in the Spanish Civil War, a Marxist who wrote for a work-ers' newspaper and was active in workers' parties. She worked in an automobile plant and as a grape picker so that she could be in solidarity with ordinary working people. Living in England during World War II, sick from overwork, she died of starvation because she refused to eat any more than the French Resistance fighters, who were living underground at the time. Weil thought of her activism in mystical terms. She spoke not of justice or power but of attention, which she defined as "a point of eternity in the soul." If we can pay attention closely enough, she thought, we will come to know the transcendent, for it lies at the center of the human heart and mind.

In terms of our story, if you practice paying attention thoroughly enough, you will see that cutting the cat in two is cutting the cat in one—that because we are all different, we are all already one. So, passionate as your views may be, you do not want to take sides in bitter dispute. Instead, you want to appreciate and understand and weep with the suffering of the world. You want to intervene in dis-putes, grabbing hold of the cat and saying to everyone, "Wake up, take a look. Let's take a look together. Let's go beyond our differ-ences and see what we are really all about as human beings." How to do this in the midst of a particular situation is not always obvious. Maybe it takes a great master like Nanchuan to have the nerve to do it. But maybe not. Maybe we all have to learn to have that much nerve, getting up from the meditation cushion to become involved in our world of twoness and manyness, with the monk's spirit of oneness.

26

On Being an Ally

2007

WHEN YOU'RE IN a group not targeted by prejudice, the experience of a group that is so targeted is invisible to you. Racism, sexism? What racism and sexism, I don't see any. You have to go out of your way to notice. When you do, it can be heart-wrenching. All of a sudden this pain you didn't know was there, but that you were actually living in the midst of, comes searingly clear. The turn of mind that can occur when you open yourself to this universe of previously unseen suffering is similar to the turn of mind you experience in dharma practice, when you suddenly realize that the world, which you took to be a certain way, is actually quite otherwise.

I've led a few retreats with Ralph Steele, an African American Vipassana teacher, on the topic of racism. This topic draws together all kinds of people who really want to look at racism. I've appreciated these retreats because they help me—a white male person—to remember my natural blindness to prejudice. Opening your eyes is not a once-and-for-all thing. You have to keep working at it because the conditions that support such blindness don't go away. And habits are strong.

I've been thinking lately about what a strange experience it is to be a Jew in America and how that might affect my relationship to people of color. Typical Jewish psychology (though of course not all Jews have this psychology) includes a sense of being oppressed and persecuted, and yet in America at this moment, Jews are among the most privileged people. Still, you can easily find powerful and wealthy Jewish people who feel inside as if they were members of a persecuted minority. It's a weird thing. I, too, have that Jewish psychology. I always feel surprised to find myself included among privileged, powerful white people. Even though I know I am privileged, it's still weird. Inside, I'm still a Jew who's an outsider and liable to be an object of persecution.

I just do not identify with white males, for example, even though I am one. Whenever I hear that I'm a member of a privileged group, I always cringe at first because I think, "What are you talking about? I'm a Jew!"

This feeling doesn't come from any experience of being discriminated against or persecuted, because I never was, even though I was literally the only Jew in my class at school. But certainly people of my parents' generation experienced anti-Semitism a lot, and my parents constantly reminded me that I was a Jew and that I was different.

I realize that from the point of view of people of color, my Jewishness is largely irrelevant. I don't feel a need to speak about it. If someone looks at me and sees a privileged white male, I know that's a fair assessment, even though I don't feel that way inside. It's an odd contradiction.

I think it's typical for people to feel powerless. It's just human. Even a rich and powerful person knows deep inside that the wealth and the power are temporary and unearned. We are all pathetic temporary vulnerable creatures. Somewhere in us we all know this.

Even the stereotypical brutish white male who's throwing his weight around—well, if he lives long enough, he will realize how flimsy his bravado is, and that realization is never really far away, however much it may be unavailable to him at the moment. At the deepest level, we're all in the same boat.

But there's no denying social realities. We may have a deep connection to the bottom of the ocean, but we live mostly on the surface. We have to deal with the waves of social power and the pain that is caused by conceptions of social power and the individual and collective behavior that comes from those conceptions. Actual choices and material and psychological consequences. Maybe we can't afford to, or are unable to, get down to the level where we are all vulnerable, sorry, human beings.

In most dharma communities now, you won't find people who are saying that racism and privilege are irrelevant issues and that we should just get down to dharma. But twenty years ago, many white people did say that, and they felt uncomfortable with the idea of diversity training and consciousness raising in the sangha. Years ago I wrote an article called "Buddhism, Racism, and Jazz" (the following essay reproduced here in a revised version) for *Tricycle* magazine. My argument was that American culture is African American culture—American culture without reference to African American culture is incoherent. To have any idea about America, how it works and lives, you have to understand and appreciate this, otherwise you are missing the most salient point, the point that influences all other points. So if you have an American Buddhism it has to be deeply aware of the African American experience and its many brilliant and troubling cultural manifestations.

White Americans need to go out of their way not only to be allies to African American people but to make an effort to understand African American culture and experience, because that is part of our experience as Americans. Understanding ourselves requires that we understand African American contributions to and experience in our lives. That's why we should listen to jazz and recognize it as something at the heart of our culture, not only our musical culture but our literary culture as well.

We need to study other minority cultures in America as well. To be an ally to someone from a culture subject to prejudice, when you are from the dominant culture, it's not enough to feel magnanimous and say you will be open, you will be helpful. You have to stretch. You have to educate yourself. You have to listen. I'm trying to do that. I have to keep reminding myself. And since I am in a position to speak about the Buddhist teachings, I have to speak about this, because the teachings tell us that love and compassion for all beings is something we have to practice, and this may be more difficult to practice than we thought.

27

Buddhism, Racism, and Jazz

1993

THE OTHER DAY I picked up a world religions textbook my twin sons were using for their freshman high school history course. The chapter on Buddhism had a subsection entitled "Western Buddhism," and here you could see pictures of life in an American Zen Buddhist monastery, along with thoughtful text on the subject. I was surprised. Apparently, with the accelerated pace at which everything moves these days, American Buddhism has arrived at a point of establishment while still being formed. Looking at this textbook—at the same time that I've been taking a self-directed crash course in jazz, listening to Charlie Parker, Duke Ellington, Louis Armstrong, Thelonious Monk, et al.—got me musing on connections I hadn't noticed before. Buddhism. Racism. And jazz, perhaps the most American of all things.

To think about the origins of American Buddhism I suppose you start with Europe. (In this essay, by "American Buddhism" I mean "convert" Buddhism, as distinguished from "heritage" Buddhism, as practiced by Asian immigrants and their descendants in America.) Europeans encountered Buddhism as part of their colonial expansions in Asia and, in the nineteenth century, projected onto it the staid and sober, if tragic, point of view that was then culturally ascendant. This version of Buddhism had a big impact on German philosophers like Schopenhauer, Schleiermacher, and others, and through them on many subsequent thinkers including Nietzsche, the force of whose thought was a great challenge to conventional

European philosophy and religion. By the early twentieth century, and especially after the tremendous shock of the Great War (World War I), European culture was becoming frayed, and Christianity was less compelling to intellectuals than it had been. All over Europe, intelligent and thoughtful people were questioning their cultural roots, and many found Buddhism intriguing, as it seemed psychologically astute and fully compatible with science. A good number of such people—people like Lama Govinda, Bhikkhu Nyanamoli, Nyanaponika Thera—spent the greater part of their lives in Asia, steeped in the languages and traditions of Buddhism, and provided the first modern European look at Buddhism from the inside.

In America, Buddhism was also, if differently, influential by the mid-nineteenth century. Emerson, Thoreau, and Whitman were deeply affected by their reading of Buddhist and other Asian classical writings. But unlike in Europe, with its long-standing and influential intellectual traditions, the energy of American culture was popular and materialistic. Thinking of foundational American figures, one is more likely to picture inventors, entrepreneurs, capitalists, or entertainers than philosophers: Thomas Edison, who invented stuff, or Henry Ford, who figured out how to manufacture stuff quickly and efficiently. Our Schopenhauer is the musical theater genius George M. Cohan, our Schleiermacher the comic Bob Hope. Though the Transcendentalists' absorption and Americanization of Buddhism and Asian thought prepared the way for the next great wave of Buddhist influence, the real power behind that wave was economic and popular.

The wave crested a century later, in the 1950s and '60s, with the explosion of pop culture. The Beats and the Beatles made Buddhism cool. The cultural foment of the period spilled over into big bold movements, rather than thoughtful efforts to translate, digest, and studiously absorb Buddhism. Buddhism was seen as mystical and exotic, Asian thought wild and poetic, and in almost every way the obverse of American life in the 1950s. So it was not that white

Americans (mostly young white Americans) understood Buddhism and wanted to take it up. No, exactly because we didn't understand it we could take it as the answer to an underlying impulse, a contradiction within us that had always been there but was only in this period beginning to be felt. By the midsixties it felt clear to my generation that America needed to break out of something, and Buddhism appeared, to some of us, as a way to help us do that.

And what I'm contending here is that this impulse, this need to break out, which eventually became a deep undercurrent in the culture, had everything to do with the experience of African Americans: a group that was, and is, marginalized—and yet has been, at the same time, from the beginning, at the center of American life and culture, however denied and attacked this centrality has been.

▶◄

The American Buddhist movement can be said, more specifically, to have begun when Jack Kerouac and Neal Cassady made their frantic trips across America in the late 1940s, kindling the Beat movement. Many of the Beat writers—Allen Ginsberg, Gary Snyder, Philip Whalen, Amiri Baraka (then called LeRoi Jones), Michael McClure, Diane di Prima, and others—were influential cultural figures for the youth movement; almost all of them were practicing Buddhists, and all of them were deeply inspired by African American culture, specifically jazz. Read *On the Road* for its mystical, almost guru-like worship of black jazzmen. Outsiders and iconoclasts, the Beats (who were, except for Baraka and a few others, white) naturally identified with that part of American life that was always lively, always embattled, always underground.

You can't understand American culture without understanding jazz. Jazz (and its sister form, blues) accounts for most of the creativity that has sprung from American soil. Jazz was the roar of the twenties as much as it was the howl of the sixties. All the breakout energy of American artistic culture—the stuff that is exported and lusted after all over the world—comes from or is associated with the energy of jazz (which later became the energy of rhythm and blues, then rock and roll, then pop).

But the jazz of the Beats, the jazz of the late thirties and forties, was different from what had gone before. It was more Beat than upbeat, as the earlier music had been. The early jazz giants—like Duke Ellington and Louis Armstrong—played their music initially in black settings for black audiences, and later became acceptable and even essential to white American audiences, for whom they played graciously, excellently, without ever publicly expressing the alienation and disconnect that anyone with their life experience would have felt. Not that they were unwilling to express it, but at that moment it was more or less impossible for the white world to hear it, and they understood that, as did most black people at that time. By the late thirties things were changing. Younger black players were getting restless, perhaps tired of the long silence on race oppression, and began to reflect this in new forms of music—a trend that accelerated after the Second World War, when many of them came home after fighting side by side with white Americans, to find that nothing had changed. Racism may not have gotten worse; it just got harder to take. The new breed of musicians, the beboppers (Monk, Parker, Miles, Dizzy, et al.), wore dark glasses, funny hats, and goatees; they played what they wanted; white audiences were welcome to listen, but the music was not to be compromised for them. Many of the (white) jazz critics definitely did not like it.

This great generation of jazz musicians, like their predecessors, were geniuses of the first rank. And it is really impossible to separate their musical breakthroughs from the cultural and social revolution that went along with them. They knew what they were doing. They understood the forces that had formed America. They saw exactly how the inspiring tale of "liberty and justice for all" depended on denigration, economic oppression, and invisibility for them, and always had. They insisted on their Africanness and their historical American bondage as gritty, valuable, and revolutionary facts of life; they took charge of their imposed marginality—and made art out of it.

It is no accident, I think, that so many of these jazz players died young, in many cases from alcoholism and drugs. What they saw, what they understood, what they expressed, burned them up.

The African American experience, in all its painfulness and nobility, so clearly seen and expressed by these jazz players, is not simply that of a minority against whom great wrong has been done. In fact, it is the American experience—it is ours, all of ours, white and black alike. It is and it has always been central to who we are as a nation; therefore it is crucial for all of us to appreciate and understand it.

———— ►◄ ————

America still fascinates the rest of the world because it remains a unique social experiment, anyone's secret childlike aspiration: to start fresh, to begin again from scratch, to have things as you want them, without having to put up with patterns from the past. Anyone who has done meditation for any length of time realizes that this is impossible. The mind is full of history and formative patterns. And anyone who is born into or lives for a span of time in a coherent culture with deep historical roots also knows this is impossible. Nevertheless, everyone at least sometimes wishes it were possible. In America it is—or so the story goes.

But the real truth is, America does have a past, and that past has always had as much to do with slavery as with freedom. The first enslaved African people landed on American shores in 1619, in the colonial era, over 150 years before the Revolutionary War. This same span of time saw the displacement and killing of Native Americans on a massive scale, which would continue throughout the nineteenth century. Slavery continued until 1865, with its near equivalent, sharecropping under Jim Crow laws, continuing well into the twentieth century. Yet the white American impulse toward a national definition based on "freedom" was so powerful that it persisted through all of this. This mental contortion was possible only through evolving forms of legal, cultural, and intellectual white supremacy, foremost the (variously articulated and unarticulated) conviction that nonwhites, and especially blacks, were "other," less than, inhuman, and unworthy of attention.

Hence the particularly cruel and twisted character of the American institution of slavery, predicated on the enslavement of a people totally unknown, from a place far away. African slaves in America were not viewed as people. Serious literary and pseudo-scientific speculation of the day posited all kinds of theories to show that they were an inferior race. In the nineteenth century, social Darwinist and other forms of evolutionist thought doubled down on this direction, arguing—with little serious engagement with Darwin's actual work—that African-derived peoples were a degraded subspecies. As such, they were considered fortunate to have been brought to a place where they might be improved upon, even eventually Christianized and civilized. To this end they were outlawed from using their language, playing their music, worshiping their gods—and from reading and writing. Their families were not viewed as real families, so they could be broken up as it suited their white owners to do so. Their bodies were brutalized, and there was a consistent effort to dismantle them spiritually.

The ongoing effects of the experience of slavery—some 250 years of trauma—are still a dominant factor in the African American experience; that this is so little understood and appreciated is one reason African American culture, in all its richness and sadness and complexity, seems so baffling to white people. There is simply a tremendous gap in understanding of what is actually going on, what the real nature of the African American community actually is.

African Americans from slavery times until World War II carried this psychic, as well as social and economic, suffering in secret; they were literally invisible to white society—who they were, what they felt, could not and would not be shown to the white world. This was the condition for which W. E. B. Du Bois coined the term "double-consciousness," the necessity, as a black person, of always knowing how one appears through white eyes and conforming one's behavior to white expectations in order to try to stay safe. But after World War II this invisibility was no longer possible. And the effort to gradually come out of the shadows into the light—an effort that has not yet reached fruition—illuminates not only African Americans, but the white world as well.

———— ►◄ ————

I believe, and I get this from my own contact with the African American community (though in a limited way, from teaching at a local high school and volunteering to teach meditation in a day care center), that there is a sanity and a depth in the African American community that American society as a whole needs to recognize and learn from. White culture hasn't seen it; it isn't available to the camera or the reporter; it doesn't fit into the journalistic form. We get the problems and the tragedy, which surely are there, but the complexity, ambiguity, and nobility never surfaces. White America simply doesn't get it; it doesn't have the eye or the mind or the language to understand.

But it is there in the music. African music has the most complex rhythmical structure of any music in the world. It is a music that depends entirely on improvisation, on the human voice and human feeling, and on sincerity and presence: it has values that lean into a kind of friendliness and easy connection with things, not a description of them. Since African captives were not allowed to use their native music in America directly, they created it anew, using American folk and church singing, and the conditions of their own lives, to craft their own saving way of expression. This was gospel, and also blues, which had its origins in the work song or "field shout," and which later emerged, when instruments were introduced, as jazz. Jazz as the preeminent product of American denial. Jazz as the distilled elixir of the suffering that has run secretly through the night of the American Dream. As LeRoi Jones (now Amiri Baraka)

says in *Blues People,* a classic of jazz and blues that influenced a lot
of my own thinking:

> The poor Negro always remembered himself as an ex-
> slave and used this as the basis of any dealing with the
> mainstream of American society. The middleclass black
> man bases his whole existence on the hopeless hypothesis
> that no one is supposed to remember that for almost
> three centuries there was slavery in America, that the
> white man was the master and the black man the slave.
> This knowledge, however, is at the root of the legitimate
> black culture of this country. It is this knowledge, with
> its attendant muses of self-division, self-hatred, stoicism,
> and finally quixotic optimism, that informs the most
> meaningful of Afro-American music.[1]

Denial, rage, hurt of all kinds, taking care of karma buried so
long you almost can't see it any longer—this is the stuff that dharma
in America seems most firmly based on. At first it was the colorful,
exotic face of Buddhism that was attractive to white people, that
or the intellectual or aesthetic satisfaction of the teachings and
the culture they implied. But beyond this is the very real suffering, often the hidden, unacknowledged suffering, that meditation
practice brings to the surface, that sustains the practice over time.
And I think that to some extent the sexual abuse and power abuse
scandals that have created so much confusion in American dharma
centers over the last decades have come not from any selfish or evil
intention on the part of the teachers, or students, but rather from
a failure to understand this point—a failure to appreciate, in other
words, the fragility and hurt that are so central to the experience
of so many dharma practitioners. This is why I am arguing that
African American people are, in fact, our ancestors in the American dharma, as much as, and probably more than, Padmasam-
bhava, Buddhaghosa, and Hui Neng. As white Americans, we've

come to Buddhism in the end, I believe, not because we had some mystical transport or deep faith or understanding. We've come to it because we need something to help us look at the suffering we have caused and the suffering we experience. We can't go on any longer without it.

———— ▶◄ ————

American Buddhist groups are now at the point of looking around and noticing that there are few, or no, dark people of color in the meditation halls, and are wondering why this is so and trying to figure out what to do about it. (This is true at least in the Bay Area, where a few interracial Buddhist convocations have been organized to look at the issue.) It's traditional to point out that it takes a body, leisure to practice, and an encounter with the teaching in order to begin to practice in any given lifetime. A good number of white middle-class Americans have these requisites; probably fewer African Americans do. And even if they did, would they be interested in participating in a movement that looks like it is predominantly white, and therefore likely not really open to African Americans?

This is something the American Buddhist movement needs to work on over time, to make sure they are fully available to everyone, African American people and all others. What's crucial to me, however, as a white American practicing Buddhism, is that to understand myself as a Buddhist practitioner, or, for that matter, as an American, it is necessary that I understand the African American experience. African American people have understood the roots and branches, the dynamics and undercurrents of America—they've understood it, been formed by it, in turn formed it, and expressed it in many ways. But white America has not heard these expressions because its ears have been shut by long habit, ignorance, and willful avoidance. Hearing what has never been heard requires a new listening skill. Which you don't develop until the pain of separation, of nonhearing, becomes so great you are finally motivated to begin. At first you hear grunts, groans, noises, gestures, questions, hopes, that come as much from inside as outside your ear. Later you can hear words, sentences, paragraphs. The other begins to speak, and you can hear. At least a little. And then, finally, you are willing to truly see what you couldn't see before, to acknowledge your fear, guilt, and shame, to admit in shock and horror that the immense sins of the past are not left in the past, they continue into the present, and that you did not wish to know this.

In such difficult yet necessary ways a bridge will be built to reach across so that for the first time it perhaps becomes possible for white people to begin to comprehend what it means to be an African American. And to whatever extent it is, it will to that same extent become possible for white people to begin to see themselves. For white Buddhists, who know that the first noble truth is "all conditioned existence has the nature of suffering," this self-seeing must be the beginning, and the essence, of the path.

28

The Sorrow of an All-Male Lineage

2018

ONE OF THE most profound spiritual awakenings I have ever experienced happened when I was abbot at Green Gulch Farm Zen Center. In those days it was my daily practice to sit in my room conducting practice interviews (called *dokusan*) in the early morning hours, while the community did zazen and chanting service in the zendo. One dark morning a young woman came to see me. She was a short-term student, someone I hardly knew. She was impressive: I remember her as large and tough-looking, with lots of tattoos and piercings. Maybe I am making up this detail, but I recall she had arrived at the temple on a motorcycle.

She sat down in front of me and began weeping, which surprised me as she seemed so tough. I asked her what was the matter. She told me she was weeping because she had just come from the service where the Zen lineage was being chanted, as it has been at morning service since the founding of Zen center—and before, in Japan.

I was confused by her reply. I said, "Why would chanting the lineage make you cry?"

"Because every name is a man's name," she said.

Of course, I was well aware of this. Some scholars say it's possible that a name or two on the list could be a woman's name. But yes, by and large the Zen lineage is a male lineage, because like all organized religions Zen has always been dominated by males. I had long recognized the injustice of this, but what can you do? It was just a fact. That someone could be emotionally overcome by chanting this list had never occurred to me.

But when I saw this woman weeping I suddenly felt the pain she was feeling. The all-male Zen lineage wasn't just an unfortunate piece of history. It was a symptom of a much larger outrage, a far deeper sorrow. It was as if the entire human history of men overlooking, oppressing, and committing violence against women washed over me all at once. I was overwhelmed.

In Mahayana Buddhism, awakening isn't personal liberation. It is awakening to the reality of others and the fact that the lives of others are our own life. From earliest times, Buddhism's key insight was that self as we normally conceive it is an imprisoning illusion, causing all our suffering. In Mahayana Buddhism this teaching takes the form of radical compassion, which flows from the heartfelt understanding that we are the sufferings and joys of others. As a Zen practitioner, I had long appreciated this. But it took on a more profound reality for me on the day that young woman wept.

I practice zazen, study teachings, and go to retreats not just to find some peace but to open my heart a little wider, to expand my capacity to be unsettled by suffering. When I practice *metta* or *tonglen*, I am quite specifically hoping to extend my love and compassion.

Prajna wisdom, the practice of transcendent understanding, shows me a point of peace at the heart of suffering that enables me to sustain my caring. It isn't always easy—it is not supposed to be—but it can be beautiful to extend a caring heart. Yes, to care about others in pain is to increase one's suffering. But compassion is the most liberating, the most wonderful, of all practices. It comes from the life-changing experience of true empathy—of really feeling how someone else experiences their life.

I have thought of this lately while reeling from the public outcry that has resulted in the #MeToo movement—that spate of revelations of sexual harassment, to the point of callous brutality, by powerful men in politics, entertainment, journalism, business, and elsewhere. Recall that this is only the latest round: this stuff has been happening for a long time (and male Buddhist teachers own their share of the guilt).

Although the stories are all different, there's a pattern. Powerful men intoxicated by their privilege, and assumed charm and genius, imagine that women exist as characters in their distorted fantasy lives. It's an illness, but not a rare one, given the norms and values of our world. And it is no news: males in male-dominated societies have always dominated and abused women, and we all bear the scars. The full equality, dignity, and inclusion of women is not only just and long overdue, its absence over the centuries unspeakably sad—it is a necessity. The abuse, violence, psychological brutality, has to end. Otherwise what world do we have?

It's unsettling. Let's be honest: these revelations stir up disturbing feelings long buried. All men have soul-searching to do. Have we done the same, or something like it lately or in the past? Have we knowingly or unknowingly colluded? How thoughtful and careful have we been about the privilege we enjoyed? What man can say that he is free of his own perhaps less spectacular but equally unfair and belittling words and deeds? Any man takes the moral high ground with trepidation. Who can claim virtue or innocence?

That early morning at Green Gulch, I got up from the interview and immediately began insisting that we find a way to begin the chanting of a women's lineage along with the male lineage. Others in the community joined me in this. We met resistance (from some women as well as some men), but within a few months we researched a list of women's names and began to chant them in daily service. Today, as far as I know, most if not all Western Zen centers chant a women's lineage along with the male ancestors.

And that tough tattooed Zen student? She soon disappeared and I never saw her again. I wonder whether she was real, whether I made her up, or whether she was a goddess, like the ones you read about in Mahayana Buddhist sutras, sent to awaken an ignorant abbot.

———— ▶◀ ————

In addition to the lineage names chanted in daily service, there are also lineage documents given in Zen lay and priest ordination ceremonies. These documents are considered sacred, are carefully prepared by preceptors for each ceremony, and are kept as precious by ordainees. Though we were able to add women's names to the chanting list fairly quickly, it took far longer to figure out how to add them to these traditional documents. Eventually a group of us (including especially the lay Zen teacher Peter Levitt and the priest Grace Schireson) designed a document that was approved by the Soto Zen Buddhist Association—a Western organization with no official ties to Japanese Soto Zen—and is now, in various formats, used by many Western Zen centers. In our groups we now bundle both documents—the traditional lineage that we have received from Japan (and that still contains mostly male names but, as the generations go on in the West, includes more and more women) and the "women's lineage" document—together in one package we call Complete Dharma Heritage. I feel very good to offer this document to people in our ceremonies.

There is no doubt in my mind that ancient religious traditions, despite all their baggage and painful histories, are valuable— perhaps even more in this present era when human confusion abounds and the search for sustainable meaning seems more difficult to come by than ever. There is simply no way to match the experimentation, discussion, literature, history, tradition, doctrine and know-how that is embedded in these age-old discourses and institutions. Secularizing the old practices, inventing new ones, reinventing doctrine, mixing and matching teachings and practices, is good. But I believe that preserving the richness that remains in the old is also necessary.

We can't ignore that all the great religious traditions (Buddhism included) were created in feudalistic contexts, in which women were oppressed, gays and lesbians vilified, and social injustice of all sorts supported. These things have to change. Religion has to be updated drastically, and it seems to me that the issue of full inclusion of women is pivotal in this process.

In American Soto Zen (though not in Japanese Soto) we have maybe for the first time in any continuous ancient religious tradition full inclusion for women. In American Soto, women serve as fully ordained priests, abbots, and senior teachers and take their places side by side with men, sharing status and leadership equally. And now, finally, women's names are chanted in daily temple services and handed out in official lineage documents to all ordained Zen Buddhists—men as well as women.

29

On Difference and Dharma

1999

I OFTEN READ THE online news so that I can be mindful of what's going on in the world—or at least what some people think is going on in what they consider to be the world. Doing this can get me disgusted, agitated, or sad, sometimes bored, but I realize all this is a distraction one way or the other. No doubt I would be more peaceful if I did not read the news. But I read it anyway. It's good to be peaceful, but sometimes peace is not the most important thing.

I have been reading about the NATO bombing and the war in Kosovo, about Iraq, and Pakistan. I have also been reading about yet another case of racially incited police brutality in the United States. I respect police officers, and I believe that out-and-out racial hatred is becoming rare, and yet, in our nation, institutional poverty and racism is common, though seldom reported in the news. People of color are quite aware of this. The rest of us, I am afraid, are naive.

The U.S. prison population is expanding at a tremendous rate, and there are many more bond issues on our ballots for building new prisons than for building new schools. The prison population in the U.S. is overwhelmingly made up of people of color whose presence there is a direct or indirect result of drugs, which are directly related to poverty and racism. Most citizens of the U.S. see this as a lamentable but normal situation.

When the U.S. and China meet for talks, the U.S. brings up

human rights violations in Tibet, and the Chinese say: Yes, but let's talk about prisons in the U.S. To us this seems like an avoidance tactic by the Chinese, and maybe it is, but they are not wrong. We are blinded by our viewpoint; we can't see what is going on around us. Just a few miles from our peaceful zendo is San Quentin, a large prison, in which executions are carried out more and more frequently. Some nights while we are sleeping peacefully in our beds, the state is killing one of our brothers a few miles away. The two people executed so far in 1999 were both men of color.

In our city streets there are many homeless people, among them many homeless youth. Of these young people, the overwhelming majority are gay, because when their parents discover they are gay they either are thrown out of their homes or feel so alienated in them they leave. We all know about the murder last fall in Wyoming of a gay man whose crime was apparently that he *was* a gay man. A Protestant clergyman and his organization regularly picket the funerals of gay people who have died of AIDS, carrying signs and chanting slogans that demean the deceased as evildoers. Such a protest took place at Matthew Shepard's funeral in Wyoming.

This is the world we live in. When we meditate, we have to breathe it in with each inhalation, and accept that this is how it is. And when we breathe out we have to breathe out relief and hope. Zazen, Zen meditation, is not an escape or a denial of the world we live in. It is a profound love and acceptance of it, and the cultivation of the mind that wants to heal it and is, ultimately, capable of healing it.

Conditioned coproduction—that things arise in cooperation with each other, and coproduce each other; that no thing can be alone or isolated—is a cornerstone of Buddhist teaching. There are no separate entities—only the mutual and continuous arising of interrelated patterns. This means that what happens in this world is our responsibility and our sorrow. We have to expand our mind and heart big enough to see it and to accept it as our own.

———— ►◄ ————

When we meditate we see our mind very intimately. So much that we have not wanted to acknowledge comes into view. We see how the patterns of greed, hatred, jealousy, and fear are deeply rooted in us. The problem isn't somewhere else. Over there is also right here.

The point of Buddhist practice is transcendence. In other words, we are not trying to improve ourselves; we are trying to go beyond ourselves. But this can't be done by jumping over ourselves. "Me" means all of my confused and nasty mental states. "Me" means all my misapprehensions, and my constant conceptual faux pas. That is what "me" is. We need to breathe it in and breathe it out. We have to come to accept and appreciate what we didn't want to know was there at all.

The more you look at your mind, the more you see your mind isn't just your mind—it's your parents' mind, your culture's mind, the mind of your racial group or gender. We want to be free of all this, and in a way we are. It all comes and goes of its own accord. Nevertheless we have to notice how it all comes over and over again in us. When you first take up meditation, you may think you are going to get beyond all this. You may think that when you sit in meditation you are going to go beyond being a woman or a man or a white person or an Asian person. There is just going to be breathing going on. It's true. But it's just as true that your conditioning is still there—you are still a man, a woman, gay, straight—and that this identity is rooted even more deeply than you thought. We are bound to our conditioning. In the present moment, all of the history of oppression passes through us. The mind that arises now contains the whole history of our culture or family lineage. Meditation practice is not a way around, it's a way through. Each moment is a chance to liberate all that has happened. To turn all of it around for the good. We have to practice this both on and off the cushion.

It's a tremendous shock to realize you are a human being. You feel empathy, remorse, and a desire to be compassionate. You have a moral sense. You are also capable of enormous hatred, and violence. You have to respect that and not forget it. It makes you very humble. Anything anyone has ever done, good or bad, you could do. You see this if you look long and carefully enough at your own mind.

The mind is like a great ocean—everything can be found in it, and, like the ocean, in some places it is very deep. In your mind you see greed, hate, and delusion, and you see the power of history —your own history and the history of your family or gender or race. You see how all of that is working itself out in your own thinking right now. And you know that Vietnam and apartheid and Rwanda and Kosovo and Iraq are blood emblems of your mind of suffering as it touches history and the world. This is what we have to investigate, grieve over, accept, and dedicate ourselves to liberating. Only when we have appreciated all of this can we awaken to the real nature of things.

In the bodhisattva path there is a stage called omniscience. Omniscience means that you can see everything. But it's not a supernormal power, like clairvoyance. Omniscience means that you see all things in their true aspect, the fluid cooperative pattern of emptiness. When you can see one thing truly then you are seeing everything. Whatever is in front of you is all things, and each thing is complete. So if you are a woman, you can see that woman is empty and includes everything. If you are an Asian, you see Asian is empty and includes everything. When we can see things in this way, we can celebrate our own history without needing to denigrate other people. A Jew who can appreciate the true universal and empty nature of being a Jew can see that being a Palestinian is included in that. There is no need to hurt anyone else.

The Buddha did not promise that suffering would disappear. He did not promise permanent heaven or endless peace to anyone. As long as there is consciousness there is going to be suffering, and in a human world there will always be the suffering of death and disaster, of loss, of love that is unfulfilled, the suffering of economic setbacks, of wanting things that you do not get. But we don't need to make this suffering worse. There can be suffering, but we can be free of it. Hating is absolutely unnecessary. We don't need to create this kind of suffering. It can be reduced and even eliminated by the wisdom and courage of our own activity.

Each of us is different from every other one. We say there are men and women and Asians and Africans and white people. But if we get closer, we see that there aren't any Asians—there are Chinese and Vietnamese, Cambodians and Thais, and they are all quite different. And there are no white people either—there are French and German and American people, there are women who are different from men, and gay people who are different from straight people. If we get closer still, each man will see that he is not like other men, each Jew that they are not like other Jews, each African American that she is not like any other African American.

In the end, most intimately, each one of us is completely different. Each one is a universe of difference, and each universe of difference is impossibly deep. When you really look at your mind, to its ocean depths, there is nothing you can say about who you are. What a strange thing it is to be someone, to speak about this world as though it were something, to want anything, to find something or to lose something; all of this is very strange.

I think that if we appreciated the real nature of our minds, we would not be able to hate one another. Knowing that we do not understand one another, we would be curious about one another, and all the strangeness of the world. We would want to know all about it and enjoy it. This is how children are. They want to know about everything and to enjoy everything. They have to be taught to hate.

Why is hatred so common? If it is just something in our minds, why don't we get rid of it easily? People hate one another for what they consider to be very good reasons. Because they have wounded one another out of their own woundedness; and everyone wants and needs satisfaction for their hurts. The Palestinians who hate Jews have good reasons. They have been terribly wronged. Their families and friends have been oppressed or killed. So hatred is not simply something in the mind that will go away if we are nice. It can become our identity; to give it up can be a form of suicide.

We all want to practice in order to be happy, but it is not possible to be happy without seeing that our lives are implicated completely with all other lives. If we practice thoroughly, we see that we are happy only with everyone and we suffer with everyone.

I am often surprised by the narrowness of my world. This is why I make an effort to look outside my small world and see a bigger world. I know I must do this for my practice. I must do this so that I can understand my own mind. I hope everyone will reach beyond the narrowness of conditioning to touch a bigger world, the great and real world of sorrow and joy, a world that leaves nothing out and knows that in actual life, the actual life of liberation, nothing ever can be left out.

30

On Forgiveness and Reconciliation

2001

I WATCH MORNING television—a practice I would recommend. You can learn a lot from it: what people are buying and selling, what they are thinking and talking about, what they are afraid of, what they hope for. The other day a woman appeared on television who had worked out a good method for achieving happiness. Her idea was that you would write in a journal every day, as a way of keeping track of yourself in various areas of your life, like physical health, relationships, and spirituality. Through the writing there would somehow be an improvement. I was impressed that in the category of spirituality she included forgiveness as a regular daily topic: that every day you would write in your journal about your efforts to forgive yourself for what you had done that was harmful, and to forgive others for what they might have done to you. She had her own personal story to tell, about how her life had changed dramatically for the better because of this journaling practice.

It seemed quite startling to me to imagine that there was so much hurting going on in the world that every day every person would need to spend some time actively forgiving people, including themselves. But I quickly saw that yes, this is probably true. There are so many possibilities for hurt! There is the explicit hurting through anger, violence, deprivation, and oppression, but also the more subtle hurting that comes from failing to love enough, failing to acknowledge and appreciate oneself and others—the kind of hurting that goes almost unnoticed and yet is a powerful negative factor in our lives. So yes, it would make sense that if you were going to take care of yourself well, take your vitamins, eat a low-fat diet, and so on, that you would also, as a hygienic discipline, take on the daily practice of forgiveness.

But forgiveness is difficult. It's painful.

If you have hurt yourself or someone else, you are responsible for having created pain. Whether conscious or not, that pain is there in you. And if someone else has hurt you, then of course the pain is there. The first step in forgiving yourself or another is to let yourself feel the fullness of that pain. So forgiveness, at least in this first stage, doesn't feel good.

Nobody likes to feel pain. Naturally, we want to distract ourselves from pain, and we will latch on to something else, anything else, to avoid it. Our economy depends on this human tendency—companies that market the drugs that keep us pain free, the products that distract and amuse us, the entertainment that absorbs our attention so we won't think of anything that matters—all this is essential for our prosperity.

But the most compelling form of avoidance of pain is blaming. When you can't entirely eliminate the pain by distraction or oblivion, you get around it by blaming it on someone or something—even if it is yourself. Blaming is a smoke screen for the pain itself. You focus forcefully on blame so you don't have to notice the horrifying weight of your suffering.

So forgiving has to begin with allowing yourself to drop blame, distraction, and oblivion and actually feel the pain of what has happened. This is hard work, especially since much of the time the pain isn't within the immediate frame of your awareness, and you need to do something to evoke it, to bring it forth into your heart. It's rare that anyone is willing to sit still for this, but forgiveness requires it. This is one reason meditation practice is sometimes not so peaceful: if you meditate with a sense of openness to what comes in (and this is really the only way to meditate), it does tend to evoke all of this hurt. Meditation practice itself in this way can bring you toward a sense of forgiveness.

The next step toward forgiveness, which comes with the thorough completion of the first step, is to go to the root of the pain, beyond the story that comes associated with it and beyond the dismay and the fear.

Pain's true root is always the same: existence itself. Because you are alive, there is this pain. With being, there is always this pain. You've been hurt, yes, it's true. Someone has done something to you—that may also be true. But if you didn't have a mind, a body, an identity, it wouldn't have happened. Since you do have a mind, a body, an identity, it is guaranteed that you will be hurt when the conditions for your being hurt come together. So the person who hurt you, you yourself personally, and the story of the hurting are all actually incidental to the ultimate fact of your existence. Forgiving follows naturally when you see that we are all in this together and that we are all victims of hurt. This is a tall order. This is forgiveness as a profound religious practice.

———— ►◄ ————

So I agree with the expert on television that forgiveness must be a daily practice—a path that we have to keep walking, probably for our whole life.

To forgive *yourself* seems the hardest form of forgiveness. In Zen practice, simply allowing yourself to be yourself, just as you are, is considered the mark of awakening. Short of this, you are at best slightly embarrassed about who you are, and at worst, tortured by it.

Forgiveness of another person is also an internal act—it is something you do, in the final analysis, for yourself. After all, if you harbor resentment for another, it is you yourself who will suffer for that. The other person may be just fine, completely oblivious to how you feel about him or her, while you are eating yourself alive with anger. You think: *I'll never forgive him—he doesn't deserve it.* This is a little like hitting yourself over the head with a hammer and refusing to stop because the other person isn't worthy of your stopping. So forgiveness is for yourself. In a way, it doesn't really affect the other person. If you forgive someone, it doesn't get them off the hook for what they have done. They are still responsible for their actions. No one can ever escape the consequences of action; everyone has themselves to answer for and live with. When you know that, you can feel free to forgive. And to do so in order to open your own heart, so that maybe one day you could actually learn how to love others completely. So forgiveness is something you do inside yourself and for yourself.

Reconciliation is the effort you make to reach out to those who have wronged you or whom you have wronged. Because reconciliation involves others, it is much more complicated. With reconciliation you try to understand things from the other person's point of view, to express that understanding, and to make peace based on that mutuality of understanding. It is like reconciling your checkbook—you balance one side with the other, until there is a sense of mutual identity.

This also is not so easy, and you can't expect too much. When there is already pain between two people, or groups of people, there is a risk that more talk will actually lead to *more* hurting. Sometimes reconciliation is impossible—or impossible now. Maybe a lot of time has to go by. Sometimes the best thing is to agree that nothing can be said without causing more trouble, and to part company for a while.

The other day there was yet another horrible bombing in Israel, at a disco, and the victims were teenagers. And I've been thinking about how Jews and Palestinians persist in hating one another, and hurting one another over such a long time, at such tremendous cost to all involved. People think it's irrational—just a matter of blind prejudice. Why can't they be more reasonable, more kind, like the rest of us? This is a naive view.

The fact is, hatred is not irrational. People have very good reasons for hating each other. They hate each other because they fear each other. And they fear each other because they feel that the other is a direct threat to their identity. And since fear is a disempowering emotion, it is usually covered up with hatred.

Although Buddhism's genius is to deny the reality of identity, and to offer a thoroughgoing path that takes us beyond fixed identity, still, for most of us in this world, including Buddhists, identity is experienced as a fact. Gertrude Stein famously said, "I am I because my little dog knows me." And I am I because my beliefs and associations speak my me-ness to me. If your beliefs and associations seem to deny mine, then I am frightened for my very lifeblood, and I feel I have no choice but to hate you. Your existence threatens to blot mine out.

And this hatred isn't made up: it is rooted in external events. Members of your group have killed members of mine, my brothers, my sisters, my countrymen. They have taken away our land, forbidden us to speak our language, and withheld our rights. And they have done this not only to some of us but to many of us, and have done it not only once or twice but repeatedly. How can I be who I am, a Jew or a Palestinian or a Basque or an Irish Catholic or Protestant or a Lebanese Christian or Muslim or a Serbian or an Albanian, if I can forgive such things? If I were to forgive you, how could I face myself, and how could I face my community?

When I visited Northern Ireland last year, I saw how in some situations not to hate the enemy is an unthinkable possibility. In Northern Ireland everyone must be either Protestant or Catholic, and if you are one it means you must deny the other. I was there with the Dalai Lama, and believe it or not, people wanted to know whether the Dalai Lama was a Protestant Buddhist or a Catholic Buddhist. They accepted that he was a Buddhist—but which kind of Buddhist was he? So in certain historical situations it becomes almost impossible to let go of your cultural identity. Some years ago, when I was in Israel, I tried to speak to people there about Zen practice and about the Buddhist sense of reconciliation based on emptiness. I found I couldn't even get the words out because it was simply an inexpressible thought in that culture at that time.

Tremendous emotion builds up over a long time, and myths are created. As we tell the story of what has happened, it becomes not so much the story of what has actually occurred as the story of our pain and our fear. With these stories conditioning our views, how can we ever reach out to one another in reconciliation?

I have seen this happen in personal conflicts among my own friends. Without the practice of forgiveness, which commits us to feeling the naked truth of our pain and simply allowing it to be what it is, the effort to reach out fails every time. In political conflict involving generations and multitudes, the situation becomes far worse. If you listen to what Jews and Palestinians say about what has happened in the past, it is astonishing. They describe events in which both peoples have participated, but the descriptions seem to have nothing to do with one another. Even the very names of the places over which they contend don't jibe. There seem to be no facts whatsoever—only myths that are accepted, almost on faith, as facts. So there is no way to sort things out. And at the root of this tremendous dissonance is the fear of loss of identity.

Years ago, in Israel, I ran into an old settler who said to me, with utter confidence and cheer, "Peace will come. The momentum is always for peace." At the time I was in despair about the situation, and I was astonished by his comment. He was not a naive, sentimental person but someone who had seen tremendous hardship in Israel, and in Europe before he came to Israel. But now I believe that he was absolutely correct—that the momentum is always for peace.

I suppose this is nothing more than a species of faith. The human capacity for bitterness and hatred and delusion is tremendous, and that energy is by no means played out in this world. And yet, people still fall in love, still have children, and still love those children. People still hope for peaceful homes and neighborhoods. They hope for beauty.

Identity and fear are powerful motivators, and they need to be respected. Probably the single most important realization that would lead to peace in the world would be this one—the recognition that we are all afraid of ceasing to be what we imagine we are. This is what motivates most of our political activity.

So yes, we need to respect fear and identity; they are strong. But stronger still is the desire for peace. Peace is the end of every story, just as it is the end of every life. So peace will come, and people want it to come.

———— ▶◀ ————

When I was in Northern Ireland at the peace conference with His Holiness, I listened to a panel of victims of the Troubles, all of whom, in different ways, had been devastated by what happened. What was inspiring about their presentations was that each of them had had a change of heart. Each had gone through enormous hurt and bitterness to find that place where hurt is just the hurt of being alive, and there is finally no one to blame and nothing to regret. In a way, for each of these people, the worst had happened. What they had feared and dreaded, with a fear and a dread that had previously motivated them to hatred, had actually taken place, and there was nothing else to do but let go of identity and fear, and accept a new life as a different person.

The alternative is to shut down internally. But these panel members had done the opposite; they had opened instead of closing. And they were cheerful people, natural and at ease with themselves, and every one of them was actively and passionately involved in peace work.

As long as there is more than one of us, there are going to be conflicts and tragedies and the need to work things out in the midst of difficult situations. So we will always need the skills of hard-nosed and realistic negotiation, of tradeoffs and strategy. But I am convinced that real reconciliation depends ultimately on forgiveness, which is internal, spiritual work that all of us have to do.

31

We Have to Bear It

2002

This essay grew out of a dharma talk given on September 16, 2001.

IN THE *Shurangama Sutra* we read of Kwan Yin, the bodhisattva who hears the cries of the world with a still and perfect serenity, understanding them as manifestations of the perfect light of enlightenment. Because of this she remains peaceful, despite her tears, and is able to offer the right kind of help to beings, each according to their situation.

I suppose we all are Kwan Yin, or aspire to be her. But also we aren't Kwan Yin. We are human beings who confront the stark realities of human violence and pain, and we cringe. We aren't serene. We are jittery, angry, confused. We feel grief and anguish, terror and disorientation.

I don't think we want to get rid of these feelings. We feel them and we want to feel them. Maybe we have to be both Kwan Yin, who accepts what is with perfect and effective equanimity, and also poor human beings, who find what happens sometimes unbearable and unacceptable. And yet we have to bear it and accept it, because there isn't any alternative.

The day before the terrible tragedy of September 11, 2001, I was helping to facilitate a meeting about racism and diversity in the Buddhist community. In the meeting we heard many expressions by people of color about their frustration and their suffering. This suffering often is hidden to people of the dominant culture, who have no idea what their brothers and sisters go through in the course of any ordinary day in America. One African American woman said to the group, "Racism isn't just eye-holes cut into white sheets. In its most insidious form it is simply privilege itself. When you live in a world structured so that some races dominate over others, some races enjoy peace and prosperity while others suffer terribly, then simply enjoying your privilege unthinkingly is itself a form of racism."

I do not doubt that something needs to be done in response to these terrorist events. Exactly what needs to be done I do not know—as a religious person I have no experience in this field, and it is not my job to defend the nation. I do not know what I would do if I did have the expertise and the responsibility. But if the actions taken come out of a wrong understanding of the situation, out of a blindness to the social and spiritual forces that have given rise to it, then those actions will be twisted and ineffective, driven by emotion and distorted views based on bad information. I have seen this so many times in my lifetime: violence inspiring violence that gives rise to more violence. Wars that end temporarily, only to produce new wars.

The people who hijacked those airplanes and murdered so many people were themselves people. They did what they did because of the condition of their hearts and minds. But the condition of their hearts and minds came from somewhere; it came from what happened to them and how they understood what happened to them. There isn't any separate evil out there that I can find, blame for all this, and root out of the human family. There's just one world, one human race. The evil that happens happens for a reason.

I heard a Catholic priest speaking about this on television. Someone asked him to explain how God could allow such things to happen. He said, It's a mystery, we don't know. But I think we do know. Terrible things happen because human beings act with violence, aggression, and delusion. And they do that because they have been hurt, because others have acted with violence and aggression and delusion against them and their families. People do what they do because they are terrified of confronting the pain and anguish in their own hearts. The violence in the world is an outer projection of the violence and pain we feel inside.

When we externalize such events and their perpetrators, scapegoating them as some outside force, some independent evil in which we have no part, and then, to alleviate the grief and the impotence we feel, try to stamp out that evil once and for all, we make matters worse. It is so perfectly clear. The result of this will be more and more violence. Soon after the crisis began, His Holiness the Dalai Lama wrote a letter of condolence to President Bush. "It may be presumptuous of me to say this," he said, "but I hope that the American government will not try to correct the situation with further violence."

But of course there will be further violence. We must be strong; we cannot allow violence to go unanswered. We have been thinking this way for so long it seems like forever. This disaster in New York and Washington and Pennsylvania was horrible. But there have been so many horrible things. Almost every nation in the world has experienced horrible things like this. The dropping of atomic bombs on Hiroshima and Nagasaki. The bombings of London, of Dresden, of countless other cities. Vietnam, a country decimated. The Holocaust. The genocide of the native peoples of the Americas, of Africans, of Armenians. All the lives lost in those places—we cannot forget about any of them. And now, so close to home, we are feeling the pain of such useless deaths.

There are some people who wonder how there could be such evil in this world. How human beings could generation after generation perpetrate such acts. But I do not wonder. To me it seems clear why there is such violence ingrained in who and what we are. To speak in theological terms, it's not that evil is out of God's control and that we, on God's side, have to overcome it with violence. Good and evil exist on the same plane and operate by the same calculus. Evil is good covered over. Wherever we ourselves, in our confusion and in our unwillingness to look at life as it actually is, with all its pain and difficulty, commit acts of evil, we add to the covering. And whenever we have the courage and the calmness to be with life as it is, and therefore, inevitably, to do good, then we remove the cover. We transform evil into good. This is the human capacity. Evil is not a part of reality that can be excised, cast out, and overcome. Evil is a constant part of our world because there is only one world, there is only one life, and all of us share in it.

There are times when life becomes so stark, so absolutely real in and of itself, that there is nothing to do but bear witness to what is. Meditation practice is not going to take care of violence or make us feel better about it. Meditation is so precious, too precious, all its sensitivities and refinements and developments that can get so artistic sometimes. Stark and tough reality blows all that out of the water. Meditation practice seems foolish when the world is on fire. Screams drown out the silence.

But bearing witness is itself the essential meditation practice—stepping back, being quiet, listening to ourselves, to the world, with an accurate ear, allowing, opening to what we hear—this practice, the fruit of our time on the cushion, is more relevant in times like these than ever. There are, in a crisis, a million ways to help, and we should help in whatever way we can. But beyond help, we need to bear witness to what is happening. To take it in, imagine it, feel it, grieve over it, accept it, not accept it, understand it, fail to understand it, and comfort each other in that. To do that we need the expansiveness of our sitting, of our chanting, and of our prayers.

32

The Religion of Politics, the Politics of Religion

2005

O N JANUARY 20, 2005, a few hours before I needed to leave for the airport, I was exercising on my ski machine while I watched the president's inaugural address on television. I confess to being fascinated by our president, whose sheer nerve amazes me. Besides, I love national spectacles and am easily swept away by the emotion of the occasion, however cooked up it may be. So I sped along on my skis (going nowhere), mesmerized by the black-suited president walking down the aisle toward the podium, the crowds, the pomp, the solemnity of the occasion. I momentarily forgot about my flight.

All my past skepticism about the president's actions and statements was suspended as I listened to his inspired opening words. As he went on, though, I was sweating more and more, and not just from the exercise. The president's address was making me nervous, even as it thrilled me. Truth is, it was a noble speech. Had it been delivered by someone else, I probably would have cheered, gotten off my machine, and stepped outside to contemplate the dawning of a new and glorious era. But these words were coming out of the mouth of George W. Bush, a man whose policies had caused me no small amount of grief—a man for whom I would never have dreamed of voting.

Referring to the terrorist attacks of September 11, 2001, the president spoke of a "day of fire." "We have seen our vulnerability," he said, "and we have seen its deepest source. . . . There is only one force of history that can break the reign of hatred and resentment . . . and that is the force of human freedom." He went on to say that "the survival of liberty in our land increasingly depends on the success of liberty in other lands," and that the task of spreading liberty was the "work of generations. The difficulty of the task is no excuse for avoiding it," he said.

The president repeated the words *freedom* and *liberty* many times in his speech. Though he didn't give us his own definitions of these words, his voice conveyed a confidence that everyone knew what he meant by the words, and that everyone was as inspired by them as he was. Coming from a man whose idea of preserving freedom includes full-scale invasion of a foreign nation on false pretenses, such words make me nervous. But I applaud the sentiment: the idea that no one can be free of tyranny till all are free is a noble thought, one that lies at the heart of all religious teaching.

The speech also challenged young people to "serve in a cause larger than your wants, yourselves," adding that "self-government relies on governing the self." The president was making a plea for a sense of discipline, morality, and personal responsibility as the basis of public life.

How could I object? As a Zen Buddhist priest and teacher, I am constantly advocating these same values.

The president vowed to take America forward to promote "goodness" everywhere in the world, beginning at home with compassion for people through social programs that, he said, would give everyone a chance at "ownership." Never mind the details: this was a high-minded speech, full of vision; a speech that went, in a sense, beyond politics. Yes, this was a religious speech.

I think about religion all the time. I'm convinced there's a human need for religious expression and practice. Some people find ways to engage it, others don't. For me, religion isn't something imposed from the outside; it comes from within, an indelible aspect of our human nature. I find the religious expressions of some people a bit abstract, theoretical, and ideological, rather than personal and soulful, but I have an open mind. I keep listening, trying to find out what people really feel, and what difference those feelings make in their lives.

I think the president's sense of religious mission is sincere. I think he had a genuine conversion experience, changed his inner life dramatically, and is a sincerely devout person who feels moved by his faith to pursue his political goals. Although my political instincts are not the same as his, I can appreciate his passion, for I, too, have a sense of an inspired social mission that comes out of my religious practice. Like President Bush, I care deeply about the world and wish for its inhabitants universal well-being and freedom from oppression. I realize that this is an impractical and possibly even foolhardy wish. The historical record certainly does not support the possibility of its ever being anything more than a dream. Nevertheless, I try my best to work toward it, to see my personal life and my political life as one seamless whole, and to let my actions in both be motivated, as much as possible, by the desire for good. It may be that our president sees his actions in precisely this way. It may be that his vision and mine are not so far apart in essence, however far apart they may be in execution.

But, as inspiring as religion-based politics can be, it is also dangerous. Some of history's worst offenses can be attributed to it. So it is no wonder that I was sweating so robustly on my ski machine. We all ought to break out in a sweat when we hear any hint of religion and politics mixing. There's nothing worse than a political (or a religious) leader who sincerely feels God is on his or her side. The results of such immense confidence are usually disastrous. This is what we are seeing right now in Iraq: a religiously motivated force meeting an immovable religious object. Who knows where it will end?

On the other hand, politics as mere rational management doesn't satisfy either. It's too sheepish, too colorless. It lacks vision. Maybe there was a moment, sometime in the mid-twentieth century, when politics as rational management seemed the wave of the future, but that moment is past. In a world that's changing so rapidly, a world that's full of immense problems and may be beyond repair, probably nothing other than a faith-based politics can satisfy. The craving for a sense of meaning in social life seems more acute now than it has been for many generations. This probably accounts for the reelection of President Bush. On a rational basis, he ought to have been voted out, because too many things had gone wrong under his watch and everyone knew it. But the president convinced many voters that the faith and vision that guided him were stronger and truer than his policies and actions, and that, as he said, even if you didn't agree with him, "you know what I stand for, and you know I keep my word," and so you should vote for him anyway. This is an astounding plea for a politician to make, if you think about it.

If American politics is more religious than it has been for a long time, we are not alone. The world of Islam is undergoing a tremendous religiopolitical revival. I'm not sure I understand what's behind it. I have the sense that the explanations we read in any paper or see on television are not accurate. September 11 caught us all off guard, and we still have not digested it. That spectacular act of terrorism was more than a lucky break for a bunch of marginalized fanatics. What is that kind of terrorism if not a powerful apocalyptic religion gone berserk? Suicide bombers look forward to death as a happy reward. Who among us can really comprehend this? To dismiss such terrorists as "evil" is to miss the quality of desperate religious longing that they embody. What we reject as terrorism, as pure evil, is perhaps felt and understood differently by many Muslims, who can hear in such terrible actions, however unacceptable and unjustifiable, the sadly understandable scream for a more meaningful and righteous world.

───── ▶◀ ─────

Recently a friend complained to me of a health problem. She had, she said, a pain in her heart, a heavy feeling that wouldn't go away. After consulting many doctors, none of whom could find anything wrong with her, she concluded that she was literally heartsick at the state of the world, exhausted with the politics of the last few years. She was feeling paralyzed and impotent and too emotionally numb to address it, so the despair came out physically.

Many people I talk to these days are experiencing similar despair or depression. They are feeling listless, vaguely frightened, and unenthusiastic about their futures. The frenetic activity that preceded the November presidential election is now over, and for the moment everything is more or less quiet on the Left. People are perhaps too exhausted to go on being contrary, and their efforts seem futile in the face of a triumphalist and hermetically sealed administration in the White House. Among the people I know— and I suspect this is true of progressive forces across the country— there is a lot of fear. The program of the current administration is truly radical. There seems to be no lively alternative. So we sit and hold our breath, facing the direst of prospects: an American fascist state; economic collapse; environmental catastrophe; World War III, to be fought against proliferating bands of terrorists all over the globe. People are aware of these things, but they don't want to think about them, so the awareness comes through as an unconscious dread, bad dreams, a pressure on our hearts, an almost physical weight we bear.

These frightening possibilities cannot be denied, but neither can they be taken as facts. The only fact is that we don't know what will happen in the future, and to imagine that we do is foolish. It is not unusual for history to proceed by a process of reversal: momentum going in one direction is unexpectedly replaced by momentum in the opposite direction. The Buddhist teachings on karma are relevant here. They tell us that our positive actions will always, perhaps in some unforeseeable way, lead to good results not only for ourselves but for the world. They also tell us that the warp and woof of causality weave a tapestry so complex that no one but a buddha could understand it. So hope is never out of place, even in the darkest of times.

Besides, our despair does nothing for anyone. To take action for a better future requires an optimistic spirit that is capable of seeing possibility even in seemingly hopeless situations. Our anxiety about the future is not as rational as we might think. In fact, it's a kind of personal angst we are projecting onto the world, which is beyond the influence of our projections. The world has its own path to follow, a path much more mysterious than any we could imagine.

The actions of our government, in matters large and small, can be maddening. And when we are mad, we fall back on habitual responses. It's better, though, to stop clutching and recoiling and take a more open-minded view. We should ask ourselves: Is there anything of value in what this president says? Anything to be learned from it? Can I in some way appreciate the views that are being advanced, so that my own views might be challenged? And if I must oppose them, can I do so respectfully and intelligently, without feeling that I am opposing idiots and evildoers, but rather people who might have worthwhile hearts and minds of their own?

Asking ourselves questions like these can help us to see our political choices in a new light. For example, on abortion, we might ask: Could there be some virtue in the idea of a right to life for an as-yet-unborn being? And could it be that pregnancy entails a responsibility more sacred than the right to dominion over one's own body? On gay marriage: Could it be that those who oppose it are trying desperately to say something *for* their notion of marriage, rather than merely *against* the rights of homosexuals? On privatizing Social Security, which is part of a much wider, though seldom openly articulated, argument that the government should not or cannot do much to help people in need: Could it be that personal responsibility and initiative are more powerful, and even more virtuous, than large bureaucracies?

I do not say that the forces of conservatism have the answers; only that their successes, rather than being mere evidence of the power of the rich to disregard the poor, may be pointing toward something we have not yet understood.

And there is always the possibility that wrongly motivated actions might have unintended beneficial consequences. Could we, even for a moment, indulge the fantasy that the president's faith-based policies might, despite the appearance of disaster ahead, lead to unforeseen good results? And could we imagine this even while we are working hard to oppose those policies?

In tough times one has to have a flexible viewpoint. One also needs energy, generosity, patience, focus, and wisdom. These qualities are characteristic of a religious practice that gazes skyward as well as earthward. We liberals who consider ourselves religious have been careful to compartmentalize our lives, putting politics on one side and faith on the other. It's time for us to be more forthright and serious about our religious commitments, and to see them not as private aspects of our lives but central pillars that support our public acts. This may mean, first, being more faithful to our religious practice, whatever it may be; and, second, letting others know that our political actions stem from our religious commitments. Though we have no desire to convert anyone, we need to insist on being heard, just as we are willing to listen.

Whether we like it or not, our political life is now so dominated by religious perspectives that we must all participate in defining what true religious values are, lest we allow others to do it for us. In my view, real religious values—Buddhist, Christian, Muslim, or otherwise—always involve peacefulness, generosity, and a willingness to respect views other than one's own. We ought to insist on this as we go forward, doing what we can to shape the political attitudes of a new generation. We need to develop inspiration for this task, as well as the right vocabulary, strategy, and organization—just as those currently in power did thirty years ago, when they were dissatisfied with the dominant politics of that time. We must learn something from them: that in the Western world, religion is always the basis of any powerful political consensus. Let's see to it that when the social wheel turns, the religion we are talking about will be broad-minded rather than narrow, peaceful rather than warlike, open rather than closed.

33

Contemplating Climate Change

2012

THERE'S AN OLD Zen saying: "The world is topsy-turvy." In other words, it's an upside-down, crazy world. This may seem like an extreme statement, but only for a minute. If craziness means that we keep doing dysfunctional and destructive things, even when ensuing disasters are apparent, then it does seem that the world is crazy.

Who is not aware of this? Trevor Noah makes his living off it. But after we finish laughing, we start crying: the state of the world is painful to everyone. Yet the world careens onward in its topsy-turvy course, causing a pervasive sense of inward dread we can't afford to entertain. This would explain the religious fanaticism, lunatic politics, myriad addictions, and other social and psychological aberrations that are so commonplace now. Deep down we all know the fix we're in, but we can't afford to face it. It's just too much.

At present, several national economies are dangerously teetering. Jobs and basic social services are becoming scarce, governments are bankrupt, and the economic arrangements that have served us more or less (usually less) reasonably for so long begin to seem untenable. Behind this economic crisis, and the pain and injustice it has revealed, is a looming ecological crisis. The climate is certainly changing, yet there are still people who deny the existence of human-caused climate change, though the scientific consensus is clear. We remain divided and confused.

What's the alternative to all this denial? Is there a way we can digest, hold, and live with the scale of our current problems?

The Buddha noticed that it is nearly impossible to take in all the suffering of the world, and yet there is no avoiding it. So he began his path with the insight that "all conditioned existence has the nature of suffering." The path to peace doesn't come from avoiding suffering, he taught; it comes from facing and going through, rather than around, it. You can't find peace in a troubled world by denying its trouble.

Meditation practice makes denial impossible and truth sustainable. It is impossible to sit on a meditation cushion for any length of time without noticing suffering, within and without. But as consciousness opens up little by little during the course of a practice life, it becomes big enough and resilient enough to see and withstand great difficulty. Though meditation practice may or may not help us produce rational solutions to seemingly objective problems, it does give us wide vision and deep stability in the face of difficult situations—and the courage to sustain the effort to do something about them, even against great odds. In trying times, these personal qualities may be just as important as rational solutions. Maybe even more important.

Joe Galewsky, an Everyday Zen priest from the Desert Mirror sangha in Albuquerque, is a climate scientist. A few years back, his studies took him to the polar ice caps of Peru, 18,600 feet above sea level, where he spent a full day at the margin of a melting glacier. "The overall experience of being in the presence of this glacier," he wrote in his blog, "is one of immensity, stillness, and deep deep silence. . . . The glacier is clearly melting, for sure, but I really experienced it in terms of the most basic Buddhist teaching of impermanence: All conditioned things arise, abide for a time, and pass away. As far as we can tell, this particular glacier has completely melted and regrown many times over the last hundreds of thousands of years. This impermanence is also very impersonal. It doesn't matter what we think about it, or how we feel about it, or how we vote, or what we drive. This impermanence is simply the nature of things."

This may sound like Joe is suggesting that we relax about climate change. But he's not. He's suggesting that if we're going to be able to do anything about climate change in the long run, we are going to need a deeper, more mature, and grounded perspective.

He goes on: "Don't be too concerned for the earth, which is of the nature of continuous ongoing change, or for the glacier, which has come and gone many times in the past and will likely do so into the future, but for sure, we should be concerned about our fellow humans. As people, we are capable of a great deal of suffering, and climate change is likely to create a lot of suffering for people. I think that's where we should place our emphasis in terms of where practice intersects climate change."

Political, technical, and social action will bring the changes we need. There's a lot of work ahead. Cages to rattle, courage and imagination to manifest. But we will need to sustain such effort over the long haul with compassion and clarity of vision if we hope to get anywhere with it. This is where meditation practice and other forms of serious spiritual practice really help. With it, we grow in our capacity for patience, fortitude, compassion, imagination, and love. Year by year, decade by decade, our practice helps us become mature, kind, capable individuals—the sort of people a troubled, crazy world will depend on to maintain stability and good cheer.

Beyond the personal qualities spiritual practice fosters are the valuable social skills it helps us develop. Retreat practice teaches us to live simply, enjoy quiet, be perfectly happy with only a little, and live in supportive, harmonious community. These are skills the world at large lacks and sorely needs.

I lived for a number of years at Tassajara Zen Mountain Center, San Francisco Zen Center's monastic community in the Los Padres National Forest. We kept a demanding schedule of daily meditation, work, formal meals, and a round of daily ritual, living with no electricity, no heat, and very little personal time or space.

Of necessity, we had to be self-sufficient, taking care of all cooking, cleaning, repair work, and so on.

While the life was rigorous and difficult to get used to, I felt happy and content there. I stayed long enough so the template of monastic life remains engraved on my spirit, a reference point for my life. Although my life now is more complicated, inside I still live at Tassajara. I know that if my material circumstances became reduced, I could be happy with less—maybe happier. I don't need to panic when the stock market lurches or cower when it seems that our "way of life" might change in the future.

Here's a good practice: if you have an extra room in your house, practice visualizing one or more of your friends or relatives living in that room. You may think it would be hard to live with lots of people, as our ancestors once did and people all over the world still do. Maybe so. But if—as we did at Tassajara, and as my wife and I often did later with our small children on rainy days indoors—you practice silent periods during the day and maintain simple rules for ethical and courteous conduct, then living together can be quite good. Maybe more satisfying than private living in private homes that are empty most of the time.

A few years ago I spent a day thinking about the future with a small group of engineers, social scientists, and political theorists. One of the engineers said that despite the enormity of the problem, climate change can be greatly ameliorated, because the technical solutions to do it are available. But, he said, that makes no difference, since the political possibility of applying the solutions is pretty much zero. Ultimately, climate change—like probably all our social problems—is less a technical problem than a moral one, a collective failure of imagination and courage, a narrowness of heart.

At the end of the meeting I said, "If we are in for hard times, it will go much better if our collective attitude is patience, kindness, love, and compassion, rather than panic and selfishness. So maybe the cultivation of these good qualities is really important now." Everyone in the room seemed to agree that that would not be a crazy thing to do.

34

No Beginning, No Ending, No Fear

2019

THE BUDDHA HAS many epithets. He's called the Enlightened One, the One Who Thus Comes and Goes, the Conquerer, the Noblest of All Humans Who Walk on Two Legs. He is also called the Fearless One because he has seen through all the causes of fear. His awakening moment, coming suddenly after six years of intense meditation, shows him that there is actually nothing to fear. Fear—convincing as it may seem—is actually a conceptual mistake.

What is there to be afraid of anyway? Fear is always future based. We fear what might happen later. The past is gone, so there's no point in being afraid of it. If past traumas cause fear in us, it is only because we fear that the traumatic event will reoccur. That's what trauma is—wounding caused by a past event that makes us chronically fearful about the future and so queasy in the present. But the future doesn't exist now, in the present, the only moment in which we are ever alive. So though our fear may be visceral, it is based on a misconception, that the future is somehow now. It's not. The present might be unpleasant and even dangerous, but it is never fearful. In the full intensity of the present moment there is never anything to fear—there is only something to deal with. It is a subtle point but it is absolutely true: the fear I experience now is not really present-moment based: I am afraid of what is going to happen. This is what the Buddha realized. If you could be in the radical present moment, not lost in the past, not anxious about the future, you could be fearless.

If you are suddenly threatened by an intense-looking guy pointing a gun at your head, you will likely be frozen with fear. But even then, it isn't the appearance of the man and the gun that you are afraid of. It's what is going to happen next. It is true though that in that moment you are not thinking about the future. Your experience is immediate, body-altering fear. Your reaction is biological, you can't help it. As an animal, you have survival instinct, so when your life is threatened your reaction is automatic and strong. But you are a human animal with human consciousness—a problematic condition, but one with possibilities. It is possible you could overcome your animal fear.

There are many recorded instances in the scriptures of the Buddha's life being threatened. In all such cases the Buddha remains calm and subdues the threat. Though the stories may or may not be mythical, they certainly intend to tell us that we are capable of overcoming the survival instinct and remaining calm even in the face of grave danger. The truth is, in many dangerous situations the ability to stay calm will keep you safer than your gut reaction of flight or flight.

But what if your life weren't actually being threatened. What if the only thing actually happening to you was insult, disrespect, frustration, or betrayal, but you reacted with the alarm and urgency of someone whose life was at stake. And continued, long after the event, to harbor feelings of anger and revenge. In that case, your reaction would be out of scale with the event, your animal instinct for survival quite misplaced. You would have taken a relatively small matter and made it into something much more unpleasant, and even more harmful, than it needed to be.

Impermanence is the basic Buddhist concept. Nothing lasts. Our life begins, it ends, and every moment that occurs between this beginning and ending is another beginning and ending. In other words, every moment we are disappearing a little. Life

doesn't end suddenly at death. It is ending all the time. Impermanence is constant.

Although we all understand this when we think about it, we
seem not to be capable of really taking it in. Buddhism teaches
that behind all our fears is our inability to actually appreciate, on
a visceral level, this truth of impermanence. Unable to accept that
we are fading away all the time, we are fearful about the future, as
if somehow if everything went exactly right we could be preserved
for all time. To put this another way, all our fears are actually dis-
placements of the one great fear, the fear of death.

———— ►◄ ————

These days we have fears that seem to go beyond our personal fear
of death. Climate change is a catastrophe. In the fall of 2018 we had
terrible forest fires in California. Even as far away from the fires
as the San Francisco Bay Area, where I live, you could smell the
smoke. You couldn't go outside, the air was so bad. But even worse
than the experience was the thought that this is the future, this is
how it is going to be from now on. There are going to be more and
more fires, hurricanes, typhoons; the ice caps are melting, sea levels
and summer temperatures are rising, the planet is slowly becoming
uninhabitable. This may or may not be true, but there are good
reasons to fear that it is true. So we feel afraid not for our own death
but also for our children and grandchildren and their children and
grandchildren. What will happen to them in the future?

I have a friend who is a great outdoorsman and environmental
activist. Some years ago, when the U.S. government was just beginning to become active in denying climate change, my friend got
really upset. He was upset about climate change realities, but even
more upset that people weren't paying attention to them, were
denying or ignoring climate change, because the government was
casting doubt. Here we were in a desperate situation, something
needed to be done right away, and people were going on with their
ordinary business as though everything were fine. My friend was

in despair over this, and he would tell me about it. As the years went on his despair and upset grew and grew. One day when he was telling me about it, I thought, It isn't climate change he's upset about. I said this to him, and he got really mad at me. I didn't really know what he was upset about. But it seemed to me that although he believed it was climate change he was upset about, actually it was something else. He stayed for a while, but eventually he came to me and said, You were right. So, what is it you are upset about? I asked him. He said, Yes, I am upset about climate change, but I didn't realize until you brought it up that there is something else I am upset about: I am getting old, I can't climb mountains like I used to. Who knows how long I will be able to ride my bike for hundreds of miles or do all the things I love to do. I am upset about the climate, but what makes me feel this anguish is that I am scared of my aging and dying. The planet really is under threat. And so am I.

So it may be true that the power of our fear always comes from our fear of endings—our own ending being the closest and most immediate of all endings. When we think of the world of the future, we can feel sorrow, grief, and disappointment that we human beings cannot reverse course and do better, that we seem to be unable to solve a problem we ourselves have caused.

But fear is different, fear is desolation, desperation, anguish, despair, and sometimes anger. Grief, sorrow, disappointment are quiet feelings we can live with. They can be peaceful and poignant, they can be motivating. When we feel these feelings, we can be more compassionate, kinder to one another, we can be patiently active in promoting solutions. When we understand the real basis of our fear, we can see through it. Will our lives end, will the world end? Yes. But this was always going to be the case. All difficult moments occur in the present, and the present moment, no matter what it brings, is always completely different from our projections about the future. Even if what we fear about the future actually comes to pass, the present moment in which it occurs won't be anything like the moment we projected in the past. Fear is always fantastic, always fake. What we fear never happens in the way we fear it.

There's a traditional Buddhist practice to contemplate beginnings and endings called the five reflections. The reflections gently guide the practitioner in meditating on the fact that old age, sickness, and death are built-in features of the human body and mind, that no one can avoid them. Life begins, therefore it has to end. And being subject to beginning and ending, life is inherently vulnerable.

The point of this meditation isn't to frighten; quite the opposite: the way to overcome fear is to face it and become familiar with it. Since fear is always fear about the future, to face the present fear, and see that it is misplaced, is to reduce it. When I give myself over, for a period of time, or perhaps on a regular basis, to the contemplation of the realities of my aging and dying, I become used to them. I begin to see them differently. Little by little I come to see that I am living and dying all the time, changing all the time, and that this is what makes life possible and precious. In fact, a life without impermanence is not only impossible, it is entirely undesirable. Everything we prize in living comes from the fact of impermanence. Beauty. Love. My fear of the ending of my life is a future projection that doesn't take into account what my life actually is and has always been. The integration of impermanence into my sense of identity little by little makes me less fearful.

The reflection on beginnings and endings is taken still further in Buddhist teachings. The closer you contemplate beginnings and endings, the more you begin to see that they are impossible. They can't exist. There are no beginnings and endings. The *Heart Sutra*, chanted every day in Zen temples around the world, says that there is no birth and so there is no death either.

What does this mean? We are actually not born. We know this from science, there is nothing that is created out of nothing— everything comes from something, is a continuation and a transformation of something that already exists. When a woman gives birth, she does not really give birth, she simply opens her body to a continuation of herself and the father of the child, to their parents and their parents before them, to the whole human and nonhuman family of life and nonlife that has contributed to the coming together of preexisting elements that we will see as a newborn child. So there really is no birth. This is not a metaphorical truth.

If no beginning then no ending. There is no death. In what we call death the body does not disappear. It continues its journey forth. Not a single element is lost. The body simply transforms into air and water and earth and sky. Our mind travels on too, its passions, fears, loves, and energies continue on throughout this universe. Because we have lived, the world is otherwise than it would have been, and the energy of our life's activity travels onward, circulates, joins and rejoins others to make the world of the future. There is no death, there is only continuation. There is nothing to be afraid of.

35

The Problem of Evil

2015

BEHEADINGS. Drone attacks. Suicide bombers. Mass shootings in malls, movie theaters, and office buildings. Religious fanatics slaughtering innocents, sometimes by the thousands, in an effort to purify the world according to their lights.

The world today seems more filled with evil than ever. But no doubt people felt this in 1918, 1945, and afterward, as they reeled with the shock of then-contemporary events. How could our reasonable, scientific, enlightened, and progressive culture, in its most promising century, have produced two world wars, the Holocaust, mass starvations, and the long, terrifying shadow of nuclear weapons?

We have been trying to digest this crisis of culture for a hundred years, to understand the perceived failure of modern Western civilization, and the horrors, confusion, and despair it has left in its wake. Meantime, the planet is heating up every day—with as-yet-unknown but certainly dire consequences—and humanity can't seem to find the political will to do anything about it.

And all of this is perpetrated by people, ordinary human beings like you and me. How do we understand human nature in the light of these sobering realities? How do we reconcile our hope that people are basically good with all the evil in the world?

Zen Buddhism is usually characterized as a nondualistic tradition. In the realm of the absolute—of oneness, self-nature, true nature, buddha nature, and so on—good and evil are aspects of the one reality. There is no fundamental difference between them.

As the Sixth Zen Ancestor challenges: "Without thinking good or bad, what is your Original Face?" All things, no matter what they are, are as they are; they can't be some other way. And what they are is buddha, the absolute reality beyond good and evil (and every other dualism).

It is true that in Zen there are precepts that describe moral rules not unlike those followed by any religion or ethical humanistic program—not killing, stealing, lying, and so on. But Zen teaching distinguishes three different levels of precept practice: relative (or literal), compassionate, and absolute. On the relative or literal level, we try to keep the precepts as written and simply understood. On the compassionate level, we sometimes violate a precept in order to benefit others. The absolute level proposes that there is ultimately no way to keep any precept, and no way to break it. All precepts are always broken and kept. This is nondual morality— beyond good and evil.

Or so it seems.

When the precepts are deeply considered, it's clear that literal, compassionate, and absolute are only words, distinctions meant to help us appreciate aspects of the precepts we might otherwise miss. In the actual human world, we can't avoid the choice between good and bad, because there is no absolute level apart from the relative and compassionate levels. Relative, compassionate, and absolute are ways of talking about the moral choices we make with these human bodies and minds, in an actual, lived, physical world.

Of course there is a difference between good and evil. But we notice that not everyone agrees on which is which (though I believe that as a human family we are getting closer to unanimity on this point). Nor can we help noticing how much evil is perpetrated in the name of combating evil.

In Zen precept practice, the fundamental, absolute ground of ethics is being itself. Because we and the world exist, there are precepts. Things are. Life is. And in this, *not* being is also included. A moment of time arising is a moment of time passing. Being born is the beginning of dying. This is sad, tragic, and probably impossible for us to fully appreciate. Yet we can and do feel the immensity of being itself—and the strangeness of unbeing. Grounding our lives in this fundamental truth is the fruit of our practice. This is where the teaching of "no difference between good and evil" comes from. It is essential. But it can't be taken out of context.

When evil is perpetrated it becomes a fact of existence. When ISIS militants behead people in Syria and Iraq, or when children are used as suicide bombers, evil is being perpetrated. This becomes something that *is*. It is undeniable. We have to accept that this evil has actually happened. We have to somehow take it in, difficult as that may be, because it is now a part of our world, of our human life.

This doesn't mean we have to condone it or accept it in a moral sense, or that we shouldn't do everything we can do to prevent it from happening again. It only means that we have to accept it as having happened. This acceptance is how I understand the absolute level. When evil exists, we accept it as existing, just as we have to accept a loss that's happened to us, even as we grieve it. If we deny or refuse to accept reality as it is, we won't be able to cope with it. We will keep on making the same mistakes again and again. Our losses, if we don't accept them, can destroy our lives. To attempt to relieve our pain by identifying evildoers and vowing to wipe them out, as if that will remove the loss's stark grip on us, won't work. It will only add to evil's mounting pile.

───── ►◄ ─────

What does *nondual* mean? I am not sure I entirely understand the concept. Some years ago I was invited to make a presentation at a conference whose theme was nondualism. I was surprised to find that to many of the speakers nondual meant "oneness." I guess this makes sense—either it's dual (which means two or more, like dual headlights) or it's not dual, which means it's one (or "One," as most of the speakers seemed to understand it). By this logic, good and evil as separate things would be dualism, two different things. Nondual would mean that good and evil aren't different; they are one thing.

But to me the concept of oneness is also dualism, because you have oneness on the one hand and dualism on the other hand. And they seem like two different things: "I agree with oneness. Dualism is a mistake." This seems like dualism.

Sometimes reality arrives as one, sometimes as more than one. Nondualism must include dualism. If nondualism doesn't include and validate dualism, then it is dualistic! Saying it like this seems odd, but in actual living it simply seems to be true.

Oneness would be: yes, this happened. A man was tortured to death. A child was born. Like all that happened or ever could happen, these are true, living facts, and as such I must accept them as real—good or evil, whether I like it or not. Dualism would be: wrong is wrong, and I am committed to doing what is good and right, not what is evil or wrong.

In actual living, I can't see any way but to embrace both of these ways of seeing. How else could we live a reasonable human life?

Zhaozhou once asked Touzi, "When someone who has undergone the great death then returns to life, how is it?" Touzi said, "She can't go by night, she should arrive in the daylight."[1]

In Zen language, "the great death" stands for the nondual sense of life as one. All things, good or bad, desirable or undesirable, express that oneness. To experience the great death is to see, face to face and for oneself, that everything is real, everything is true, everything is just as it is. Such an experience, if it is an experience, is certainly important in Zen practice, if not all-important. What does that—and this story that speaks of it—imply for our collective moral lives?

A commentary to this story cites another story about this same monk Touzi. In this story Touzi asks his teacher Cuiwei to explain the most mysterious and essential aspect of the Chan teachings.

In response, Cuiwei turns and looks at him. Touzi says, "Please direct me," and Cuiwei says, "Do you want a second ladleful of foul water?"[2]

The great death, oneness, enlightenment, total acceptance of reality beyond good and evil—this is a necessary step in Zen or any other profound spiritual practice. But although this may be ultimate, it is only a step. Zen calls it "the great death" for a good reason. It *is* a kind of "death." It requires a complete letting go, a complete relinquishment, in trust, of everything that one has identified as one's life.

To be truly alive, as Zen practice sees it, one has to die—to let go of life. But until we are physically dead we can't remain dead. We have to be alive. We can't remain in the darkness and purity of beyond-good-and-evil. We have to arrive in the daylight of this physical, limited world of distinctions and moral choices. Difficult though it may be, there is no escape and no alternative. And yet we celebrate. Having died the great death, we know what a miracle it is to be alive, and how strange and marvelous it is—even with its difficult and sad challenges, which are themselves miraculous.

Almost all Zen stories are encounters between individuals, and therefore essentially dualistic. When Cuiwei faces Touzi he is saying to him: I am me, you are you. We may be one, we may be inherently empty of any difference or separation, but as long as we are alive we are different people. This essential difference—even though it is, in the light of the great death, unreal—is our life. "Appreciate and understand this," Cuiwei is wordlessly teaching his student.

But Touzi requires a bit more explanation, so Cuiwei says to him: "Do you want another ladleful of foul water?" To be alive in this world of human beings, plants and animals, flesh and blood, earth, sky, fire, and water, is to be immersed in trouble, in essential imperfection. "All conditioned existence is suffering, unsatisfactory, dukkha," the Buddha originally taught. In its purity, being is beyond good and evil, beyond moral dilemmas. And it's not. We all want to escape to some ultimate goodness, some ultimate certainty, some ultimate peace. We hope, as Touzi hopes, that our religion can give it to us. But all our religions, all our explanations, all our moralities, are mixed and impure. To accept and embrace this is what brings an end to our suffering.

The story continues: after Cuiwei says this, Touzi gets it. He is, as Zen stories always say, "enlightened." He bows and readies to leave. As he is going, Cuiwei says to him, "Don't fall down!"[3] Meaning, "In this sad world of birth and death, do your best to remain on your feet and do the right thing." And also meaning, "Of course, you won't be able to do that. You'll be constantly placed in moral dilemmas, you'll make mistakes all the time. So when you fall down, get up as gracefully as possible."

To die the great death is to see and feel life as being/nonbeing itself, sadly and beautifully beyond good and evil. But death is useless; it can't produce anything in this world. You have to come back to life, and, as Touzi says to Zhaozhou in our original story, you can only do that in the daylight, not in death's darkness.

Yes, "life and death are one" is a deep and ineffable truth. Killing and being killed, one. All victims of violence would have died soon enough anyway. All of them were, like us, more or less already dead—impermanence, emptiness, means that we are all already dead, losing our lives (evanescent as smoke) moment by moment anyway. Our having an actual possessable life has always been a painful illusion. The change of state from life and death is slight, the curtain between them far thinner than any of us believe. From within the great death everything is acceptable; everything is all right all of the time. Things are just as they are, not some other way. But this, monstrous as it sounds, is so only when you are dead—only when you have entered the samadhi of the absolute, which is stasis.

We can't stay dead. We have to come back to life because this is our condition, privilege, and obligation. We enter the world of face-to-face encounter, of the difference between us. Oneness isn't anything other than this. There is no difference between oneness and manyness. These are just ways of speaking. In the light of life there's only me and you, Touzi, Zhaozhou, and Cuiwei, and what we and they can do together to bring some goodness to our lives. Following precepts is very clear. There are no two ways about it: don't kill, never kill, don't support killing, try to prevent killing when and however you can. Support and promote life and do what you can to nurture it. And when killing happens anyway, grieve with bitter tears the innocent death, because you are a human being, and it is very sad and terrible.

A person who's died the great death before reentering the light understands how all this happens, and knows that in some form or another it will always happen as long as we are human. Of course, it can happen more or less drastically, and one needs to work daily and tirelessly to make it better. But there will never be an end to this work of making things better, because it is our human birthright to make things worse and to make them better.

———— ▶◀ ————

Are human beings basically good or basically evil? This isn't a sensible question. Human beings are buddha, because life is buddha, all-inclusive. Understanding this, you know you have to forgive, although not forget. You know that you can't go forth with vengeance and hatred, or with a sense of moral superiority. Because you are you and not someone else, you know that there will always be foul water in your mouth—that the evil deeds of others are yours as well, that they are ours collectively. So you protect and defend as you can, but you don't condemn. Evil is part of all of us—and part of buddha too, according to the Zen teachings.

There's a line about this story of dying the great death that appears in the *Blue Cliff Record*, a Zen koan collection: "Where right and wrong are mixed, even the sages cannot know. . . . She walks on thin ice, runs on a sword's edge. . . ."[4]

Moral choice is fraught. The more you know and the more you appreciate about a given situation, the more fraught it is. At the beginning of this piece I mentioned drone attacks. Are they good or evil? Do they kill innocent civilians? Yes, they do. But even when they don't, are they targeting the right people? Who are the "right people"? If someone is forced, by social pressure and the threat of murder, to harbor a so-called terrorist, or even to commit so-called terrorist acts, is such a person worthy of being targeted? Is anyone? And who decides? On what basis?

Can anyone, in this corrupt, unjust, unfair, confused world, claim a position of moral superiority? Is there anyone who can sit on a pristine throne of moral rectitude from which to proclaim the judgment of who shall live and who shall die? According to this commentary, not even the sages can say. They, like us, are walking on thin ice that might break through at any moment. Yet we must walk and run; we must make ethical choices based on our best understanding of and firm commitment to precepts and the goodness they represent.

A verse on this story says: *Even the ancient Buddhas, they say, have never arrived / I don't know who can scatter dust and sand.*[5]

In Zen, teaching is a dubious proposition. That's why it's called "scattering dust and sand." Like Cuiwei, with his "ladleful of foul water," Zen ancients recognized that all religious and moral systems, however necessary, must be taken lightly. They will always be partial and therefore potentially destructive in this checkered world. Even the buddhas, as Zen sees them, are still working on being able to understand their own lives, and ours, well enough even to be able to spread the half-truths that constitute Buddhist teaching.

The three pure precepts of Zen come from the earliest Buddhism, long before Zen. They are: "To avoid evil, to do good, to benefit all beings." We may not really know what this means. We may not know how to do it. But it is our commitment, the effort of our lifetime, to be carried out with energy, appreciation, forgiveness, noncondemnation, understanding, and grief.

Acknowledgments

WHILE WRITING may seem the last lonely occupation, in fact a published writer has many collaborators. Certainly this is so for me. In addition to my wife, Kathie, who supports me in all things, my Zen teachers Sojun Weitsman and Zentatsu Baker, and my many Zen colleagues with whom I am in dialogue, I am deeply grateful to my many supporters, transcribers, editors, and friends who have aided and abetted this and others of my literary efforts. My editor Cynthia Schrager was an enormous help with this collection. She not only gathered the texts from far and wide, but she also thought about them, organized them thematically, and provided careful editorial suggestions, often saving me from some of the more outrageous and possibly unconsciously offensive things I might have said, left entirely on my own. My good friend Sue Moon, Zen teacher and beautiful writer, gave much advice and review. As editor of the engaged Buddhist magazine *Turning Wheel*, Sue also was involved, years ago, in soliciting and editing some of the pieces. So too were the good editors at the Buddhist magazines *Tricycle* and *Lion's Roar* (formerly *Shambhala Sun*), where editors Melvin McLeod and Andrea Miller have long been supporters of my writing; and the editors at *The Sun*, that great and very unusual magazine. Matt Zepelin and Emily Coughlin, my editors at Shambhala, are so good at what they do that they make it nearly impossible for a stubborn writer to complain. I also thank the editors at the University of Alabama Press, where several of the pieces appeared in my essay collection *Experience: Thinking, Writing, Language, and Religion*. I am grateful to Anne Johnson, Barbara Byrum, and Cynthia Schrager for their transcriptions of my talks. Lindsay Edgecombe, my longtime literary agent, has become a good friend, always clear and kind. Finally, I would like to thank the many practitioners of the Everyday Zen community, a far-flung group of people, whose reading of my books and listening to and appreciation of my endless dharma talks have kept me going these many decades and given me the feeling that my writing is worth the trouble it takes to do. A deep bow to all.

Notes

CHAPTER 1: WHEN YOU GREET ME I BOW

1. Eihei Dogen, *Treasury of the True Dharma Eye: Zen Master Dogen's Shobo Genzo*, trans. Kazuaki Tanahashi (Boulder: Shambhala, 2013), 288.

CHAPTER 4: LEAVING HOME, STAYING HOME

1. Adapted from John Strong, "A Family Quest: The Buddha, Yaśodharā, and Rāhula in the Mūlasarvāstivāda Vinaya," in *Sacred Biography in the Buddhist Traditions of South and Southeast Asia*, ed. Juliane Schober (Honolulu: University of Hawai'i Press, 1997), 113–28.

CHAPTER 6: WASH YOUR BOWLS

1. Dogen, *Treasury of the True Dharma Eye*, 474.

CHAPTER 7: ON SPIRITUAL FRIENDSHIP

1. Ralph Waldo Emerson, *The Laws of Nature: Excerpts from the Writing of Ralph Waldo Emerson* (Berkeley, CA: North Atlantic, 2010), 47.
2. Thomas Cleary and J. C. Cleary, trans., *The Blue Cliff Record* (Boston and London: Shambhala, 2005), 428.

CHAPTER 11: IMPERMANENCE IS BUDDHA NATURE

1. Dogen, *Treasury of the True Dharma Eye*, 243.
2. Dogen, *Treasury of the True Dharma Eye*, 237.
3. Dogen, *Treasury of the True Dharma Eye*, 236.
4. Dogen, *Treasury of the True Dharma Eye*, 243.

CHAPTER 13: EVERYTHING IS MADE OF MIND

1. Yoshito S. Hakeda, trans., *The Awakening of Faith* (New York: Columbia University Press, 1967), 28.
2. Hakeda, *Awakening of Faith*, 46.
3. Hakeda, *Awakening of Faith*, 46.

CHAPTER 15: BEYOND LANGUAGE

1. Wallace Stevens, *The Collected Poems* (New York: Vintage, 1982), 345.
2. Paul Celan, *Collected Prose*, trans. Rosmarie Waldrop (Riverdale-on-Hudson, NY: Sheep Meadow Press, 1986), 50.
3. James Green, trans., *The Recorded Sayings of Zen Master Joshu* (Boston: Shambhala, 1998), 89.
4. Robert Aiken, trans., *The Gateless Barrier* (New York: North Point Press, 1990), 42, 90, 155.

CHAPTER 16: PHRASES AND SPACES

1. Thomas Cleary, trans., *The Book of Serenity: One Hundred Zen Dialogues* (Boston: Shambhala, 1998), 352.

CHAPTER 17: ON DOGEN'S *SHOBOGENZO*

1. Dogen, *Treasury of the True Dharma Eye*, 29.
2. See Dogen's "Twining Vines," *Treasury of the True Dharma Eye*, 478–84.
3. Dogen, *Treasury of the True Dharma Eye*, 29.

CHAPTER 25: QUICK! WHO CAN SAVE THIS CAT?

1. Eihei Dogen, *Record of Things Heard: From the Treasury of the Eye of the True Teaching*, trans. Thomas Cleary (Boulder: Prajna Press, 1980), 5.

CHAPTER 27: BUDDHISM, RACISM, AND JAZZ

1. LeRoi Jones (Amiri Baraka), *Blues People: Negro Music in White America* (New York: Morrow, 1999 [1963]), 136.

CHAPTER 35: THE PROBLEM OF EVIL

1. Adapted from Cleary, *Book of Serenity*, 264.
2. Cleary, *Book of Serenity*, 264.
3. Cleary, *Book of Serenity*, 264.
4. Cleary and Cleary, *Blue Cliff Record*, 249.
5. Cleary and Cleary, *Blue Cliff Record*, 251.

Publication Credits

1. "When You Greet Me I Bow" originally appeared in the September 2011 issue of *Shambhala Sun*. See more at LionsRoar.com.

2. "No Teachers of Zen" originally appeared in the Spring 2017 issue of *BuddhaDharma*. See more at LionsRoar.com.

3. "Falling in Love" originally appeared in the July 1999 issue of *Shambhala Sun*. See more at LionsRoar.com.

4. "Leaving Home, Staying Home," originally published as "The Sacred and the Lost," first appeared in the Fall 1997 issue of *Inquiring Mind* (Vol. 14, No. 1).

5. "Stages of Monastic Life" originally appeared in the Winter 1997 issue of *Wind Bell* (Vol. 31, No. 1).

6. "Wash Your Bowls" originally appeared in the June 2005 issue of *The Sun* (Issue 354). See more at TheSunMagazine.org.

7. "On Spiritual Friendship," originally published as "Making Friends on the Buddhist Path," first appeared in the May 2016 issue of *Lion's Roar*. See more at LionsRoar.com.

8. "Beautiful Snowflakes" originally appeared in the May 2006 issue of *Shambhala Sun*. See more at LionsRoar.com.

9. "What Is Your Body?" originally appeared in the July 2013 issue of *Shambhala Sun*. See more at LionsRoar.com.

10. "A Mother's Death," originally published as "Into Emptiness," first appeared in the Spring 1992 issue of *Tricycle: The Buddhist Review* (Vol. 1, No. 3).

11. "Impermanence Is Buddha Nature" originally appeared in the May 2012 issue of *Shambhala Sun*. See more at LionsRoar.com.

12. "Suffering Opens the Real Path" is excerpted from *Solid Ground: Buddhist Wisdom for Difficult Times* © 2011 by Unified Buddhist Church with permission of Parallax Press.

13. "Everything Is Made of Mind" originally appeared in the May 2019 issue of *Lion's Roar*. See more at LionsRoar.com.

14. "On Looking at Landscape" originally appeared in *Five Fingers Review* (1993) and reprinted in the Spring 1994 issue of *Turning Wheel*.

15. "Beyond Language" originally appeared in the Summer 2011 issue of *Tricycle: The Buddhist Review* (Vol. 20, No. 4).

16. "Phrases and Spaces" originally appeared in the March 2008 issue of *Shambhala Sun*. See more at LionsRoar.com.

17. "On Dogen's *Shobogenzo*," originally published as "Plum Blossoms Open Early Spring," first appeared in the Spring 2011 issue of *Tricycle: The Buddhist Review* (Vol. 20, No. 3).

18. "The Place Where Your Heart Is Kept" originally published as the introduction to *A White Tea Bowl: 100 Haiku from 100 Years of Life* by Mitsu Suzuki, translated by Kate McCandless (Boulder: Shambhala Publications, 2014). Reprinted in the Winter 2014 issue of *BuddhaDharma*. See more at LionsRoar.com.

19. "Why Do We Bow?" originally appeared in the Spring 1997 issue of *Tricycle: The Buddhist Review* (Vol. 6, No. 3).

20. "Applied Dharma" originally appeared in the March 2009 issue of *Shambhala Sun*. See more at LionsRoar.com.

21. "Putting Away the Stick" originally appeared in the Winter 1998 issue of *Tricycle: The Buddhist Review* (Vol. 8, No. 2).

22. "On God for Sue," originally published as "God is a Three-Letter Word," first appeared in the Fall 2013 issue of *Inquiring Mind* (Vol. 30, No. 1).

23. Introduction to *Opening to You: Zen-Inspired Translations of the Psalms*, published by Penguin Books (New York, 2002).

24. "The Two Worlds" originally appeared in the April 2007 issue of *The Sun* (Issue 376). See more at TheSunMagazine.org.

25. "Quick! Who Can Save This Cat?" originally published in the Spring 2003 issue of *BuddhaDharma*. See more at LionsRoar.com.

26. "On Being an Ally" originally published in the Summer 2007 issue of *Turning Wheel*.

27. "Buddhism, Racism, and Jazz" originally appeared in the Summer 1993 issue of *Tricycle: The Buddhist Review* (Vol. 2, No. 4).

28. "The Sorrow of an All-Male Lineage" originally published February 26, 2018, on the *Lion's Roar* website. See more at LionsRoar.com.

29. "On Difference and Dharma" originally published in the Summer 1999 issue of *Turning Wheel*.

30. "On Forgiveness and Reconciliation," originally published as "Impossible Possibilities," first appeared in the Fall 2001 issue of *Turning Wheel*. Reprinted in *Not Turning Away: The Practice of Engaged Buddhism* edited by Susan Moon (Boulder: Shambhala Publications, 2004).

31. "We Have to Bear It" originally published in the Winter 2002 issue of *Turning Wheel*. Reprinted as "In Times of Trouble" on the *Lion's Roar* website on November 9, 2016. See more at LionsRoar.com.

32. "The Religion of Politics, the Politics of Religion" originally appeared in the May 2005 issue of *The Sun* (Issue 353). See more at TheSunMagazine.org.

33. "Contemplating Climate Change," originally published as "Topsy-Turvy World," first appeared in the November 2009 issue of *Shambhala Sun*. See more at LionsRoar.com.

34. "No Beginning, No Ending, No Fear," originally published as "El origen del miedo" [The Origins of Fear], first appeared in the September 2019 issue of *Revista de la Universidad de México*, translated by Clara Stern Rodríguez. First English publication here.

35. "The Problem of Evil" originally published in the May 2015 issue of *Shambhala Sun*. See more at LionsRoar.com.